The Political Art of Greek Tragedy

The Political Art of Greek Tragedy

CHRISTIAN MEIER

Translated by Andrew Webber

The Johns Hopkins University Press
Baltimore

Copyright © C. H. Beck'sche Verlagsbuchhandlung (Oscar Beck), München 1988.
First published as *Die politische Kunst der griechischen Tragödie*.
This English translation copyright © Polity Press 1993.

First published in 1993 by

The Johns Hopkins University Press
2715 North Charles Street
Baltimore, Maryland 21218-4319

ISBN 0-8018-4727-3
LC93-78142

Catalog records for this book are available from the Library of Congress and the British Library.

CONTENTS

TRANSLATOR'S NOTE

The translations cited in this book are as follows:

Aeschylus, *The Oresteia*, translated by Robert Fagles (Penguin, Harmondsworth, 1979)
Prometheus Bound, The Suppliants, The Persians all in *Prometheus Bound and Other Plays*, translated by Philip Vellacott (Penguin, Harmondsworth, 1961)

Aristophanes, *The Clouds* in *Lysistrata, The Acharnians, The Clouds*, translated by Alan H. Sommerstein (Penguin, Harmondsworth, 1973)
The Frogs in *The Wasps, The Poet and the Women, The Frogs*, translated by David Barrett (Penguin, Harmondsworth, 1964)

Sophocles, *Ajax* in *Electra and Other Plays*, translated by E. F. Watling (Penguin, Harmondsworth, 1953)
Antigone in *The Three Theban Plays*, translated by Robert Fagles (Penguin, Harmondsworth, 1984)

Line numbers refer to the original texts.

1

WHY THE CITIZENS OF ATHENS NEEDED TRAGEDY

The entire spirit and culture of Greece are in the closest relation to the polis.

Jacob Burckhardt

Greek tragedies were meant for the citizens of Athens, not just for a theatre-going minority, but for the whole citizenry of the most powerful city in the Greek world. Such was Athens in the age of Aeschylus, Sophocles and Euripides, in the fifth century BC.

Could the presentation of these tragedies, which took place once a year, with new plays on each occasion, have been mere theatre? Could Athens have allowed itself such an extravagant luxury? 'O but the history of Greece runs at such a pace', writes Nietzsche, 'Never again has life been so prodigal, so unbridled.' We might indeed concur with this observation when we survey the legacy of the Athenian, or Classical, century. But was it really like this? Or did the economic imperative, which asserts that societies should primarily suit production to needs, hold sway here too? Did the Athenians *need* tragedy? Indeed, did they perhaps need it almost as much as they did the Assembly, the Council of the Five Hundred and all the other institutions of their democracy?

It is undeniable that the citizenry of fifth-century Attica was exceptional in its constitution and that it found itself in a most unusual situation. For the first time in world history, broad sections of the population achieved a regular and forceful voice in politics and ultimately came to play the key role. The conditions under which this could have happened must have been extraordinary; we know that some of these conditions can be explained by a lengthy intellectual history and by the fact that the Greeks set public prestige above all other types of human motivation. But perhaps there were other factors, which have so far eluded us.

Around the time at which the oldest extant tragedies were produced, the Attic citizenry, mainly men of little education or experience who had hitherto existed within the confines of a provincial horizon, gained wide dominions as a result of the Persian Wars, assuming virtual primacy in the Aegean. Shortly afterwards they toppled the aristocratic Council of the Areopagus and adopted sole responsibility for Athens and its empire. This demanded a long arm and considerable boldness in the making of policy and the conduct of war over a domain that stretched from the Black Sea to Egypt and was soon to take in the west of Greece. As a result, undreamt-of fields of activity and expectation opened up, so that in every area things could be perceived, shaped and mastered anew, initiating a great torrent of change.

How did the Athenians cope with this? Power can be a thing of glory or of oppression, a source of great pleasure or of anxiety for those who wield it – particularly when life and death are concerned and the plotting of momentous decisions into the unknown. This is no reason to surrender it, quite the contrary. But it can cause problems, and nowhere more than in Athens at that time, where it fell all at once into the collective hands of the citizens, whose position in the political sphere had perhaps been prepared at an intellectual level, but who quickly found themselves faced with problems that would have defied all anticipation. In the late eighties of the fifth century BC a fleet had been constructed to confront the Persians, and it had triumphantly defeated them. This was the result of the utmost rationality both in those who thought out the requirements and drew up the plans and, in a different way, in those who adopted the plans and carried them out. But what then occurred was another matter: the Athenians had to engage in politics on a grand scale, to exercise sovereignty; they had the responsibility, that is, they were faced with the necessity, of having answers ready for all the conscious and unconscious questions and doubts which arose, and of addressing themselves to all the consequent demands.

The Athenians had no state, no government, no institutions on which (even if they had known any different) they might have relied. They had no police to speak of, no administrative apparatus, no public education. Everywhere responsibility lay with and among the citizens; only the implementation of decisions was ever delegated to individuals, and even then with multiple checks. How could such a citizenry be equal to such tasks, such practical demands, such responsibilities, above all at a time when these were all so new? It certainly needed the knowledge and the capacity to judge the speeches and proposals of politicians. To some extent the Athenians also appear to have developed new sets of standards by which to assess and settle their thoughts and aspirations. But we must ask whether it was as simple as that. What about the old ways of thinking? Could they simply pass away, fall into neglect or be, as it were, written out of the agenda, perhaps, even at this early stage, handed over as a plaything to the poets? Once the Athenians had known the fear of the 'envy of the gods', now they governed a mighty empire. Once they had continually invoked justice and the 'customs of the Greeks'; now they offended these not just here and there but as an inherent consequence of what was becoming a system of power politics. Question upon question was bound to arise, questions which could hardly be aired before the Assembly without arousing suspicions of vested political interests and which required a constant concern for practicability and for the constraints of rational argument.

Could tragedy step into this breach, not maybe in its original form, but in the form that it was to assume? Perhaps it contributed far more than this to the mental infrastructure of this so successful and in a way so adventurous society, this most powerful but also most insecure part of a world which had yet to test its potential and its frontiers, a world suspended in the first instance between the old and the new.

In tragedy the received, mythical way of thinking engaged with a new rationality, folk culture engaged with high culture. Might it not have served to play out recurrently, by way of myth, the concerns of the citizens as citizens? It may be that they sought in the plays, in the festival of the Great Dionysia, renewed confirmation of their order and its principles, and of the justice of the world. Perhaps early democracy gained through this channel the sort of support which early monarchies derived from their world-views and early aristocracies from tradition. Was tragedy – like, for instance, the human image cast by the sculptor, like temples and styles of dress and appearance – perhaps the specific beauty in which democracy (and that which led up to it) found its sustenance?

The festivals of the gods at that time were not merely pleasurable leisure activities relieving the workaday routine, but, in all probability, the necessary foil to everyday existence and its essential complement. We can have little idea of what the festivals meant to the Greeks, what it means to a society to cultivate the 'restrained intoxication' of the festival. Perhaps we have just not yet recognized how much Athenian democracy needed tragedy.

It seems possible that we have here a rather special example of a social body carrying out quite publicly the maintenance and development of its mental infrastructure. In the public arena of the festival the Athenians may have found an ongoing guarantee for the sort of precise balance which is so indispensable for political life. Surely we see here how the political is based within those imaginations and beliefs, within that deeper knowledge, according to which we situate our experience when we wish to be sure of it. The mental underpinning of such a daring society can certainly have been no simple matter.

We know that for the Greeks festivals were of importance in binding the citizens together. Did they perhaps also need tragedy in order to gain distance from the everyday, to find equilibrium and clarity and to keep open the principles of their existence, indeed to evolve these further? They certainly found themselves in an unusual position. Notwithstanding sometimes serious conflicts, the citizenry of Attica was relatively homogeneous and unified. Belief and art appear to have still found succour in one another, in such a way that both the need and the possibility arose to make sense of events, plans, experience, thoughts, motives and conditions in the context of the world at large. To be more precise: such a need, which humans invariably have, could not yet have been blunted in this society, but must on the contrary have been both actively felt and communal, as things were experienced, enacted and suffered collectively. However diverse, indeed divergent, had been the political positions with regard to the upheaval of achieving full democracy, the question of how such a break with an order sanctioned by the gods might be assimilated into the traditional world-view was probably common cause for concern.

This was the case with all the problems which the greater rationality of Athenian politics raised with regard to inherited wisdom. For this citizenry, politics was nothing less than the most vital element of life, attracting enormous energies, while all other areas were subsumed or simply neglected. For a time this must have brought about an extraordinary intensity of experience. But did it not mean that these problems, too, had to be tackled in the alternative public arena of the tragedy festivals?

It seems most likely that it was essentially *as* citizens that the citizens saw and heard tragedies, just as it is likely that the tragedians were part of the Greek tradition of political thought, combining a healthy measure of independence with a strong authority. This need not mean that their works were consumed by politics. Nor need the tragedians have adopted a stance on topical political issues, most likely just the opposite. But the evidence certainly suggests that they did have a political function, which must warrant investigation.

This book works on the premise that tragedy and politics were most closely connected in the fifth century. First and foremost it delineates the particular character of the Attic citizens and their political situation in the time between the Persian and Peloponnesian Wars, the time which saw the birth of democracy, a new empire and the predominance in Athens of generations still relatively strongly rooted in, or affected by, the old ways. The book further provides a guide to the function of the festivals and in particular the tragedy festival in Athens at that time. Above all, however, it gives an interpretation of several tragedies, primarily those of Aeschylus and two early works of Sophocles, in terms of the ways in which they might have mattered to the citizens as citizens. The concentration on tragedies dating from the period before the Peloponnesian War is justified by what I hold to be the close involvement between the literary works and their time. To do justice to the almost seven decades from which tragedies survive would have demanded a colossal study.

The question arises as to how the modern reader is supposed to obtain an insight into the needs of the citizens of Attica. Historical accounts which provide a guide to the politics of the period are of little help here. In these we find the Athenians simply occupied with the conduct of politics and especially of war. Such were the conventions of this new form of writing, and such were no doubt the facts of the matter as far as the aspect of life in the polis described by the historians is concerned. This period must none the less also have seen a considerable development in the history of the mind. To overlook this is to commit the error of understanding history too narrowly, but to attempt to reconstruct it is to risk a false view. The risk seems to me less dangerous than the error, not least because it can be contained by indicating hypotheses and open questions as such.

I believe that tragedy itself can provide many of the answers to the questions posed here. Tragedy is of particular interest because in this genre alone – and, of course, comedy – we find the middle and lower classes 'present' in the literature of that time; they may only participate as audience, but in a certain sense they set the agenda. Thus we can learn from the tragedies what concerned and indeed motivated them. The question then remains, why it is that something written for such a specific body of citizens, one so extraordinarily alien to us, should have anything – should indeed have so much – to say to us. This in turn brings up the general problem of the relationship between what appears foreign to us with the Greeks and what familiar, as well as the whole problem of Greek Classicism; and here the best path to understanding is via the direct relationship between this art and the politics of its culture.

This book aims to set out a thesis. Its interpretations seek to view the tragedies as a whole, but do not in the least pretend to supply an exhaustive account, even of essential matters. Political and dramatic points of view are not seen here as alternatives. The playwrights, at least those whose work is known to us, were far too good at their art to run the risk of making what concerned them politically go against the grain of the action. Such, at least, was the general rule.

The book is not specifically addressed to experts, but is aimed at all those who can perceive a problem in what went on in the deeper dimensions of thought and imagination, morality and belief, during this most important phase of Athenian history, one of the most significant in the history of the world. Such readers may see why what Ernest Renan has called the 'Greek miracle', astounding and in many respects 'fortuitous' as it may have been, can ultimately be explained, as long as the unique character of the Athenians of that time is properly recognized. The explanation will also shed light on what was a singular achievement for art as a whole, the unique way in which it was embedded in society. This may be of interest, impossible though it may be to reproduce.

2
ATHENS

The Athens of the fifth century, the era of tragedy, was an exuberant and disconcerting city, a city in extreme ferment. Fascinating, feared and admired, it would have stretched the understanding of many.

Both inwardly and outwardly the Athenians so disturbed and whipped up the Greek world, breaking through the accepted limits of action, thought, order and the execution of power, within such a short time and so radically, that not only others but also they themselves must have had great trouble in coming to terms with the new state of affairs. What had always been taken to constitute reality was now largely made invalid. In its stead there burgeoned new possibilities, which were not so easily delimited. There was an upheaval such as had never before been seen. And along with everything else that was opened up to the Athenians, there must also have been an element of insecurity, a sense of the uncanny. The words of Sophocles' chorus 'numberless wonders, terrible wonders walk the world, but none the match for man' mirror contemporary experience.

In one way or another Athens became a foreign body within the Greek world, and yet it was also its centre, its most powerful and interesting city. The centrality of Athens was due to the control it exercised over the Aegean, to the fact that for decades it played the role of a great power alongside Sparta and in opposition to Persia, to all the changes that it underwent, but not least to the coming together of all manner of goods and above all individuals in its ports and within its walls. The outsider as sovereign, the unbridled city setting the agenda: it sounds some-what paradoxical, but this is exactly how it must have been, and it is not least for this reason that this city provokes such interest, now as then.

Before the resultant internal problems for the citizens of Attica can be sketched, however tentatively, a clearer picture of Athens and its situation at that time must be established.

The sudden rise to power

In the Archaic era (*c.*750–500 BC), although – or perhaps because – its population was by far the largest in Greece, Athens remained relatively insignificant. It had barely taken part in the great move-ment of colonization. While Sparta conquered Messenia and gath-ered most of the cities in the Peloponnese into a system of partially dependent alliances, Athens may perhaps have expanded (Eleusis was taken, for example), but even in the conflict with the much smaller Megara over the island of Salamis, the Athenians suffered severe defeats, and they seem to have made little impression beyond the borders of Attica. Athens was simply of a different order of importance, compared with the much less populous Corinth or the little island of Aegina, not to mention Miletus and other Ionian cities.

The great crisis of the Archaic era, signalled by indebtedness, widespread enslavement of peasants, uprisings, civil wars and coups, reached Athens rather late. At the start of the sixth century Solon sought to reassert order in the city, but although he was an important political thinker and statesman, his work and character in many ways admirable, he had only limited success. At any rate, around 560 BC Pisistratus was able to tap sufficient dissatisfaction to establish a tyranny. It was one of the last in a long line of usurpations that had characterized Greece since the middle of the seventh century. Here too Athens rather lagged behind the others.

Shortly after 510 and the fall of the tyrant, however, Athens made up lost ground in the shape of reforms introduced by a man who was evidently as power-conscious as he was open-minded: Cleisthenes, the son of Megacles and scion of the powerful Alcma-eonidae. He recognized that he could best realize his ambitions for political influence by getting the people on his side, and he was shrewd enough to see that this was most likely to be achieved by extending their political rights. The situation in the past had been very different: then it had been necessary to promise the general populace economic advantages or more security before the law, if they were to be mobilized against the leading families. The political profit had gone only to those few who stood to gain power. In the meantime, though, things had changed.

The political order which Cleisthenes established was a prototype for democracy, which is now generally known as 'isonomy', under which at least the middle classes had a regular voice in politics. The actual conduct of political matters was still vested in the aristocracy and still concentrated for the most part, as in Athens, in an aristocratic council. But there was an attempt to strengthen the popular opposition in such a way that the aristocrats were bound to take its wishes into account and to temper their own despotism accordingly.

Athens was not the first among the isonomies, as other cities such as Corinth and Argos appear to have led the way. But under the new order an exceptionally high number of its citizens achieved collective influence for the first time, and this meant that the city became both powerful and self-assured, ready to get involved in Greek, indeed in world, politics. All at once it was playing a key role, and circumstances, as well as its own achievements, set it on entirely new paths. Political history could move quickly through extraordinarily radical mutations at that time, for politics stood at the centre of the world, and many possibilities, either the result of long gestation or the product of the inconceivable fluidity of power structures, could be realized from one year to the next, with profound consequences.

Soon after Cleisthenes' reforms the Athenians went to war against the Chalcidians on Euboea and against the Boeotians, beat them and annexed part of Chalcis for their own citizens. Of this Herodotus writes, that it shows to what extent a city in which political rights are evenly shared gains in outward strength. This seems undeniable. We also know from Herodotus that towards 500 BC Athens was the most powerful city in Greece, next to Sparta. And having become so suddenly conscious of its power, it seems to have tended towards more active and aggressive policies. In any event the Athenian Assembly was tempted into supporting the uprising against Persian rule started by the Ionian cities of western Asia Minor in the year 500.

So it was that Athens entered world politics, and things moved quickly thereafter. The Ionian rebellion was put down in 494 BC, and in 490 the Persians despatched an expeditionary force to punish the Athenians for their part in it. This force was defeated at Marathon. The Athenians' success was all the more surprising, given that they stood almost alone, for the Spartans had been prevented from setting out to their aid by the need to celebrate a festival.

Around 483, after a short period of tranquillity, the Persians began to arm themselves on a grand scale for a renewed onslaught, aiming this time to conquer all of Greece. At just about the same time the Athenians, following the advice of Themistocles, decided to construct a fleet such as had never before been seen in Greece. The whole city must have been transformed. Not only ships but also wharves had to be built; huge amounts of materials were required, experts had to be brought in or trained and all of this at great speed, for time was short. It was a great feat of organization. Above all, at least half of the adult male citizens had to devote much time and effort to learning how to row. It was not only a matter of propelling the ships (which was hard enough in itself, as the oarsmen had to sit in three rows, practically on top of each other, handling their oars powerfully and with strict precision, in spite of the extremely cramped conditions); they above all had to practise manoeuvring, for the superiority of a ship with three banks of oars (trireme) lay in the fact that it could turn suddenly in order to ram an enemy ship from an advantageous angle. It was later said that Themistocles made 'sea-creatures' of the Athenians, and this is indeed what the change amounted to. They not only learned new skills, but also took on a new element. And this was of great significance.

When the Persians advanced, the Athenians made a second phenomenal decision, namely to desert Attica with their families. The entire citizenry took to flight – flight into complete uncertainty, and not in order to find sanctuary elsewhere, but to take the improbable risk of gambling everything on one chance: that, together with their allies, they would overcome the superior Persian fleet in a battle at sea.

The gamble paid off: in September 480 the Greeks routed the Persian fleet at Salamis. The Athenians did not do this single-handed, indeed they were arguably not foremost in the fight, but they had the lion's share of the Greek fleet, and there could have been no victory without them. Their commander Themistocles was also responsible for the battle taking place, and under such favourable conditions. The Persian king retreated in haste to his realm, fearing that news of his defeat might spark off revolt.

For the Greeks, victory posed a new question. What was to become of their kinsmen in western Asia Minor, who had in part joined forces with them and were now clamouring for freedom from Persian rule? The Spartans, who led the Greek alliance, proposed that these compatriots should be resettled. However, the Athenians, who felt that theirs was the oldest Ionian city, self-confident and in possession of their fleet (which would otherwise be more or less redundant), were prepared to carry the war over into the Persian empire. In 478 BC an alliance was formed, the so-called Delian League, which in the course of a few years enabled Athens to become the major force in the Aegean.

Thirty years earlier Athens had been an insignificant and self-sufficient polis, one canton among many. It now emerged as the most important city in Greece. It had created policies out of the new state of affairs and with great pluck and good fortune had taken advantage of the various, admittedly quite extraordinary, opportunities for ascendancy which the times had offered. After having made barely any impact beyond its own borders for so many years, it had now become a great power, able to take issue with the mighty Persian empire. Of course Persian rule stretched from the Balkans to the Indus and from Egypt to the Caspian, with the Aegean as only one of its many frontier regions. And the empire had lost its momentum, and was thus occupied with all manner of problems, so that it could not devote serious attention to the Greeks. Even so, it was remarkable that Athens was now in a position to challenge Persia on an equal footing.

The subsequent history of the city can only be understood if we first understand how it came to make its citizens effective as a group. For, apart from the enormous advantage which it gained through its fleet, it was this factor that accounted for its greatness.

Identity as citizens

With the introduction of isonomy the Greek citizenries, and above all the citizenry of Athens, underwent a relatively swift and significant transformation in anthropological terms. This was not just a rhythmic wave-movement of 'involvement and disappointment' (A. O. Hirschman), but a genuine transformation. Otherwise isonomy would simply not have been possible. It is probably no exaggeration to say that the Athenian citizenry only then came into existence as a true political force.

Clearly the Greek isonomies (but above all the ensuing democracies) were founded on the substantial, regular participation of an extraordinarily high number of citizens in the political process. The Council of the Five Hundred, which since Cleisthenes' time had been designed to represent the general will in Athens (and to prepare motions for the Assembly), contained about a sixtieth of the citizenry, and Cleisthenes probably had already introduced a provision that the councillors should be replaced annually. In addition, the assemblies needed to be held more frequently and to be well attended, if the Council was to fulfil its intended function of lending effective voice to the broad populace, for it was clearly subordinate to the aristocratic Council of the Areopagus, and therefore reliant upon the active support of the people.

Democritus was later to declare that if a dignitary avoided politics, he would get a bad name, even perhaps have 'something to suffer', as if there might be psychosomatic consequences. Pericles even held that, in terms of the radical democracy of his time, 'we are alone in regarding one who takes no part in these things, not as an idle, but as a useless citizen.' Even allowing for the element of exaggeration in all such generalizations, they bear witness to a considerable pressure to play an active role in politics. Such pressure must have been compounded by strong expectations and counter-expectations on either side.

This means that a fairly large group of men, in the first instance those of moderate wealth who were thus not able to make a career out of politics, were none the less prepared to become seriously politically active. They accordingly had to neglect their own affairs to some extent, investing considerable time, energy and concentration in their existence as citizens. The question is, how did this come about?

It certainly came about as a consequence of the extended process that was responsible for the creation of isonomy (as indeed for the particular character of the Greeks). The most decisive characteristic of Greek cultural development can perhaps best be explained in negative terms: it happened by and large without the real involvement of a monarchy and the consequent authority of priests. In this sense Greece is an exception to the rule of world history. The tyrants may have made no small contribution to the consolidation of the citizenry, but they only, so to speak, functioned as catalysts, no part of their system of rule survived them.

The reasons for this curious 'lack' in early Greek society are obscure; nor are they of relevance here. In any case during the great crisis of the Archaic era no individual had the strength to impose the solution of his own rule on any city or region for any length of time. On the contrary, power remained relatively broadly based, within the cities and above all between them. The small scale of the communities was at least as much a consequence of this situation as its cause, for if power had become more concentrated, the opportunity would doubtless have arisen to conquer further areas.

Equally, in the course of the great crisis, such significant fields of activity and ambition had been nurtured, transgressions against established rights had become so commonplace and at the same time such a degree of rebelliousness had developed in the ranks of the exploited, the dispossessed and the deprived, that, for the most part at least, even stable aristocratic regimes became unviable.

This resulted in a virtual vacuum. Neither the old aristocracies nor the new usurpatory regimes could inspire loyalty for any length of time, nor could they order the world of the polis in such a way as to establish a secure power base. This would have required the setting up of reasonably serviceable and unequivocal notions of just and unjust, right and wrong, creating a more or less self-contained world-view. While such a world-view may not be an invariable political requirement, it surely becomes necessary when what was hitherto self-evident is irreparably confused, and there is no possibility of a solid pluralism.

In this situation an autonomous brand of political thought developed, which could not be bound to any single faction and was used by many parties. It was a way of thinking that produced a new image of just order for the polis. Given the barely containable despotism of the rulers and the potential for disorder among their subjects, the conclusion was reached that the members of the middle classes should be given institutional powers to counter the excesses of the nobles. In this way the injustices which had so often provoked uprisings could be nipped in the bud. The polis could thus gain some sense of equilibrium.

We hear of many attempts to move in this direction during the sixth century. In all probability a series of political thinkers helped by spreading insights, knowledge and also encouragement, arousing among the general populace the idea that they too, they in particular, were responsible for their city. They also sought to create favourable institutional conditions. It was a question of transforming discontent with the way things stood into political demands. The opportunity to do so grew with the gradual economic consolidation in Athens and elsewhere, not least thanks to the tyrants. The fact that Cleisthenes, and others before him, found that the people were best won over by granting them a greater say in politics shows how well the new trends could take hold.

But insight and good will alone were not sufficient to ensure lasting and regular political participation from the people. However great the interest of the individual in communal order (thereby guaranteeing a level of security in the law), it generally has to take second place to those interests that have a more direct bearing. The new perceptions and calls for change therefore had to join with, be rooted in, vital impulses, if life in general, the system of interests of a large proportion of citizens, was to be changed. Yet this was what came about.

A particular trait of Greek polis society comes into play here, determining that the 'political', that is existence in the sphere of communal life, could potentially be far more important than other areas and directions of life, as soon as an opportunity presented itself for this.

The poleis were small, so that an overview was possible. Being part of the citizenry could be fairly easily experienced, at least among the subdivisions out of which every citizenry was made up. These represented the most important level of communal relations above the house, the village and smaller social circles. The mass of citizens had neither economic nor social relationships of any consequence. Religion was primarily a matter for the polis, with the subdivisions of the citizenry forming cult communities. In this sense belonging to the citizenry was of extreme importance, and it increasingly became a privilege, for there were relatively sharp demarcations between male citizens and their wives, non-citizens and slaves.

Within the citizenry and its subdivisions, the worth of a man was measured on a comparatively simple scale. The society was essentially agricultural. Members owned land. This general rule may have been breached in favour of artisans and merchants early in the sixth century, but they had not been able to make their way of life, their activities and interests, seriously comparable to those of the landowners. Also, if no tyrant ruled the city, military service was not to be entrusted to specialists, but was the business of the landed citizens, as far as they could equip themselves. Both the financial situation and the practical organization of the polis demanded this; it would have been too dangerous to put a mercenary force in the hands of some official.

Thus the ideal for the citizen to attain was established. It was fairly clear: he had to be a landowner and a warrior and one or two other things which were of importance for life and competition between the citizens; he should, for example, be a sound counsellor, eloquent, of good appearance and practised in certain sports. So the ideal personality was remarkably fixed, with no plurality of values; it was purely a matter of striving after the one ideal. Indeed specialists were not particularly valued. To be precise, their abilities and works were deemed worthy of respect, but they were primarily perceived as persons with no land, not earning their keep in established ways. Later they were even seen as being essentially aloof from the lives of the citizens, neglecting the general good in order to achieve something special; and this was not appreciated. This shows how binding the general ideal was, how much pressure there was to conform in the exclusive male societies.

At the same time there were naturally still great distinctions and contrasts between the non-specialist citizens, in particular the differences between the upper class – that is, the nobility – and everybody else. Their effect was concrete and tangible, for rights and privileges were most likely unevenly distributed within the subdivisions: among them were official appointments, access to communal property, surplus income, military service and not least the share in offerings, which were as a rule communally enjoyed. People were given a palpable and public feeling of what they were worth.

Such inequalities can be regarded as self-evident, and so they will have been in the early days. But then the foundations which had supported them collapsed. After the continual experience of injustice, leading to tensions, oppositions, uprisings and conflicts, new yardsticks were applied to political thinking. These made it possible to distinguish clearly between just and unjust, challenging the methods by which the aristocrats enforced their rule. There was a new awareness of the nobles' weakness *vis-à-vis* the tyrants, and as demands for a just order grew, so their despotism, their failures and their limitations were seen for what they were.

Thus the tension between the inequitable *status quo* and the potential for equality through solidarity with the citizenry had to come to a head. As such serious doubts were cast on the superiority of the nobles, the idea of equality was bound to develop. A series of duties, such as military service in the phalanx, had after all long been evenly divided between middle and upper classes.

The watchword was now isonomy, and it became a powerful motivating force. As communal existence was of such importance, it was here that men established their rank and value. There were few real opportunities for accumulating wealth, most areas of economic activity being deemed inferior. It was politics alone that provided the chance for many to rise above their station.

Admittedly this opportunity existed in the first instance only for those who had no need to earn their living, that is, dignitaries of the second rank. And they could only improve their situation collectively. For as individuals they remained subordinate to the nobles in terms of wealth, education, bearing, connections and experience. The aristocratic Council was also generally kept on, as in Athens, and the influence of the people's Assembly had to be tenaciously fought for. The most important weapons were the new boards of the Council, which regularly changed their members. Only through unity could the middle classes match the influence of the nobility. This was precisely the *raison d'être* of isonomy, the precondition for perceiving and upholding their claims on equality.

This solidarity was evidently present. Various motives had conspired to bring it about: the tenet of citizens' responsibility; the awareness that perhaps they could genuinely serve the city better than the nobles; the exhortation to political involvement; the conviction that there was no other answer to aristocratic despotism; the importance of public status; and finally the fact that it was now possible to participate in what had hitherto been the preserve of the nobility, namely, the realm of honour, freedom from want and the communal domain.

We might do well to set the singular development of the polis within a further perspective. It is characterized first by the severe upheaval of established order in Greece, such as happens at the beginning of any process of cultural development. Entirely new spheres of activity and thought were opened up; received norms became increasingly deficient and were finally called into question. This is what distinguishes Greece from Rome for example, where there was no such profound shock to tradition, but a sustained extension of the ruling class's domination. The citizens therefore deferred largely to the aristocracy, who essentially held sway over public life. Status could be asserted only within the framework of the given order, primarily in the military sphere, and otherwise rather in particular domains than in the ever-expanding whole of the republic. A strict social hierarchy was preserved.

Disruption of the process of cultural development did not, however, lead the Greeks to introduce the sort of hierarchical society that generally arises in such cases. First they took advantage of the greater scope for activity by initiating more poleis of the conventional kind: colonies, with predominantly agricultural citizenries. Greater differences in level of wealth did arise between citizens, but not the form of differentiation which was the rule in the great cultures that predated or lay outside Classical Greece, that is, the organization of the whole society around the monarchy at its centre. This would have meant the constitutional subordination of the masses, grounded in a fixed world-view. A further likely consequence would have been a manifold specialization and re-evaluation of status, not least in terms of the usefulness of individuals for a social body which was to operate like clockwork.

As this did not arise, the cohesion of citizens' organizations, the links forged by concrete and common allegiance to defined groups across class barriers, could never really be broken, in spite of great pressures. Nor were the small scale and independence of the poleis vulnerable. In other words the old and tried structures of communal life, the old yardsticks, were retained, and old institutions like the people's Assembly, efforts to establish autarchy for households, and much else, which would usually fall victim to cultural development, could survive in the case of the Greeks. And despite all the profound disturbances, the potential for equality between citizens was maintained by the fundamental and concrete fact of the sharing of rights and duties, even if the shares were not equal.

Greek societies found their specialists either among the ranks of non-citizens and slaves or, on the margins, so to speak, of the citizenry, that is, among individuals who were not so strictly governed by the political ideal. As neither monarchy nor aristocracy could really set its seal on Greek society while the conditions for equal political rights were upheld (in world-historical terms an exceptional fact), demands for forceful and regular political involvement could genuinely be grounded in the citizens' system of interests – providing, that is, that the economic situation allowed.

This ready potential could be reinforced by introducing suitable institutions. The way this happened is best evidenced by Cleisthenes' reforms, whereby a sort of grass-roots democracy developed in the small areas or demes, which generally encompassed several hundred men at most. At the same time the larger sections or phylai enabled middle-class citizens to become acquainted with each other and prove their solidarity through political co-operation. Through these developments and the Council of the Five Hundred, which represented the villages and small city areas proportionally, the citizen body could achieve a sense of self-awareness and give its will a presence in Athens. Citizens gained independence from the mediation of the nobility, which had hitherto been their only means of access to the polity and its institutions. In this way the indicators of political life as a whole were transformed.

Among the middle-class citizens at least, a quality became important, which had until then been registered more or less passively: they met, presented themselves and treated one another *as citizens*. And as they had to show solidarity in order to stand up for their rights, in the small, narrow, inescapable conditions of the polis there resulted that pressure for political involvement witnessed by Democritus and Pericles, without which the isonomic, not to mention the democratic, systems would have been unthinkable.

What occurred is best understood as the institution of the individual citizen's identity: allegiance to the polis became the first priority. Beyond the family unit this allegiance met with little competition and was consequently highly secure. Different sorts of motivation were united under this allegiance: to have citizen status was of such importance precisely because citizens had equal status, and conversely, because it was of such importance, this equality became a decisive factor. Because public service was deemed honourable, they were proud of it, and it was so honourable because it was principally here that they could gain respect. They became so involved in politics that it in its turn got them involved. In this way their identity as citizens became stronger and deeper through the active practice of politics.

It is symptomatic that the Greeks took up the call for equality before the call for freedom. In the minds of citizens from the middle and lower classes it was indeed a matter of achieving equality with the nobility. They had taken the measure of the nobles politically and demanded recognition in accordance with their own increased sense of responsibility for the city. This was the foundation, the essence of their solidarity. All else – the limitation of aristocratic despotism, independence from their lordships, a voice in politics – would come with equality. And because this was the crux, the citizens could not allow themselves to be represented by others in the political arena, except where this was absolutely unavoidable. Equality must also have determined the character of the citizen among the population in general, for with such a fixed and attainable ideal, it was a case of all aspiring to one thing: the model of citizenship.

Accordingly, not only were relations between different classes of citizen transformed, but there was a sea change in anthropological terms. A new identity was created.

Thus it was that the citizens became politically involved. It would be wrong to attribute to them a particularly keen interest in politics, which would be to judge by our own unpolitical standards. What those Greeks did was rather to attune themselves fundamentally to politics. They were concerned with taking part. They understood themselves to be parts of a city, which was their sum, not as in the workings of a clock, but as a composite of equal elements. They therefore viewed the world through political eyes. The opportunities for perceiving themselves as citizens were thus at a premium; new opportunities were created, old ones expanded. Besides the subdivisions of the citizenry, the people's Assembly and the Council, this meant the festivals; the Agora not merely as a place for meeting, but also as the original site for theatre. It is surely clear that politics, when it becomes the very stuff of life for a citizenry, is not limited to its commonplace definition. Rather it becomes the realm of the universal, of higher things, beside which all else pales into insignificance. What the Greeks denoted as politics (*tà politiká*) were literally the 'affairs of the citizen' (the corresponding adjective being derived from *polítēs*, the term for citizen). These were the public affairs of the citizens, what the French would call the '*espace civique*'.

As so much attention, ambition and jealous energy were concentrated upon this public space, it stood at the centre of life in the polis. This led to a significant split between the two spheres, domestic and political, in which the normal citizens moved. At home they were masters, but in public all were equal. At home they had various private interests, but in public they were principally citizens, and they had to be so, not only because of the ongoing need to present a united front to the nobility, but also because there was such a clear boundary between their public and home lives. For their existence as citizens sprang from a strong emphasis on common identity. This did not by any means exclude egoism, vested interest and contrasts of all kinds, but it did modify them.

A highly developed rationality held sway over public life in the polis. Even the order initiated by Cleisthenes' reforms was based on a fairly unconventional conception. It did not accord with the social class structure, since it was only in the political field that the citizens could counter the still prevalent superiority of the nobles.

However, isonomy was not only a highly rational structure; it also lacked the support of a world-view, let alone a basis in myth. It waṣ relatively defenceless. And the thinking that went with it was not developed in universities or in rationalized citizens' organizations, nor was it taught in schools; it had to come about in the course of many a discussion, in the marketplace and public squares and in the houses of citizens. This was the first time that such a rational way of thinking was experienced by broad sections of society in the political sphere.

So the isonomies represented a fairly bold enterprise. They may have been politically well-grounded, but they were also based both upon most unusual conditions in world-historical terms and upon exceptional effọrts, energies and achievements. Just to draw level with the superior nobles cannot have been easy for the citizens. However, the demarcation *vis-à-vis* women and non-citizens will have caused problems, for the superiority of the dignitaries of the second rank over everyone else was not as clear as that of the nobility. The truth is that, seen as a whole, the polis societies were oligarchies whose members were not oligarchs.

And it is a teasing but doubtless also most important problem to determine further the foundations of this order. What, for example, was the relationship between the rational language, which must have characterized public discourse, and the language learned and spoken in the home, or the ideas, the myths, with which the men had grown up, and which their wives were probably still passing on to their own children? Surely considerable discrepancies and tensions must have arisen, and these must have been particularly severe where public life was fundamentally determined by broader sections of society. And what is to be made of a political order which had no doubt largely developed side by side with the customary ideas and myths?

By reconstructing the rational aspect of this organization and its derivation, we all too easily run the risk of deluding ourselves about the irrational aspect and only getting half the story. What was the relationship between the public existence of these citizens and all that lay outside it? The aristocratic world had already strongly cultivated the spirit of gaiety and the rational, and now an artificial order was being created. Certain things – ideas, desires and aggressions – must have escaped their control. Could for instance the strict demarcation between the citizens and the rest have been sustained without profound tensions and psychological ramifications? And what was uppermost in the minds of these citizens: the security of their order, or the risks and dangers, perhaps even the chaos from which they had won it? If, as we shall see, tragedy was so careful to respect the demarcation between different domains, did this perhaps reflect the situation of the citizenry, which had to draw lines on every side?

At any rate, within the institutions of Cleisthenes' new constitution, numerous impulses and energies could be both liberated and focused, at once establishing an intense way of life for the citizens, and turning their attention outwards. Within a very short time the Attic citizenry underwent a thoroughgoing and lasting transformation. It became assured of itself and of its power, and able to put that power into effect.

Of course at first the Athenians encountered severe limitations. When the Persians first invaded Attica in 490, Athens could muster only 9000 hoplites, that is, citizens from the middle classes who were able to equip themselves. They were still shackled by the past. What a great step forward it was then when, by the year 480, the city was perfectly able not only to man its fleet with the entire citizenry, but also to evacuate everybody and to risk everything – in order to win it back if all went well. Thucydides has Themistocles, in Sparta shortly after 480, explain what had changed: he resists any suggestion of subordination and declares that the Athenians are second to none in their insights. If the Spartans should wish to send envoys in future, then they should do so in the knowledge that the Athenians were well able to recognize what was in their own and the general interest. There can be no doubt that this ability represented a new way of thinking, which no longer simply took its cue from convention.

Large-scale politics, radical democracy and accelerated change

The history of Athens after the Persian Wars is marked by extraordinary activity. The city's fleets would often set sail in successive years, taking a sixth, a fifth, even a quarter of the adult male citizens with them, in order to do battle with the Persians, renegade allies or others. And the army also had to be deployed from time to time in neighbouring states or overseas. Athens' activity was not limited to the Delian League, which took in most cities and islands in the Aegean, the Sea of Marmara and the Bosporus, but it also extended to the Black Sea, along the southwest and south coasts of Asia Minor as far as Cyprus and Egypt, to the Greek mainland, the realms of the Macedonians and Thracians and, at times, as far as Sicily.

Nothing remotely resembling such activity had ever been seen in Greece. Sparta's horizons were limited to the Aegean, and anyway its strategy was defensive. Cities like Miletus and Phocaea may have traded and colonized as far afield as the South of France and northern Spain, or Odessa and Egypt respectively, so that they must have been highly knowledgeable and far-sighted, but they only ever had to focus on individual points and lines of activity at any one time. Their influence was not extensive; they would not have thought on a grand political scale, but would have concerned themselves at most with securing certain monopolies, strategic points and routes. Neither had the Greeks ever experienced anything like suzerainty on the scale that soon developed through the Delian League. It was hardly credible that around 40,000 adult male citizens, aided by several thousand non-citizen conscripts, were able to maintain suzerainty over hundreds of cities for almost three-quarters of a century, even finally through the increasing trials of the great Peloponnesian War, not to mention the fact that they were able to hold Persian influence over the Aegean at bay for most of this war, and that they were also at war with Sparta and its allies around the middle of the century.

Athens obviously had from the start a huge advantage over all others in the guise of its fleet, which it was able to expand progressively. Its rule clearly afforded certain benefits to its 'allies', and it could rely on support from many of the cities, which frequently were democracies cultivated by the Athenians and depending on them for their survival. By the time the necessity of the League against the Persians was no longer so palpable, the Athenians had already developed such skill, such refined methods and at the same time such determination and daring, that they also enjoyed sufficient intellectual superiority over the others to surprise them again and again and set the rules for action.

The interior politics of the city underwent no less phenomenal changes. The fleet had from the first conscripted its oarsmen from among lower-class citizens. Each trireme had a crew of 170, which meant that any sizeable fleet was manned by over 10,000 oarsmen, and that over 20,000 had to be mobilized and trained for the Persian War. The city thus had the lowest class, the thetes, to thank for its success at sea. Their self-respect and their consequent wish for an active voice grew accordingly.

There was nothing in the laws to prevent this; the thetes were, to be sure, admitted to the people's Assembly. Yet, if they appeared at all, they can have had little effect at first; poverty and lack of status would have ensured this. Politicians probably therefore avoided addressing them specifically since there was little to be gained by courting their support. One argument could however secure political power for the thetes: their military achievements on behalf of the city. What they needed were vigorous advocates.

These emerged around the middle of the 460s in the shape of a group of politicians who then came to the fore. They wanted radical action against Sparta, but above all else to deprive the aristocratic Council of the Areopagus of its political rights, so that policy would be determined by the people's Assembly alone. In unleashing great agitation over this matter, they must also have mobilized the thetes.

The result was a profound revolution in political conditions. For the first time (as far as we know or can judge) a city disposed of the institution of aristocratic leadership. In future all important decisions were to be made in the people's Assembly and the Council of the Five Hundred whose members were annually replaced. After open disputation between the various politicians, policy was made by a majority of simple citizens, lacking education and experience, and liable to be borne away by any speaker, atmosphere or passion. This was the true beginning of democracy in Athens. And that meant that the question of who should hold ultimate power in the city was posed in real earnest for the first time. In place of the limited exchange of power between individuals, or between tyrant and aristocracy, came the most extreme imaginable alternative: should the people rule, or the city's traditional leaders? Isonomy had merely curbed the rule, or government, of the nobility; this government was now abolished. The centre of the political order, and everything which moved around it, was put at the disposal of the citizenry.

Athens, indeed all of Greece, must have experienced profound shock at that time. That a city, the most powerful and important of Greek cities at that, should actually pass into the hands of the people, must have been regarded as a freak or a temporary interruption of the proper state of affairs. How could it possibly succeed? And on top of this, how could it be squared with the will of the gods and the order of things?

The Athenians therefore met with great distrust. And they immediately set about implementing a foreign policy which must generally have been viewed as foolhardy: the conflict with Sparta, the assailing of central Greece and an expedition to Egypt supporting the uprising against the Persians which had started there. To render the city impregnable, the Long Walls were built, linking it to Piraeus. Old men and youths could look after its defence, as the fleet ruled the waves. Athens became free to undertake bold and extensive deeds. In the city itself, however, there were fears of conspiracy and civil war, and the initiator of the toppling of the Areopagus was assassinated.

Astonishingly enough, this democracy confounded all the prophecies of doom and held firm. Its policies were rash and there were severe setbacks, but it was certainly not as irrational as had been feared, though not everybody recognized this straight away. The internal order of the city was further extended. Allowances ensured that poorer citizens could also sit in the Council and take up office, and so partake in the 'honours'. This would have seemed rather perverse to many, but it worked. The *petit bourgeois* of Athens gained political experience, and while they may have relied on experts to provide technical know-how (as do modern politicians), they clearly were not lacking in political judgement.

In addition, the drawing of lots for places on the Council and for filling most offices ensured that these were largely in the gift of chance. As little power as possible was to be vested in institutions other than the people's Assembly. The number of public servants therefore rose sharply. Thousands of citizens were now regularly active not only in politics but also in the large jury courts, and of course at intervals in military service. The city, its thoughts and conversations, must have been full of this. Conversely, a number of prominent politicians assumed considerable authority through their collaboration with the Council and the people's Assembly, not the least among them the man responsible for the new order: Pericles, son of Xanthippus. For a long period he practically governed Athens. According to Thucydides, it was government by the people in name only; in fact, the top man could take charge on condition that this was not too obvious, and that it served the interests of the majority. Pericles kept a low profile, letting the citizenry believe that they were making the decisions. And so they were, under the repeated prompting of their great statesman.

The policies that Athens followed, or had to follow, in order to meet the crop of new situations, could not be formed by convenient and stable maxims. The Athenians therefore had to rely for the most part on novel perceptions and judgements, free of intellectual presuppositions. These policies which so determined the citizenry, the city and thus the Greek world introduced a plethora of problems and insights, doubts and possibilities.

It was in no sense merely a question of political tactics or strategy; such an enterprising, innovative and successful citizenry ensured these were frequently difficult enough in themselves. The Athenians often operated beyond rather than at the limits of their powers, lured on by their superiority and boldness and by the fact that their limitations were not easily felt. For the geostrategic space in which Athenian politics moved was at first more or less a power vacuum, since it had not as such existed before Athens mapped it out. Before then the lives of, and relations between, the Greeks and their neighbours had focused on disparate points. Now the space in which they operated formed an uncharted whole, as all power relations in its extensive framework had to be reassessed.

It is true that shortly after the middle of the century there was another swing in foreign affairs. Athens and Sparta agreed on a *status quo* between the two great alliances. But while the Spartan alliance had matured through many decades and served only to protect the mutual interests of Sparta and its allies and their respective systems, its young Athenian counterpart was conceived to engage with the Persians, but now was no longer at war with them. It perhaps made sense to its 'allies' in the Delian League that Athens should preserve its military might and police the seaways, but otherwise its dominance was purely in its own interest. While Sparta conferred with its allies before mounting joint military action, Athens alone determined military matters in its 'alliance'. While the Spartans and their allies were brought together only by necessity, Athens regularly claimed 'contributions' from its allies, increasingly as a type of tribute. And Sparta was passive, while Athens was always itching for activity. Sparta's alliance was self-contained, while the Delian League constantly sought recognition and espoused intervention. Its cohesion was secure, but not to be taken for granted, so that Athens was continually tempted not only to maintain it, but also to take every possible step to improve it. This state of affairs was therefore precarious, as witnessed among other things by the disaffiliation of various cities.

Thus the city led a very tense existence and derived from it an extraordinary dynamism. It made constant claims on its citizens. Thucydides has a Corinthian politician characterize the Athenians before the outbreak of the Peloponnesian War: incessant innovators they are swift both in planning and in the execution of policy; accustomed to taking risks which exceed their powers, and to flouting common sense by courting disaster; confident even in dangerous situations. When they overwhelm the enemy, they pursue them relentlessly, and when they are defeated, they retreat as little as possible. They are alone in equating hope with attainment in all their plans, and quick to act on every decision. Their notion of a holiday is to do what is necessary, and they think idleness a crueller fate than hard labour.

They give up their bodies to the service of the city, as if these meant nothing to them, but treat their minds as the key element, that is, the special, individual contribution, in their civic achievement. So what is generally spared as the most essential thing, they relinquish, while they stretch, each in his own way, the faculty with which nothing individual is ever achieved by most. This is what the Corinthian, at least, maintains, and it seems true that the Athenians regarded the achievement of an independent intelligence in civic affairs as their most essential quality – compared with other places, where people did only what they were used to doing. This is a measure of their commitment as citizens, but also of the release of phenomenal inner potential.

Pericles' funeral speech in Thucydides, his great hymn in praise of the city, even suggests that the Athenians fulfilled their many tasks 'with grace'. This evidently refers to an unparalleled effortlessness and lightness of touch. Even allowing for exaggeration and viewing the statement relatively, there most likely remains a grain of truth in it. Such lightness would be accounted for by the extremely propitious situation, which was rapidly opening up such rich possibilities for the city.

It was probably necessary that a city whose citizens devoted themselves so fully to citizenship should increase its demands on their services, cut back on domestic and consequently on traditional moral considerations, even entrench itself against them, and set up unconditional political interests as the ultimate benchmark.

However, Athens' activity, its new way of thinking things through, was not to be limited to foreign policy. It was bound to be turned inwards. Apart from reports of developments in the constitution, historical sources tell of one particular consequence: Pericles' policy of construction, which was responsible most notably for the extension to the Acropolis. The aim was not only to beautify the city, but surely also to make up for a deficiency. The *petit bourgeois* of Athens were necessarily less refined than the aristocrats, who could value the cultivation of grace so highly and whose peers still reigned over most of Greece. Now, by representing the citizenry in the form of the Panathenaic procession to the Parthenon, they were able to show that, even if they were no more 'graceful' than the others, they could certainly appear so in art.

The building policy was financed with surpluses from the League's treasury. Pericles was of the opinion that it was up to Athens how to dispose of this money, as long as it did not neglect its military responsibilities. A fine alliance this, collecting payments regardless of whether the money was all needed! And what self-glorification, as, having equipped the fleet sufficiently and set aside a large sum for emergencies, the city spent the rest on decking itself out! The argument that it was for all Greeks to restore the Athenian shrines destroyed by the Persians cut little ice, and even within the city voices were raised against the programme, with many believing that this was going too far. But Pericles won the day.

Shortly before this, in 451 BC, Pericles had brought in a law that ruled that only those of Athenian descent on both sides qualified as citizens of Attica. It was not aimed merely at the marital politics of the aristocracy, but more importantly at restricting numbers in general. It countered, in particular, marriages with children of the metics, the free non-citizens, thousands of whom lived in Attica, providing some of the oarsmen for the fleet in wartime and making important contributions to the economy and armament of the city. Citizenship was to be a special privilege. This accorded with the Greeks' intense efforts to mix only with fellow citizens, the basic wish for utmost homogeneity. Given the power of the Athenians, it was also an expression of their claim to general superiority.

Apart from internal and foreign affairs, the economic ascendency and intellectual life of fifth-century Athens were also unparalleled. Artisans, merchants and goods from all over the world came together as never before. Techniques and know-how could be compared and exchanged, leading to what must have been great progress. The best indication of this is that artisans and craftsmen gained the conviction that they were capable of using completely new methods, and this spurred them on to greater heights. At almost the same time, the arts experienced the same phenomenal freedom of expression as politics had. A 'tide of textbooks' (Albrecht Dihle) appeared. Rhetoric, music and various sciences thrived. The Sophists believed they had found totally new methods of education and also of pleading in the courts. All of this combined to form an extraordinary sense of capability, equivalent to the sense of progress in the eighteenth and nineteenth centuries. It did not indeed reckon with a broad development of all-embracing progress, but rather with the perfection of the different, specialized forms of dealing with problems. To what extent this new consciousness depended upon the individual and the level of his technical ability is best illustrated by one of its most vigorous manifestations: the orator who was able to make the weaker (or worse) side of an argument into the stronger. Admittedly it was at first unclear how much the individual's new ability would benefit society as a whole. The only common denominator in the new awareness of know-how and progress was the faith in the potential for decisive improvements in the conditions of human life and activity. I know of no third example of such a consciousness in world history.

New abilities developed all over Greece at this time. But they were particularly concentrated in Athens, so that the city was famed for its 'wealth of experience'. According to one contemporary observer, the 'change in all conditions' meant that 'thought was goaded on'. So conscious were the Athenians of their constant accumulation of new methods, that, according to Thucydides, Alcibiades could justify attacking Sicily by the fear that the city might otherwise stagnate with regard to knowledge and expertise of all kinds, whereas by doing so it could continue to accumulate 'constantly new experience'. This is telling evidence that Athens gauged its superiority not least in technical terms. In addition, the city's success was in itself a compelling argument for the potential of human capabilities; after all, few matters were more technical than marine warfare.

Of a piece with this consciousness of ability was the opinion that there was no such thing as chance, that all things were calculable. Pericles himself was more cautious; for him sufficient superiority meant licence to neglect chance. And in view of this superiority, he felt able to plan war on a massive scale. This was what came to be known as the Peloponnesian War: Attica was to be abandoned, and the entire population ensconced within the Long Walls. Rather than risk going into battle, they would simply look on as the Spartans ravaged the land. Meanwhile the Attic fleet was to assail the Peloponnese, cut off supply routes and make life so difficult that the Spartans would eventually capitulate. In order to conserve their energies, the Athenians would wherever possible avoid battle, and so forgo tangible success and victories. This plan represented an extraordinary intellectual achievement, but it also reckoned with the majority of Athenians being amen-able, or being made amenable, to the sort of rationality which was required for its implementation, for its demands were quite at odds with the psychology of war. When it came to the crunch, Pericles' strategy therefore met with great resistance in the people's Assembly and could not in the long run retain the support of politicians, who were too dependent upon the Assembly's acquiescence. The plan was too clever for its own good.

The discrepancy which emerged between the designs of the leading politician and the mental resources of most Assembly members was probably only the most striking example of the increasing distance between the Athenian demos and the intelligentsia of Athens and of Greece as a whole. This distance introduced many tensions, not least because the Athenian citizens encountered the enlightened, methodical new way of thinking everywhere: at the Assembly and in the courts, on the streets and on the exercise-ground, everywhere that they might be party to discussions. So much took place in public, that word got around of what was being said in the houses of the city. We find clear evidence of this above all in the comedies of Aristophanes, where the author's scoffing at the new expresses the mistrust, if not the fear, which the people felt. When, in the 430s, various enlightened friends of Pericles were tried and most of them condemned, the widespread scepticism which replaced the initial fascination with the new thinking must have made the prosecutor's job easier.

If the many transgressions in Athenian politics against received notions of justice perhaps caused few doubts, given the benefits they brought with them, the conclusion drawn by the Sophists was certainly disturbing, namely, that the question now was: what is justice anyway? And beyond this, people ought to ask themselves to what extent arbitrarily fixed laws were really binding. In the famous chorus from Sophocles' *Antigone*, the best summary of the great possibilities open to mankind are the words: 'Man the master, in genius past all measure, past all dreams, the skill within his grasp – he forges on, now to destruction, now again to greatness' (365); the alternatives to which these possibilities might lead stand side by side. On the one hand is the *hypsípolis*, the 'highly political' individual, he who is most devoted to the good of the city, characterized by his respect for the laws of the land and for the sacred justice of the gods. On the other hand the *ápolis*, the 'unpolitical', who is at odds with the polis, and is 'bad for the sake of audacity' (370), bringing the city into danger. The question which Eupolis poses in a comedy, 'Is nothing beyond the Athenians?', is open to two interpretations. But we do not know its context.

In his *Birds* of 414 BC, the time of the expedition to Sicily, Aristophanes brings on two Athenians who are fed up with the city. They want to be turned into birds. Hardly has this happened than they suggest to their fellow birds that they should found an empire. They can block the lines of communication between mortals and gods and should take advantage of this. Karl Reinhardt writes that the Athenians' spirit of uniquely audacious activity celebrates its most soaring triumphs in these heroes.

It is true that Thucydides criticizes the Athenians for always 'as it were being in search of something beyond our lives', 'slaves to the sensational' (Landmann translates this as 'the latest craze') 'and contemptuous of custom'. However, the longer this was so, and the longer it brought them such surprising success, the more uncertain they must have become, not only because their anxious expectations were refuted by continuing success, but also because they were prepared to carry on breaking new ground. Where was it to lead? And what was now to govern things? Expectations and requirements went sky-high; disappointments became inevitable. Precisely because planning was second nature, because hopes had become expectations, uncertainty was bound to breed insecurity. The ravages of the plague at the beginning of the Peloponnesian War were taken by many to be a sign from the gods; the trials of warfare and a series of defeats conspired to exacerbate internal doubts. The will to persevere, desperate evasions, above all the overturning of the political order in 411 and 404, wretchedness, failure and blindness to their own situation – at the end of the Peloponnesian War the whole edifice collapsed. Thereafter democracy had to start again, on a more modest scale, but with astounding stability. One of the first moves was the trial of Socrates.

Nietzsche's observation that Greek history ran at such an extraordinary pace is nowhere more strikingly witnessed than by the gulf between Aeschylus' *Oresteia* of 458 and Euripides' *Orestes*, which appeared exactly fifty years later. Following the upheaval in 461 through which the Areopagus lost its power, Aeschylus makes the connection between the terrible history of the house of Atreus and that of the polis, and indeed a part of the history of the dynasty of Zeus. Agamemnon, Clytemnestra, Electra and

Orestes are seen as bound up in the fate of their line. Nobody's situation is by chance, nobody acts at will, all do what they must, and the terrible history of revenge and counter-revenge which they suffer is curtailed by a trial, that is, by the triumph of the polis over all obstacles. And as the poet juxtaposes this triumph both with a great turning-point in divine politics and with the upheaval in Athens, the earthly history of the city is taken up into the grand scheme of things.

The *Orestes* of Euripides is by contrast no more than the story of an unfortunate individual after the event, quite another sort of play. The mythical mantle is far too broad for the hero. Neither he nor any other character has more in mind than his own modest existence, his advantage, his peace and quiet and his set ideas. No intrigue or dirty tricks are beneath them if such will serve the petty needs and interests which so concern them. Nobody takes up a cause, they could just as well act otherwise. They are all indifferent, random, just happen to be there at the time. Nobody can help it, nobody is quite ready to stand up for anything. Orestes shifts the blame for the matricide onto his grandfather, who conceived his mother, and onto Apollo, who ordered the murder. And when there seems to be no way out, the god comes out of the machine right on cue and shows that the whole play was nothing but absurd theatre – theatre, at that, which is often sustained by allusions to Aeschylus, having an ironic effect in isolation but amounting to a wholesale disavowal.

It is not clear to what extent the Athenians were aware of the transformation, though in a fragment by the comic playwright Plato we read that someone who is away from the city for three months cannot find his way round on his return. Plato is said to have been referring to the rapid changes in the law, but in any case the results of the transformation were in evidence everywhere.

The mental venture of politics

The Athenians' extraordinarily daring politics, the enormous successes, the radical upheaval, the new possibilities and experiences, the speed of change – all this must have had many consequences in the domain which Max Weber called nomological knowledge.

This is the general, overarching and normative knowledge to which we relate all our thinking, actions and experience, and in which these must all be incorporated if things are to seem 'right'. It is a sort of knowledge, even if it is not thoroughly conscious: through it we know, or at least we feel, what is true and what false, what is in order and what should give us grounds for concern or fear. It relates at once to how the world is (the world as a whole and the smaller worlds within which we move) and to how it ought to be. It has to do both with what we are in the world and with what is expected of us. It is partly received and partly achieved by conscious effort. It is far from being static, it can rather grow and change, but in order to give us a sense of security it must be reasonably resistant. It may embrace contradictions, tending not to be systematic or even consistent.

This knowledge serves to place experiences, thoughts and actions, to make them comply with, or at least to situate them in relation to, that which we feel to be normal and in some sense correct. Within its framework things and deeds make sense to us (if they deserve to). In it is rooted both our understanding and our judgement.

Nomological knowledge somehow brings together the most disparate things. It contains, in various degrees of development, a world-view, notions of God, the cosmos and nature, manifold ideas of regulation and chance, of what is acceptable or unacceptable, true or false, tried and tested or dubious. It can view different areas of existence, nature and civilization, politics, the economy, culture and private life, either separately or as composite. And the extent to which accepted practice and moral consciousness are mutually suffused within it also varies. The individual areas can never be absolutely discrete. In particular all political action and experience is susceptible to moral considerations. This knowledge belongs primarily to the individual, but there is also a collective nomological knowledge within society and its different parts. The knowledge of the individual and that of classes and groups, of society or indeed of the world to which they belong, cannot be conceived of as independent of one another.

It can be assumed that Athenians in the sixth and fifth centuries, at least those in the middle classes, will not have differed extremely from each other in their nomological knowledge. There was probably the legacy of a strong sense of community, and the citizens' identity which they then developed can only have reinforced this. Members of the middle classes in Athens required this community as the basis for the necessary solidarity *vis-à-vis* the nobles. In particular, the democracy which they eventually produced was founded more on intellectual prerequisites than institutional ones. Finally there was the people's Assembly which had almost unlimited freedom of action. Paul Veyne once characterized the difference between the Greek polis and modern states by comparing them to ships. The ship of state in modern times has a small crew and carries innumerable passengers. The 'polis-ship' of Classical times had, apart from the non-citizens, only sailors. It was thus all the more important that they should learn the right ways, and the value which Greek theorists laid on their education was accordingly high. And this in turn had its effect on their nomological knowledge.

The citizens of Classical times were not components of a society, fulfilling certain functions, with most responsibility being delegated to specialists. After the fall of the Areopagus, at the latest, there remained no institutions which could even lay claim to any special wisdom. Law and order could not be given over to a police force and a specialized judiciary; the complex totality of the state was not to be contained by the ingenious interplay of various bodies; the extraordinary technical resources, which enable modern societies to meet so many challenges, were lacking. The citizens of those times did not belong to a pluralistic society, whose members had centuries of practice in accepting that not all of the incalculable relations and processes of change could be understood. They had not experienced the sort of conflicts between religious and secular power which have required modern society to embrace many tensions and roles, balanced out in an extensive spiritual 'inner space', which in some sense corresponds to the complexity of the society at large.

In the era of isonomy and even more so with the advent of democracy, the Attic citizenry was responsible for itself to a quite unusual degree. Those belonging to the middle classes in particular had to show the nobles that they were capable of such responsibility; the authority of Pericles was not least founded on the fact that he recognized this capability and took it seriously. At some time or other the Athenians learnt that the city was nothing but the sum of its citizens. Isonomy and democracy must therefore be self-supporting. But how was this to work? What did it mean for the citizens, for the nomological knowledge which co-ordinated their thoughts and deeds?

One thing seems clear from the start: the questions which this knowledge posed for the citizens, the problems it caused for them, must have been intense and pressing. Their accession to a regular political voice and then to democracy was supported by a strong sense of justice and of responsibility. They had gradually developed along with the prehistory and history of isonomy; they enjoyed success, things went as they had hoped. And they were under some stress, for the new role was far from simple. Great mental energy was required of many. And their need for meaning must thus have been similarly great; there was hardly cause for the sort of resignation which generally leads people to neglect understanding and the relation to universal norms of what they do and what goes on. Where everything is so excitingly new, and a wide group is called upon to make judgements and indeed take decisions, the practices of old can no longer simply hold. In addition, the Athenians' participation in politics was a strange mixture of proximity and distance, involvement and detachment.

And the world as a whole was to a unique extent commensurable with the citizens of Greece. For what happened, or to be exact what was perceived to happen, was so to speak on a human scale. Politics came into being in front of the citizens, among them, at their very centre. The poleis were comprehensible, their foreign dealings were with a series of similar states. It was only at the margins of their world that other political configurations, such as the Persian empire, existed, and it eventually transpired that these too could be dealt with. Relations remained more or less constant. What really changed in Athens and in its influence was the work of the citizens (or of their fathers). Even the battles and naval ventures were the direct initiative of the citizenry. Admittedly the gods or chance might intervene; these were imponderables. But the citizens did not belong to a large-scale political unit such as a present-day nation; it was not a society of specialists and did not have to contend with our manifold processes of change, fuelled from all sides, beyond comprehension, and so difficult to influence.

In other words, there were none of the huge summations, or rather cumulations, of human activity, the processes and exigencies which today extend so far beyond the parameters of our thinking and actions. So, as soon as they had the city in their hands, they must surely have felt the challenge of applying great mental effort to understanding the world.

As our consideration of the isonomy posed questions about how the oppositions between the old and the new, purely rational discourse and myths, the rise of the middle classes and the concrete experience of a highly unequal social order, might be squared, so the time after the Persian Wars poses new, more far-reaching questions. However firmly politics was rooted for the Athenians in action, problems of a more general nature must have arisen continually. In the first instance there were problems about the criteria or yardsticks needed to guide their judgement; these must largely have been determined by the positions taken up in the political field and will have taken the shape of interests, viewpoints, beliefs as to how, for example, political rights should be distributed, or whether they should move with or against Sparta, follow aggressive or defensive policies. The authority of politicians must also have been a determining factor.

This was by no means all. There can have been little routine in this society faced with new situations at every turn. There was no long tradition of *raison d'état*, such as in modern times, or of dealing with sovereignty over others, such as in ancient Rome. What was built up by the Romans over many decades fell into the lap of the Athenians almost overnight: they became the leading power among hundreds of communities. The Romans learnt over a long period to cultivate alliances and to make conquered states beholden to them in various ways; they developed political maxims in tandem with military power and also procedures which lent a beneficial trimming to their rule and even mitigated it to some extent. The Athenians, however, had to establish the instruments and the positions of their power, and of the sovereignty over other states which followed fast upon it, with the utmost expediency. They hardly had to learn how to get used to the force 'without which one may not constrain others', in the words of Schiller's *Don Carlos* (2029). They were not inhibited by convention; they had to make decisions at will, governed only by the sort of pragmatic considerations that are reflected in the speeches of their politicians in Thucydides. However much the ruthless way of thinking which appears here is the work of the historian, the intellectual disposition will none the less have been fairly typical. For without self-evident premises or a gradual acquaintance with sovereignty, it was surely necessary to fall back on 'hard' rational arguments. All this was achieved through unusually open and widespread discussion.

However, over and above this, questions of a moral or religious nature must have arisen, the question for instance as to how the choice should be made between what was allowed, indeed required, by morality, and what was of benefit to the city or to sections of the citizenry. And the speed of change must have led to very different ways of thinking from generation to generation, with tensions arising between convention and the present. On occasion, the various points of view must have collided hard. The extent to which practical actions could depart from established rules and notions had to be clear. They were not used to change in the way that we are and had not learnt the many relativities which today so easily attach to our attitudes the fear that they – and we with them – may be 'outdated'.

Thus all sorts of moral inhibitions must continually have emerged. But there were also doubts and uncertainty, for what these citizens knew was always bound to lag behind what actually happened, what they experienced, did and had to do. Both inhibitions and doubts must have affected their decisions, and one wonders whether these were always simply laid to rest by the rulings of the people's Assembly. Individuals must often have been overpowered by the arguments of the leading politicians, and the enthusiastic mood of the Assembly will have carried them away on occasion, so that the doubts they might have entertained would rebound on them. The more profound the real effects of the dubious decision, the more acute must have been the self-doubts.

Behind the individual problems that arose lay the more general one of how moral imperatives are to be treated in politics as a whole. Sophocles, we may recall, defined the 'highly political' individual, who lives for the city, as one who respects the laws of the land and the divine right of the gods. Socrates was later to describe total allegiance to moral commandments as impossible in politics, which was his reason for avoiding political life. A particular variation on this question asked how freely a demand which solely served the profit of the city could be put to its own citizens and to other cities. It was raised for example in relation to the use of allied funds in Pericles' building projects. It also appears in the Sophoclean tragedies *Ajax* and *Antigone*, where it is a question of whether political enmities should be binding beyond death. How far could the city interfere in what had always been the private business of the citizens, or indeed in divine right? Socrates finally asked what justice was anyway. And even if this question was addressed only to a small circle, his doubts probably represented the most extreme point in what had become a comprehensive questioning of things which, in its turn, cannot have failed to disturb the general citizenry to some extent.

It was precisely the successes of the city that brought with them moral and religious problems. For example, could the astounding victory of the Greek David over the Persian Goliath be sufficiently explained in terms of tactics or strategy, Greek virtues or the favourable geographical conditions, or by following Herodotus and ascertaining the course of things by way of narrative? Did the victory not also have to be related to the gods, and what was known of them? Indeed, this relationship plays an important role for Herodotus, even if he made himself construct the whole process in an empirical fashion. Surely this event was great enough to encompass multiple views on the human part in it and on the gods' share in its causation. Its comprehension, its location in the world order of the Athenians (indeed of the Greeks in general) were problematic, and at the same time particularly necessary, because future policy could in turn depend upon it.

As to the extraordinary resources, daring and mastery of the city – however unfettered the pride with which the Athenians sang its praises, the awareness of this pride, or its expression, could not be free from anxiety. They were scarcely able to shake off without consequence the old wisdoms of the envy of the gods, of the blinding they could visit on men, of the fall that always follows on the rise of hubris. There was a residue of doubt, with which the Athenians somehow had to come to terms. How far did they dare to go?

Finally, what of the domestic political success of the middle classes, the toppling of the Areopagus? Even disregarding the fact that the aristocrats did not succumb immediately, that the initiator was murdered and conspiracies feared, the total exorcism of the institution of aristocratic leadership and the wilful creation of a new order was not to be realized so simply. And once realized, it had to be shown to be a secure base. The ancient ideas of the elevated and the lowly, of aristocratic superiority and of the weight of the old order, could not merely be cast off. The foundation on which they now stood at first must have been quite unstable, itself requiring foundation in the compass of traditional attitudes. Of course the rule of the nobles had already been shaken to the core in the sixth century, but having limited themselves in the meantime to playing the leading role in the city, they had superior standing, enjoyed success and could point to the aristocratic regimes throughout Greece.

It may not have been too difficult to support the motion for the abolition of the Areopagus, but peace of mind about this change at the very heart of their polity will have been another matter. As for the people, the farmers may have been able to boast a certain amount of political experience and their status as landowners, but it is unlikely that the thetes could have banished their feeling of inferiority by virtue of their incontrovertibly substantial services to the city. It seems impossible that there were really no doubts about the justification of the bold way in which they had proceeded.

All this opens up a vast complex of questions, and we should admit from the start that we thus far have precious few answers. It is certainly clear that since the founding of their isonomy, and in particular after the Persian Wars, the citizens of Athens found themselves in an extraordinary situation. There can be no question that their nomological knowledge was hard hit by this. But can we be more precise?

There is considerable evidence that in the first decades of isonomy and the early days of democracy the Athenians still thought in an archaic manner. Unlike the modern bourgeoisie they had no opportunity to develop their own disposition, their own ways of thinking, their own sense of discipline and morality, or indeed their own public awareness, before entering into politics. The area in which they constructed their order (on the basis of skilful designs) was relatively limited. Myths were still omnipresent, featuring not only in epic, in tragedy, in choral songs and on the temple friezes, but surely too in the tales they grew up with and in the images by means of which they got to know the world. For all their rationality, notions of a double causation, at once human and divine, must have held currency with the Athenians, as witnessed not only in tragedy but also in the historical works of Herodotus. Must not the belief in justice still have contained the old-fashioned association of wrong-doing with punishment? Can they have freed themselves so soon from the old idea of a guilt which is only punished in the third or fourth generation, the visitation of the fore-fathers' sins, the individual's bondage to congenital history? The only source which can cast light on this is tragedy. Ultimately, the question is whether its extraordinary burgeoning in the fifth century, regardless of the origins of the performances, corresponds to a similarly extraordinary burgeoning of problems among the Athenian citizenry. Did it represent, in a manner of speaking, the platform for an utterly unique form of institutionalized 'discussion' of the more profound problems of a population? These would not have been problems of partisanship and disagreement in particular situations, but problems which sprang from the crisis in the area of traditional ideas, ways of thinking, beliefs and the need for meaning in life.

Was the discrepancy between the old and the new perhaps so great, so clear and so compelling, that the hitherto self-evident was continually found open to question? Jean-Pierre Vernant has pointed out that tragedy did not reflect reality but rather problematized it. Perhaps myth was needed to lend foundation, confirmation and reinforcement to reality. When Plato remarks that the festival served to put people 'to rights' (or to right them), this might be directly related to the constantly changing work of renovation and development that was tragedy.

This would mean that the chaos from which any sense of order had to be won prevailed in the popular consciousness for a long time; that the questions which arose were not confined to politics and were not to be silenced; that the Attic citizenry therefore worked quite openly in response to the profound transformation of their nomological knowledge. Tragedy will thus have existed in order to play out the new within the framework of the old, to bring the two together, and so at once to keep alive the old doubts, the darker aspects of reality, and to introduce the old into the new world in new forms. In this way it would have catered for the evolution of the knowledge mankind uses for reference, in other words, for the mental venture of politics. It would have served to refresh, regenerate and further develop the ethical basis of politics, the 'store of meaning' which sustains the human need for under-standing, as long, that is, as this need is not worn away or overtaken by events (as it began to be during the Peloponnesian War – witness the tragedies of Euripides).

This would mean seeing tragedy as a buttress, a precondition for rational politics, above all in the time between the great wars. Tragedy would have prevented the Athenians from exhausting their energies in the political field and from adopting too isolated a view of politics, as detached from nature and myth, the other systems in which their notions of justice were rooted. Tragedy would have enabled the Athenians, in spite of all their successes and self-confidence, to perceive that the more certain humans are, the more mysterious human affairs become (Vernant).

So we must be open to the idea that the mental venture of politics involved a most singular task in this case. We must consider the possibility that the Athenians of the fifth century produced something so extraordinary, not because they were Greeks, not because they were encouraged by the spell of a set of humanistic (or 'Classical') ideals, but simply because they were human beings, albeit caught up in a fundamentally exceptional situation.

3

THE SIGNIFICANCE OF THE
FESTIVALS IN ATHENS

'Yet we have certainly also produced all sorts of recreation for the hard-working spirit (*gnómē*), by mounting competitions and sacrifices all the year round.' So runs part of the speech of praise to Athens which Pericles makes for the memorial to the fallen of 430 in Thucydides' account. The passage counters the criticism which Thucydides had made the Corinthian politician level at the Athenians when he had accused them of putting themselves through continual trials and dangers: 'what they have they least enjoy, because they are always occupied with getting more and their notion of a holiday is to do what is necessary.'

So the Athenians are supposed not to know truly what is the essence of the festival: the interruption of the daily grind, detachment from duty and requirements. By treating the workaday like a festival, they are seen to turn things on their head. While here, as elsewhere in the speech, there is something of the fascination which Athens inspired, the criticism remains unequivocal. Festivals which were really celebrated as such were clearly a most essential element of existence for the Greeks at that time. And indeed Jacob Burckhardt remarks upon the 'quite incalculable wealth and variety of festivals' in ancient Greece. When Richard Harder writes that 'the festival, which is so characteristic of Greek religion, makes of it a religion of joy,' he may only see one aspect, but it was an aspect which was indeed highly developed among the Greeks.

It is therefore only to be expected that Pericles should praise the city for its festivals too. He merely contradicts the Corinthian by pointing out that they have a particular abundance of festivals and that they really celebrate them. And there is much evidence that he is correct. As his Clouds look down on Athens, Aristophanes has their eyes caught above all by the 'lofty, beauteous temples' and the statues, and then by the processions, rites and dances in the city 'where no season lacks its share of festival and sacrifice; where they hold to Dionysus joyous feast at start of spring, hear the flute and hear the chorus in melodious contest sing' (*Clouds*, 306). Other sources, one from a slightly earlier date, the other from several decades later, claim that Athens had more festivals than any other Greek city. As Thucydides' Corinthian attests, they had evidently developed enormous political and military activity, putting so much into it that it might have seemed that they had substituted the means for the end, the working day for the holiday. But at the same time, and perhaps to the same extent, they increased the number of festivals – and celebrated them. They were pre-eminent in both fields. And the two things most likely went hand in hand.

We know almost nothing about the details of this. It seems probable that the Peisistratids multiplied and extended the communal festivals of the polis. The agon (contest) of the tragedies was certainly their innovation. After their fall a competition between citizens' choruses was instituted. The number and length of the tragedies would have been increased in the following years. In particular, Pericles is said to have 'conceived public plays, banquets, and processions', in all likelihood doing much to develop the 'festival culture' of Attica with, as Plutarch adds, 'not unaesthetic pleasures'. The funeral speech confirms this, for the competitions mentioned there were principally artistic agons, with the performance of poetry and song. We know that Pericles created at least one of these, the one in the Panathenaea. He also had the Odeum constructed around 440 for just such agons. The costs of the performances were met partly by the polis, but largely by wealthy citizens, each of them having responsibility for contributing to the funding of one of the festivals.

Of course there were tactical motives behind the setting up and development of the festivals. It was a case of winning the hearts of the people by feasting them on meat at the sacrifices and by entertaining them with the staging of processions and

performances, but also by making them feel that, given the importance of festivity in the polis culture, the festivals served to enhance
the splendour and bear witness to the greatness of Athens. There
can be no question but that the festival policy offered political
advantage to those who made the relevant bids to develop them.
In both domestic and foreign terms festivals were politically desirable. But there was more to the festivals than this. Pericles surely
meant more with his 'recreation for the spirit' than a demonstration
of culture as a supplement to 'bread and circuses'. And the festivals
must have had something to do with the gods to whom, without
exception, they were dedicated.

In this connection we might usefully recall a passage from
Plato's *Laws* (653d). Like Pericles, Plato speaks of how people need
'recreation after their hard work'. The gods had catered for this
by establishing 'exchange with the deities through festivals'. They
had given mortals 'the Muses with their leader Apollo and Dionysus as partners in festivity, who would put them back to rights'
(or 'right them'), and they had further granted them 'teachings'
which 'take place during the festivals in the presence of the gods'.
The context suggests that Plato saw the individual's initial education as being eroded by the daily grind, and so in need of revival.

If we are to believe Plato, then, the festivals were aimed at
regeneration not only of the body, but also of the mind, the faculty
in which, according to the Corinthian, the Athenians recognized
their essential contribution to the city. By stretching this faculty
so far, they must have laid themselves open to many questions,
confusions, impasses and strictures of meaning, and to the erosion
of moral convictions. Hence the necessity for 'teachings' in the
presence of the gods. One thinks first of tragedy because it was
here that the Athenians' nomological knowledge was refreshed,
sharpened, corrected and developed, because it was here a question
of the ethical and intellectual foundation of politics. According to
the theories of the time, and particularly those of Pericles' friend,
the theoretician Damon, music too was of great ethical significance.

Over and above all this, however, it may have been the general
qualities of the festival which offered recreation to the spirit. Given
the way things stood at that time, the festivals must to some extent
have given the community the chance to 'experience itself'. Richard
Harder spoke of 'collective gestures of taking pleasure in and

joyfully exalting communal identity'. Day-to-day differences, oppositions and conflicts receded for a time. The citizenry could primarily experience its sense of belonging. This took place both generally and within its subdivisions, among other things in the shape of the different competitions held between the phylai. Walter Burkert writes of the sacrifices: 'In the terror of blood-letting . . . tensions are relaxed, from being next to or against one another they are now together, under divine direction.' The rhythms of life and death are played out: 'In community, on one level, the people stand around the altar, experience death and bring it about, honour the immortal and, in the act of eating, affirm life in all its vicissitudes: the solidarity of mortals in the face of the eternal.' They experience their community within the exclusive 'club' of citizens. The communal festivity and the excitement of watching plays and processions will also have brought home the solidarity of the citizens.

The festivals also defused the tensions which will have arisen out of the inequality in incomes, as the richer citizens covered most of the expense. They offered to the lower and middle classes what the wealthy were able to enjoy more generally: a taste of communal leisure in the specialized form of the festival.

Festivals were a release, suspending the order and discipline of daily life and facilitating its continued functioning. They served as a safety valve, especially where they allowed, if not encouraged, the licence, the satirical songs and the hard-hitting criticism found in Attic comedy. The free rein of this public criticism, even when it came to the politics of the people's Assembly itself, is a constant source of surprise to modern commentators. Nor was it limited to comedy, where any aggression could ultimately be resolved by laughter, but it extended also to tragedy, where it was less pervasive but all the more important. This critical licence can hardly be accounted for by the fact that it was in some sense institutionalized in the detached and cultivated domain of the festivals, as happened for instance in the exchange of roles between master and slave in the Roman Saturnalia. Rather, it must have answered a real need. Attempts were indeed made to introduce new laws to curtail the freedom to criticize, but since these attempts failed, it is evidence that the people's Assembly of Athens valued that freedom.

One can probably not understand how the festivals served the cohesion of the Athenian citizenry, if one loses sight of the fact that there was no real state or apparatus of state at this time, so that such cohesion could not be taken for granted. From this there sprang a need for the confirmation of identity, and this must have been satisfied primarily by the festivals, in contact with the gods and under their patronage. However, this also involved the public airing of criticism and doubts, regardless of whether it served as a safety valve. It was after all the Greek way of dealing communally with communal questions. And there was no shortage of argument, indicating that they tended to give voice to any doubts. In addition, the excitement, the 'restrained intoxication', of the festival, will have drawn particular attention to its content. It is not without reason that early peoples repeatedly affirmed their order of things by means of festivals.

So the Greek festivals in the fifth century were anything but pleasurable entertainments or leisure activities. They did not offer idle relaxation by steering clear of politics. Politics were certainly not banished from them. But where they were present they appeared to the Greeks in an unfamiliar form, sometimes turned upside-down, sometimes dressed in mythical robes. By interpreting the festivals in this way, we privilege the passage from Plato (and indeed general postulations about the anthropological function of festivals) over the Pericles quotation from Thucydides. For Pericles was concerned above all with the various 'pleasures' which the Athenians had created for themselves. In other words, he views things from the perspective of the special achievements of the city of Athens. 'Modern', rational features are therefore rather over-emphasized in the speech. In fact it was more a matter of the general Greek principles of festive culture, which, it is true, were particularly highly developed in Athens. These principles will have been taken for granted by Pericles. They probably figured in the thoughts of those for whom he extended the festive culture as religious (and more generally anthropological) needs or at least as unconscious premises.

Admittedly, we still know far too little to be able to ascertain more precisely the significance of festivals for Athenian society. A whole series of further questions arises. Perhaps the relationship between daily life and festival within a society is of the same significance as that between war and peace, stability and change, or as the conditions of production; at any rate it is unclear for us, given that we have suspended this distinction and so many others. What is the significance of the sharp incisions into the course of the year, of the rhythm, the constant repetition of the same festivals, the strong concentration of expectations before each one and of the rapid alternation of stress and festivity? And here the Greeks are something of an exceptional case, in that they found new contents (the continual production of new tragedies, comedies and choral songs) for each new festival.

These festivals may have been part of the strong sense of presence which characterized the polis citizenries generally: in space, they were focused on the agora, and they saw time not as a *process* of evolution between past and future, but as the dimension of their present actions, a dimension in which they could feel coherent, homogeneous, free of the 'simultaneity of the non-simultaneous' (Bloch). In this way the citizenry's sense of presence also expressed itself through its individual members. One aspect of this presence was the great expense of the festivals, a type of ostentatious waste. This is very different from the often extreme concentration of our expectations on the future, or, alongside this and especially in times of disappointment, on the private sphere, with its partition of job and free time, work and 'holiday', the 'ideal leisure of an overworked century' (Nietzsche). How we abstract from the present, how we have dissolved it, and how caught up we are in the process of transformation! And in this process we are confronted with the reality of becoming different, while for the Greeks the stability of daily identity was continually supplemented by new opportunities for being different in the festivals.

To prevent misunderstandings: the Athenians were of course aware of the changes that they brought about and experienced, above all because of the constant crop of differences between before and after. Indeed the changes caused them special problems, and so became a concern of tragedy. As the *Oresteia* and the *Prometheia* illustrate, however, the tragedians sought for the most part as it were to encapsulate the problems and relegate them to the past, in order to preserve the *status quo*. Athenian perceptions thus gravitated towards the constancy of the world, and within this framework they could be taken up in the rhythm of the year, the recurrent alternation of the working day and the festival. So it seems at least to be clear that festivals were a very different matter for the Greeks than for us. Analogies with ethnological data would be most likely to yield a more exact picture.

To what extent the festivals sustained life is another question again. If it is true that daily life always relied upon the festivals, to what extent did it actually depend upon them for its very existence? If they gave the citizens the chance to experience their community, if certain festivals even served to underwrite their sense of identity, this does not necessarily mean that the tough oppositions and conflicts were not revived when the festivals were over, perhaps indeed overshadowing them from the start. And the ethical base which was renewed in certain festivals might easily soon have fallen into decay once more. On the other hand, we must ask what would have become of the Attic citizenry, its communal life and its politics, if they had had no festivals. Even a certain distance and clarity, a temporary assuaging or relativization of differences, could have a decisive effect.

One final aspect must be mentioned in conclusion. If the festival culture was so highly developed in Periclean Athens, then the notion of compensation might well have played its part. That is, the greater the success, the wealth and the power of the city, the greater the debt to the gods, to be paid in the form of sacrifices, of a share in the booty, and also of festivals. The takings had to be matched by gifts. And if this was not a religious impulse, the establishment of festivals to the gods presented the opportunity of balancing out the increased civic toil of the citizens with 'sacrifices and agons'. Both had the same purpose. And all of this led to a levelling of rich and poor, a strengthened role for the city and the fulfilling of its public role.

4

TRAGEDY AND THE
FESTIVAL OF DIONYSUS

In the second half of March the Athenians celebrated the Great
Dionysia, which was among the most important, interesting and
indeed modern in character of the long series of festivals. The
shipping season on the Aegean opened shortly before. At the
Dionysia, from the middle of the fifth century onwards, the cities
of the Delian League apparently had to bring their contributions
(which already took the form of tribute) to Athens. The city was
full of visitors, swelling the local population. And the Athenians
were clearly so confident of their superiority and glory that they
were willing to let others take part in a festival which was unique
to their city – one in which they sought to strike a balance between
their actions and experience on the one hand and their knowledge
of humankind, destiny and the world on the other.

Of course, bearing in mind the 'international' public, it is all
the more extraordinary that the contents of these spectacles were
so little concerned with celebrating Athens, but rather with posing
questions, with shedding light on problematic areas and with
voicing criticism. This, at least, is the evidence of the extant
tragedies. So, was this city capable of playing out before 'all of
Greece' all the problems which arose out of its actions and experience? Or was the 'general passion' for criticism (Karl Reinhardt)
not so much a capability as a need, even a necessity?

After the solemn bringing in of the old wooden image of the god
(which had previously been carried to a grove outside the city),
the festival of the Great Dionysia got under way with a splendid
procession, with each city under Athenian control contributing a

large wooden phallus. There followed sacrifices with quantities of meat and wine, and a further lively procession. There were choral competitions (ten men's and ten boys' choruses, each made up of fifty singers), and finally the performance of comedies, tragedies and satyr-plays. The festival lasted for several days. Perhaps as early as the fifth century various processes of law were suspended for the period. Prisoners were given temporary parole as long as they had somebody to stand bail for them.

It is not quite clear when the festival of Dionysus was first held. It seems probable that it dates back to the time of the tyrants, or, at least, was significantly developed by them. Very soon, if not right from the start, choral singing in the dithyrambic form proper to Dionysus must have accompanied the sacrificial rites of the god. The lively processions with music and pranks of all kinds (*kōmoi*) appear to have been added by the sons of Peisistratus. The first competition between tragedians took place in 534 or 533. The performances would initially merely have consisted of an exchange between an individual, often the dramatist himself, and the chorus. Thespis, the first to win the tragedy agon, is said to have been the first to make himself up in various ways and then to have introduced the use of masks. The competition probably lasted only one day at first, with each dramatist performing a single play.

The evidence suggests that different cities had a fundamental influence on the early development of tragedy, above all Corinth and its neighbour Sicyon. However, the roots and origins of the performances are obscure; the many sophisticated attempts to discover them at best offer hypotheses and exclude certain possibilities. But, whatever the importance of ancient origins, it is clear that a whole series of conscious acts and artefacts contributed to the history of tragedy. The introduction of human masks, in itself, served to distance tragedy radically from all the religious ritual of the time.

But all these questions may be set to one side in the political terms which concern us here. What interests us is less the early history or even the original sense of tragedy than its further development with regard to the requirements and challenges of the later period. It is a question of what was new, what, in the fifth century, set Attic tragedy apart from what had gone before. If certain of the changes during the late sixth century were Attic inventions, the form which tragedy adopted in the fifth century certainly was: an invention not in the sense of an individual act, but of a long series of innovations.

In the period from which the extant tragedies date, the following framework had been established (though we do not know when various details were introduced in the form in which we know them). Three days were set aside for the tragedies. On each of these days three plays by a certain dramatist were performed, followed by a satyr-play. On a fourth day comedies were put on, one by each comic playwright. The performances began early in the morning as they required daylight.

Dramatists wishing to take part in the competition had to deliver their texts to the archon beforehand, perhaps verbally. His was formally the highest office, but from 487 onwards the archons were drawn by lot from an ever wider circle of applicants. They were not necessarily politically powerful or allied to any particular party. It remains unclear how far their jurisdiction went, or even if they were able to favour certain writers because of their political tendency. We should rather assume that they and their advisers arrived at as objective a judgement as possible. At any rate, they had to be wary of public criticism. Nor is there any reason to imagine that the tragedians simply abandoned themselves to political opportunism, especially as the plays were written without knowledge of who would be archon (if we presume that little time elapsed between his selection and taking up of office). And the political scenario could be transformed overnight.

The fact that the archon had to select not one but three dramatists made things easier for him. The number of serious contenders may often barely have exceeded that of available days.

The fact that the Athenians – indeed the Greeks in general – also set store by competition between artistic achievements, that the best should strive in public view for a laurel given only on the strength of public performance, inevitably led to the drawing up of certain guidelines. On the other hand, certain writers achieved primacy in the course of time, notably Aeschylus and Sophocles, and, to a lesser degree, Euripides. Of recorded victories in the Dionysia, Aeschylus had thirteen, Sophocles eighteen and Euripides just four. They also enjoyed success on other occasions; after the middle of the century tragedies were also performed at the

Lenaea, another festival of Dionysus. While dramatists were, as a rule, only able to produce four plays every second year, Aeschylus took part in thirteen agons between his first and last victories (from 484 to 458), winning on each occasion. In any case he was the most successful and respected of the tragedians, even allowing for the fact that he first participated as early as 499.

It is worth remembering that the three pre-eminent tragedians had only thirty-five victories between them, in spite of the fact that from Aeschylus' first victory to the death of Sophocles seventy-seven or seventy-eight agons took place, and for the larger part of that time at least two of the three joined in competition. We know that Euripides submitted tragedies on twenty-two occasions and failed on eighteen of these. There must have been a large number of tragedies, over a thousand in the course of the fifth century (if there were nine per year from the beginning, this estimate is conservative). Aeschylus and Euripides are judged to have written about ninety plays each; Sophocles wrote about 113, including the satyr-plays.

The archon's decision consisted in his 'giving a chorus', as it was called, to each of the three writers. At the same time he nominated three wealthy men as 'choregoi' (literally, chorus-leaders). These were responsible for hiring members of the respective choruses, fitting them out and maintaining them for the duration of the rehearsals, and also for the pipers, indeed the whole production, including a place to rehearse. All this came out of their own pockets, but in a society where no taxes were imposed, it was taken for granted that wealthy citizens should sponsor public works. It brought them thanks and recognition, and doubtless political advantage as well. The city only regulated their selection. We do not know what considerations dictated its choice.

However, we do know that the archon nominated the choregoi shortly after taking up office, in July or August, so that they had about seven months in which to prepare the productions. This assumes, of course, that he also chose the dramatists at this early stage, in order to allot a choregos to them. But this does seem likely, especially as we know that the choregoi for the dithyramb choruses were determined only a month after the end of the Great Dionysia. So the rehearsal work evidently began very early.

Great trouble was taken in rehearsing the plays. In the fourth century the choregos was able to apply for members of his all-male troupe to be exempted from military service. They were not to be diverted in any way from the task in hand. This may well have been the case in the fifth century too. As a rule it was the writer himself who directed. Like the actors, he received a fee from the city for his services.

The tragedians were able to introduce their plays and the actors at a public meeting before the performances proper. If the rehearsals were more or less secret, these proagons must have been awaited with great suspense. It is a moot point whether the dramatists would have taken the opportunity of hinting at possible political references. For the actors it was the only chance to appear before the audience without masks. The site of the proagon was apparently Pericles' Odeum, which was erected to the east of the theatre area around 440. But the proagon may of course have been held elsewhere before this date. There is no record of how the order in which the dramatists should appear was determined; probably, lots were drawn.

The lots for places on the jury appear to have been drawn by the archon directly before the start of the performances, a list of candidates having been drawn up beforehand. The choregoi were evidently allowed to make proposals, and care would have been taken to get men with some specialist knowledge on the lists. The decisions were made by the Council of the Five Hundred, the most important government body after the Assembly. The lists probably took equal account of the ten phylai, the subsections of the citizenry. The names of individuals were inscribed on small tablets, which were sealed in urns to be deposited on the Acropolis under the supervision of the treasurer. So the lots were drawn at the very last minute. The jury consisted of ten members, one from each of the phylai. At the end of the performance they cast their votes. However, the whole vote was not considered, but just five tablets drawn, and the majority of these determined the victor.

It is worth noting first of all that the spectators were not given a vote (contrary to practice in the Greek cities of Sicily, for instance). And yet Athenian democracy had, since before the middle of the fifth century, worked according to the principle that any decision should be put to the broadest possible forum, and here was a case of many people coming together, albeit not only citizens. It was evidently the intention not to surrender the decision to popular whim, but rather to maintain certain standards of expertise. The result was not, however, untouched by the effects of audience reaction on the perception of the jurors. Plato and Aristophanes confirm what is surely self-evident. But at least a measure of independence was clearly to be maintained.

It is also striking how random was the selection of the adjudicators from the given circle of presumed experts, and hence also the ultimate decision. The arbitrary choice of the ten members of the jury may have been necessary in order to keep a rein on the sorts of political strife and nepotism inevitable in such circumstances. This was in line with the conventional procedure for filling many offices in Athens at that time; but why the ruling that only five votes should count? In an extreme case this could have meant a dramatist with only three votes prevailing over a rival with seven. This was clearly only countenanced in order to prevent bribery and to protect the jurors from accusations and blackmail. For, with this procedure, it would have been necessary to bribe not six but eight of the judges to have any certainty of success. In addition, the overall voting pattern was thus kept secret, preventing those in the know from working out how individuals had cast their vote. Care naturally had to be taken at the end to destroy the remaining five tablets unseen. How the decision was reached if two contenders each gained two of the five votes is uncertain. Perhaps again by lot. Or perhaps the votes not originally considered were then taken into account.

But, however we interpret the details, it remains unmistakable how important, how desirable and how fiercely fought over the prize was, and how much effort was devoted to bringing about as objective a decision as possible in the face of apparently insurmountable difficulties. There was doubtless also a period of experimentation. The prize was presented both to the playwright and to the choregos. From 449 onwards the best actor was also given an award, regardless of whether his were the winning plays.

From some point in the fifth century the performances were preceded by at least two political acts, over and above the ritual sacrifice of a piglet in order to purify the theatre. These are of great interest. The contributions of the League members were brought into the orchestra and sorted into talents (a talent being

6000 drachmas, a good twenty-six kilogrammes of silver). These were probably packed into earthenware jars. In addition, the orphans of war who had just come of age entered the theatre in solemn procession. They wore for the first time the armour which the city had given them, after having taken care of their upbringing. A herald announced that they, whose fathers had fallen as brave warriors in battle, would now be released from the care of the people. They were given seats of honour.

Why were these events held in the theatre? Isocrates, who comments on the matter, attributes it to the fact that, since the theatre was full, there was an unusually high number of Athenians gathered in one place. And of course there were not only Athenians, but also many visitors to the city, presumably including the emissaries who had just delivered the 'contributions' of the 'allies' – wealthy, influential citizens from hundreds of cities, which had themselves provided part of the funds for the spectacle.

So this was certainly a demonstration before an unusually large gathering, in a sense before all of Greece. A more overt, concrete and yet peaceful show of Athenian power is hard to imagine. One man after another enters with the talents, several hundred in all; the money can readily be counted, packed up as it is. It practically represents the spoils of sovereignty. Of course the contributions served to maintain the fleet, but this had long been an instrument of Athenian mastery. For a long time a part of the money had gone into the reserves which were stored on the Acropolis under the aegis of the goddess Athena. But since 447 Pericles had also secured the financing of the great programme of works, constructing the Propylaea and the Parthenon, which served as the treasury. The Parthenon moreover was a visible expression of the mastery – and the beauty, even the grace – of democratic Athens, as was, in a different way, tragedy. And the two clearly belonged together.

At the same time the generally large numbers of war orphans were testimony to the great sacrifices which the citizenry had made both for the freedom of the Greeks, their allies, and for the greatness of the city. For this too was to be demonstrated by a ceremony, which once more honoured the fallen, advertised the benevolence of the city and granted the orphans a form of reception, such as nobody else enjoyed, into the active ranks of the citizenry.

Both aspects – the power and the sacrifice – made Athenian mastery palpably present in the theatre, even before the drama began. What the allies will have made of this is another question. The Athenians clearly did not take this into consideration, neither did they tend to conceal what they openly dubbed their 'tyrannis'. In any case, all that we read of sovereignty and tyranny in the tragedies sounds quite different, when we bear in mind the prelude to the theatrical performances. It would have been difficult not to relate certain statements about tyrants and bold heroes to the city itself. This is the case even if the public display of the contributions was only introduced at the beginning of the Peloponnesian War, that is, long after the tyrant as tragic hero had taken his place on the Athenian stage.

It may well be that special honours were announced in the theatre and that the annual ratification of treaties with envoys also took place before the performances. According to the alliance of 421, the Spartans had to dispatch an envoy to the Dionysia (as did the Athenians to the Hyacinthia in Sparta).

After such a prelude, it is hard to see how politics can have simply disappeared from the stage, even if the tragedies did transport the spectators, who, typically decked out in wreaths and their best clothing, would have seen themselves as the congregation in a religious festival. Perhaps in honour of the divinity, they also brought wine and food. After all, the performances were lengthy.

As to the number of spectators, our sources only tell us that there were 'many'. The southern slope of the Acropolis, where the first theatre was probably constructed at the beginning of the fifth century, would have held between 14,000 and 17,000 spectators. This figure derives from studies of the auditorium, which must have been a less than perfect structure in the early days. But there is other evidence of the masses drawn to the theatre, the fact, for instance, that certain steps were taken to regulate admission; this job was given to an agent who would organize stewards. He may also have been responsible for setting up the auditorium, in particular the rows of seats. For this he was allowed to levy admission charges. And Pericles would hardly have drawn money from the exchequer to cover the admission charges for poorer citizens unless there was genuine interest in the productions.

Besides citizens and visitors, women may well have been present, perhaps in separate seating. The evidence on this matter is contradictory. Young people, or rather young men, were certainly admitted. Even if only half of those present were adult male citizens, this would mean a quarter of the entire citizenry in the case of a full house.

It is still a mystery to what extent the spectators could follow the plays. There were three fundamental problems. First, the acoustics: the theatre of Dionysus was not as well constructed as, for example, the structure at Epidaurus. Experts reckon with a maximum of thirty or forty metres for a modern, enclosed auditorium. On the other hand, we are not aware of complaints that large parts of the audience could not understand speech or song, such as might seem likely in the case of comedies for instance. Modern scholars have suggested various ways in which the acoustics might have been improved, but without concrete evidence. If the masks, which the actors invariably wore, were made to have a sort of megaphone effect, this would have limited the radius which the voice would reach. Only one thing is certain: that the actors evidently had voices with extraordinary carrying power, and were trained accordingly. This might explain the fact that each play had three actors at most, sharing the roles, so that relatively few would need such a strong voice.

Perhaps the seating was very tight, with the upper rows reserved for non-citizens and women. At any rate, there was more to the theatre than audible speech. The drama would have had sufficient visual appeal, with dance and body-language, which probably had to do service for facial expression. In this case the texts, which are all we have, would have been of no consequence for those sitting at any distance from the stage. Perhaps the dramatist would give at least a summary of the plot in the proagon. Other details will have been transmitted by word of mouth, but the plays can have been properly comprehensible for 10,000 spectators at most.

Exactly how much even these understood remains a matter of conjecture. They certainly knew the subjects; they were not saturated with information, and, as members of an essentially oral culture, schooled by assemblies, councils and so forth, they must have been quick to assimilate new ideas; much of what demands strenuous philological effort from us was second nature for them. If we consider how widely a culture which concentrates on just a few areas of expertise and education may be spread, then we can assume that tragedy was reasonably accessible to a large proportion of the Athenian citizenry. Also, the Athenians were reputed to be unusually discerning; attentive listening was one of their chief passions.

There remains a third problem: how much can really have been retained after enjoying nine tragedies (and three satyr-plays) in the space of three days? Must the wealth of impressions not have become confused? Did they really concentrate? Did they perhaps not attend on all three days? Or did they not only intoxicate themselves with wine but also with the plays? Was it above all just a spectacle for them? Did they leave the theatre with a sense of critical judgement or perhaps also with memories of passages which particularly engaged them? Or were they struck by some essential part of the content, by the meaning of the *Oresteia* for example? And what about the occasions when, instead of coherent trilogies, nine plays of diverse content were on offer?

In the face of such questions, we are made to realize how distant we are from these theatre festivals. We can probably assert that the theatrical culture of Attica would not have produced such great plays without a genuinely attentive audience, one whose attention span was longer than one day. This is confirmed by references to earlier plays, which would no doubt have been lost on some, but would also have stimulated the memory of many a spectator.

During the fifth century all plays were produced only once. Only in the fourth were there repeat performances, and, if Aristotle laments that in his time actors were more highly rated than dramatists, we can conclude that it was the plays themselves that were the focus of interest in the time of Aeschylus, Sophocles and Euripides. The level of production was extraordinary. They took especial pleasure in playing, in novelty, in the interpretation and recasting of mythical themes. But this was perhaps a balance, a necessary counterpoint to much of what the Athenians had to cope with in the everyday world, in political and, not least, in personal terms.

At the end of the Dionysus festival a popular assembly was held in the theatre, during which the agenda, the sacrifices, the procession and the agon were all open to discussion, including the activities of the archon, and any other eventualities. There was an opportunity to voice complaints. We first know of this assembly and its business in the fourth century. We can, however, assume that it was instituted in the fifth, for it corresponds to all that we know of Athenian democracy that everything possible should come under the scrutiny of the public eye. This is further proof that the citizenry took this festival very seriously and set great store by its proper conduct.

Above all though, this, as so many other aspects of the organization of the Dionysia, indicates an astounding idea, namely, that the citizenry of Athens was intent upon seeing tragedies of the highest order, and that those which we know are perhaps particularly outstanding but still in some sense typical of the overall standard. Strong public interest and multiple checks and balances generally lead to few risks being taken, with everybody sticking to the lowest common denominator, anxious to please and to maintain the *status quo*. But here the exact opposite is the case.

In Aristophanes we read at one point that the tragedies existed in order to teach the citizens – as adult education, so to speak. But, unless the notion of education is understood very liberally, it must be said that far more was involved: discussion, the playing through of important questions, the assimilation of new possibilities in world-view, ethics and religion and their transformation. This need not have been the reason for establishing tragedies from the very beginning, but these tasks became the lot of tragedy in the course of the citizenry's historical development, as extraordinary a period as world history has to offer.

Postscript The fact that a repeat performance of Phrynichus' *The Capture of Miletus* was expressly forbidden as early as the 490s (Herodotus 6,21,2) seems to me to suggest that after the performances in the Dionysus theatre, it was regular, or at least occasional, practice to transfer the plays to various local theatres in Attica. This would support the idea that a far greater number got to see the tragedies than the capacity of the theatre on the slopes of the Acropolis. Theatre productions and competitions are also recorded as early as the fifth century in Piraeus, Eleusis and a series of other communities in Attica.

5

AESCHYLUS

With the exception of *Prometheus*, the tragedies of Aeschylus show relatively close connections with politics. Indeed, even in the case of *Prometheus*, it is likely that, in an indirect way, the play is intensely bound up with the aftermath of a profound political shock in Athens and that it enacts one of the consequences of that shock.

There follows a discussion first of *The Persians* of 472; then, in brief, of *The Suppliants* (about 463); then of the three plays of the *Oresteia* (458); finally, of *Prometheus*, which was probably among the last of Aeschylus' works. *The Persians* is the only extant tragedy which deals with an event from political and military history. The five others belong to the period before and after the most significant internal political event of the fifth century, the toppling of the old aristocratic Council of the Areopagus. This accounts for the selection to be treated here. The seventh surviving Aeschylean play, *Seven Against Thebes*, is less interesting from this point of view.

In the case of *The Persians*, the most important historical connection is the Greek victory seven years earlier at Salamis. But it also touches thematically on the immediate reality of Athens in the 470s, for the Persian attack on Europe had been followed by various less significant Athenian incursions into Asia and the creation of an empire. The problems of rule and of the assault on another continent therefore had topical ramifications. Whether, and if so to what extent, Aeschylus' drama is also a response to the Themistocles conflict, which was reaching its climax at that point and culminated in Themistocles' exile shortly after the play's performance, is a matter of some contention. As it is at most a question of short passages in the text, we may leave the controversy to one side here.

The Persians

As far as we know, historical events were practically never the subject of Attic tragedy. However, in 494, shortly after the event, Phrynichus, one of the older tragedians, did bring to the stage the destruction of the mighty city of Miletus by the Persians. In 476 he went on to dramatize the collapse of the Persian campaign of 480, and Aeschylus followed this up with his *Persians* in 472. Apart from a play which cannot be dated concerning the Lydian King Gyges, these are the only three Greek tragedies with historical subjects. And it can be no coincidence that all three of them deal with particularly incisive and exciting events of the early decades of the fifth century. Only the battle of Marathon is missing from the sequence. But that Athenian defensive against a Persian expeditionary corps, however significant it may have been, caused nothing like the same problems for the Greeks to come to terms with. Nor did it qualify as material for tragedy, either seen as a Greek victory or as a Persian defeat. In this respect it was too insignificant for treatment.

The Capture of Miletus had been the only tragedy which had been able to depict the sad fate of a contemporary Greek city, one indeed with which the Athenians were allied. The play must have included long laments. Spectators broke down weeping. The dramatist was sentenced to a fine of 1000 drachmas for reminding people of 'their own suffering'. The play was banned from the stage as a deterrent example. And in any case, there was hardly another instance of a Greek city undergoing a fate suitable for tragic treatment: there was no other fall from such heights, no other cause for mourning or for the terrible experience of impotence. Those who suffered defeat at the hands of Athens were not deemed worthy of the honour. And anyway, if such fates were to be treated, there was no shortage of suitable mythical material, such as the fall of Troy.

The two Persian plays were at least distant from Athens in

space, just as the mythical plays were in time. Both are set in Susa, the capital of the enemy empire. Aeschylus' opening line quotes that of Phrynichus. It sounds at first as if he is paying a compliment, but the final word is transposed out of the past into the present tense. For Phrynichus the defeat at Salamis was a foregone conclusion; for Aeschylus it remained an open question, so that suspense was heightened. Aeschylus clearly set about his subject in a more fundamentally dramatic fashion than his predecessor. There is no indication of any connections with the other two Aeschylean tragedies which were performed at the same time.

The chorus is made up of old Persian noblemen, to whom Xerxes had entrusted the care of the royal seat and the empire when he marched to war. They are concerned about the size of the force which he is pitting against Greece. They are anxious for news and interpret the fear which comes over them as an ill omen.

The old men describe how the forces gathered from every corner of the empire, troops and ships, under the leadership of the impetuous young king: like a great wave which none can resist (90). But while for a moment victory seems certain, the image of the wave also introduces the thought that from earliest times the gods had determined that the Persians should fight on land. They may have learned to behold the high seas ('Confident, a million swords marched to war on hempen cords' (109)), but the chorus fears the wiles of the gods, which can so easily bedazzle men and lead them into misfortune. And so fear takes hold of them once more.

As so often when things became difficult, the elders wish to withdraw into the council chamber, following force of habit and not realizing that without information it is a wasted exercise. They act where action is senseless. Then the queen mother Atossa enters. Ever since the army set out, she has been haunted by bad dreams, but never has she had such a vivid vision as occurred the night before: two statuesque women of great beauty, the one in Persian, the other in Dorian garments – 'Sisters of one race' (185). The one had been given Greece, the other the land of the barbarians, as their respective homelands. They enter into conflict; Xerxes pacifies them, fixing a yoke onto their shoulders and harnessing them to his chariot. The one accepts her lot with pride, while the other rises up, tearing the harness and breaking the yoke in two, so that Xerxes falls.

When she arose from her bed, Atossa continues, in order to make a sacrifice to the guardian daemons, she saw an eagle flying towards the altar of Apollo, but, strangely, with a falcon in pursuit. The eagle simply allowed the falcon to tear its head to pieces. This, she adds in conclusion, was as terrible for her to behold as it is for them to hear. But she then recalls her position and her duty. She has already said too much and now brusquely declares: 'be assured of this – if my son conquers, he will be all men's wonder; but, if he should fail, no 'State' can hold him answerable. Winner or loser, while he lives he is Persia's king' (211).

The chorus advises the queen mother to pray and make sacrifices. But before doing so, she has one more question to ask: 'Where, by men's report, is Athens built?' (231). When she learns that it is far to the west, where the sun goes down, she asks whether her son has designs on the city. The answer is that with it he would gain all of Greece, and she is told of the might of Athens, of its victory at Marathon, of its silver mines in Laurium and of its citizens, who are slaves to no man.

At this moment (249ff) the messenger arrives bringing news of the defeat. He first laments the infinite suffering and the legions of the fallen; there is mention of Salamis and of Athens. When Atossa intervenes in the dialogue between the messenger and the chorus, she learns that Xerxes has survived, but there follows a long list of the names of commanders who have been slain. Their corpses swam in the sea and were smashed against the rocks; the description leaves little to the imagination. But how, she asks, did this come about? The Greeks were vastly inferior in number. It must have been a daemon that allowed them to prevail; the odds must have been loaded: 'It is the gods who keep Athene's city safe' (347). Atossa asks (as if she already knew different) whether Athens has been left intact. The messenger's response is to the point: 'While she has men, a city's bulwarks stand unmoved.' Finally there is a depiction of the course of battle, taking up over one hundred lines. The messenger once more evokes the daemon, the evil spirit, mentioned at the beginning, and wastes no time in giving material evidence: 'A Hellene from the Athenian army' (355) came to Xerxes, and there followed the cunning ploy by which Themistocles – who is not named – led the king to start the battle at a place so unfavourable for him. Then follow the

Persian preparations, the approach, the sight of the Greeks and finally the battle itself. The Persian ships come in too close, can no longer manoeuvre, bring disaster upon themselves. The Greeks encircle them and wreak havoc. They suffer such losses as never before in one day.

Yet all this is only the half of it, the messenger continues, and he goes on to describe an episode, which is all the more terrible, because it befell the most noble of the Persians. For Xerxes had ordered them to occupy a small island at the mouth of the straits, and now they find themselves surrounded, encircled once more, the first to be assailed with stones and arrows, quite unconventional weapons, before being annihilated in one fell swoop. The image is comparable with that of the ineluctable ocean wave which the chorus had used at the start to characterize the Persian assault on Greece. Now though, it is the Greeks who defy all resistance. The king can only tear his robes, pass on commands to the army, which is for the most part left stranded in Greece, and finally take flight. Even as he flees, however, he suffers further severe losses, as nature joins the conspiracy against him. Atossa and the chorus bemoan the evil daemon. The celebrated name of Athens, the city which has taken such bitter revenge on Xerxes, is heard once more. The Persian losses at Marathon had evidently not been sufficient (475).

While Atossa wants finally to turn to prayer and sacrifice, in order that the future might hold no more misfortunes of this sort, the chorus sings of the suffering which is the lot of the widowed women of Persia. They have been in the thoughts of the chorus, and shall often be so again; they also mention the parents, but not the children, of the dead. Then the old men openly turn upon the guilty party: 'Hear this accusing groan that rises now from every Asian land laid bare of men: Who led them forth, but Xerxes? Who sealed their death, but Xerxes? Whose error sent our all to sail in ships, and lost it all, but Xerxes'?' (548). His father Darius had only ever fought on land and had never been defeated. Xerxes on the other hand . . . , and so the lament recommences, now taking up the fate of the ships which were captured or destroyed. And finally there are the consequences: the nations of Asia will no longer look to Persia for leadership; people will no longer suffer bondage, but will speak their minds freely, now that the yoke of power has been broken. The chorus itself has set the process in motion.

When the queen mother returns, on foot this time and stripped of her jewels, she explains that when the floods of catastrophe break in upon mankind, any small thing provokes fear. Just so, when the floods of fate are at bay, we think the wind will always hold fair. She intends to make an offering at the grave of Darius. The chorus sets about invoking the spirit of the deceased king. When he indeed appears, and the old men are transfixed with terror, Atossa tells him of the crushing defeat. His first reaction is to ask whether Xerxes undertook this foolhardy venture by sea or by land. He learns of the bridge of vessels which his son had constructed over the Hellespont, and is of the opinion that some great daemon must have robbed Xerxes of his senses. Finally, he attempts to square the events with his knowledge of things. In his initial horror, the worst possible thing occurs to him: he recalls an ancient prophecy that had evidently spoken of the end of the Persian empire. Apparently it was being fulfilled far earlier than Darius had ever imagined. This was thanks to Xerxes, who had accelerated the natural course of things through his youthful arrogance! The fundamental error was the bridging of the Hellespont, the attempt to stem the 'holy stream' and make a slave of the sea: 'He in his mortal folly thought to overpower immortal gods, even Poseidon!' (745).

After Atossa objects that it was Xerxes' advisers who had given him the idea that he should further increase the legacy of his father, the ghost of Darius once more relates events to the overall course of Persian history. He recounts the series of kings, who had fulfilled the will of Zeus by submitting Asia to the sovereignty of a single man, and who had maintained that sovereignty, until 'Xerxes, my son' who 'is young, and has a young man's mind' (782) threw his father's caution to the winds.

The chorus asks how 'after this reverse, shall we and Persia now take action for the best?' (788). To this he answers: 'By taking none. Even if your force be twice as great, never set arms in motion against Hellene soil. You cannot win; the land itself fights on their side' (790), because its soil is too meagre to support a great army. The chorus retorts that a select, well-equipped force might be despatched, but they are told that even the army which Xerxes has left behind will not return from Europe unscathed. The spirit of Darius refers to the words of the gods which would thereby come to pass, for the Persians would have to atone for the hubris of sparing neither temples nor shrines in Greece. He foresees the battle of Plataea, which will seal the process in the next year (479 BC). Burial mounds would remind subsequent generations that mortals should never set their sights too high. For this can only lead to folly and punishment. The old men should take this to heart, and ponder upon Athens and Greece: 'let no man, scorning the fortune that he has, in greed for more pour out his wealth in utter waste' (822). The elders should impress upon Xerxes the need for reason and for respecting the will of Zeus. This being so, the empire might yet be preserved. Darius' initial doubts have given way to sober counsel. It is a matter of limiting the damage and ensuring survival. But Atossa should meet the king bearing new robes for him. He must now show outward signs of his debasement, if the continuation of his rule is to be assured.

The spirit of Darius withdraws. The chorus sings the praises of the halcyon days of the reign of the godlike old king, when the army was glorious and laws and customs were respected. They claim that Darius never crossed over the Halys (the river marking the border) with the long-conquered territory of Lydia). This is surely a veiled, ironic reference to the Delphic oracle of 550, which had pronounced that he who crossed the Halys would destroy a great empire. The Lydian King Croesus had received the oracle and thereupon declared war on Persia, duly losing his empire in the process. The implication is that Darius did not fall prey to such foolish hopes. In fact, however, he had indeed crossed the Halys, but the chorus is speaking of other enterprises here, which he had delegated to his minor generals. His armies, they claim, had always returned unscathed; there is no mention of the different fate of those led by these generals. The chorus only has eyes for success: the generals conquered cities all around the Hellespont and in Thrace, and they took possession first of a series of Greek islands from the northern Aegean to Cyprus, and then of all Ionia. There is no mention of the fact that a good part of these victories only served to reclaim territory which had been lost in the Ionian rebellion.

Finally, Xerxes returns. He laments his destiny and the antagonistic daemon. The chorus joins in the lament, listing the ranks of heroes whose fates must be divulged. Xerxes can only answer that all are lost, that he has filled 'Hell's hungry jaws with Persian dead' (923). An immensely mournful long lamentation is intoned. The Persians are defeated, defeated. This is repeated in dialogue. Of the huge army with which he had set out, the king can show them only one empty quiver. The chorus interrupts, wanting to know what it is. A container (literally a 'treasury' (1021)) for arrows, the king explains. Not a symbol of sovereignty then, but a mere, vain object. After all the losses, it is devoid of value. We sense, as Darius had said, that the Persian king is being taken to task, not only by Zeus, but by his own subjects. The lament once more touches upon the Persian flight from Salamis, and the courage of the Greeks is praised. In the last lines the triremes are recalled, for it is they that played such a decisive part in the Athenian victory.

So the phenomenal, the improbable, Greek victory over the Persians, which will still have been barely comprehensible to many, here confronts the Athenians in the theatre in the shape of a devastating defeat, through the perspective of the enemy: as premonition; as a picture of expectation, of battle and finally of flight; as lament; and as interpretation. Only from the Persian point of view could all of this be represented as tragedy.

The scale of the events could not have been more impressively realized. Aeschylus hardly pulls his punches: the great legions of the fallen, all of Asia crying out in agony at the losses; the mastery over the whole continent, which one king after another had built up according to the will of Zeus, now put at risk. The premonitions are gloomy, the anxieties infectious and the laments moving; invoked again and again is the sad fate of the women left behind. The audience is made to feel a strange interplay of identification with, or at least sympathy for, those who are so terribly steeped in suffering before their eyes, and of enmity for those who had waged war against them, and had barely been repelled.

The messenger repeats the chorus of cries which could be heard before the battle of Salamis: 'Forward, you sons of Hellas! Set your country free! Set free your sons, your wives, tombs of your ancestors, and temples of your gods! All is at stake: now fight!' (402). But while horror and the memory of triumph were awoken in the Athenians, they were also confronted with the messenger's resounding account of the Greek forces bearing down on the Persians from all sides in the straits of Salamis, just as before in the case of the little island (this may not have been quite what happened, but we can imagine that the Persians experienced it much like this). It is difficult to assess how the spectators must have felt, as all of this passed before them, but seen from the other side.

The glory of Athens is powerfully underlined: it is the only city in the alliance which is mentioned by name, several times at that, and not simply in order to locate the action. Its liberty is praised, as is the support which Athena gives to her city. The memory of how they had given up their city for lost, and how the men still protected them even from afar, so that it was won back, will doubtless have met with appreciation. And with what pride must the Athenians have listened to the long catalogue of Greek cities which had been conquered by Darius only to be liberated by Athens!

However, it is not Athens, but the fate of Persia, which assumes centre stage in this play. Aeschylus shows respect for the enemy of 480/79. The Persians' concern for their own empire, for their honour and glory, is taken quite seriously. Both the queen and the chorus are depicted in a sympathetic light; Darius appears as just and thoughtful, worthy of Zeus' favour. He is able to say that Zeus was not angered when his predecessor, Cyrus, took Ionia by force, for his intentions were good. Atossa's dream, we recall, figures Greece and the land of the barbarians as sisters from the same stock.

Aeschylus is clearly distinguishing between East and West. The barbarian woman is proud to bear the yoke of the king. Faced with the ghost of Darius, the chorus is seized by 'remembered fear' (703). Free speech would threaten the empire; the strikingly abrupt assertion that Xerxes has nothing to account for, indicates a clear difference from Athens and other Greek cities. The kings are characterized as 'godlike' with significant frequency. The grandeur of the empire, the sovereignty over all Asia, is everywhere in evidence. Various strange expressions, the preoccupation with ornament, a symbol of rule such as the quiver which Xerxes tenders at the end, and of course the costumes, the whole appearance of the characters: all of this was calculated to represent the foreign nature of the Persians.

And yet, the action is on the whole portrayed in such a general way, that it appears to have more to do with the character of human destiny in general than with the Persians in particular. Not only is much of the play taken up with defeat, suffering, mourning and lamentation, but all of this might so easily come about in a Greek city. And curiously enough, among general thoughts of the empire, Susa repeatedly comes to the fore, as if it is specifically a matter of the experience of defeat within a city, the sort of experience, that is, that might occur anywhere in Greece. The elders' transformation from councillors and guardians of the state, as they abandon themselves to grief and ultimately become aggressive critics of their king, must have made considerable impact. The queen too provokes genuine sympathy. And how impressive is the candour of Xerxes' self-condemnation at the end, how effective the whole ignominy of defeat, all the more so because there is no time to present the king with new robes before his arrival, as Darius had counselled! These Persians were more or less as close to the Athenians as the heroes of mythology who usually graced their stage. It is hard to imagine that, apart from isolated instances, there was any real opportunity here for *Schadenfreude* on the part of the victorious Athenians.

But the Persians also exemplify the general human lot by virtue of the contrasting portrayal of Darius and Xerxes. Darius may be represented as King of Persia, but there is no trace of the tyrant about him: his rule is fair and considered; he has the character of a good father who is concerned for his heritage, the wealth that he has taken so much trouble to acquire. This means that Persia is not simply to be identified with Xerxes. The Greeks may well have believed that Xerxes could only have made so many mistakes because he did not have to take account of his people (though the Athenian Assembly had been known to act rashly on such occasions as their decision to take part in the Ionian revolt). But Atossa's account of Xerxes' irresponsibility is directed not at the system, but rather at the king's personal foibles. The play is thus in a sense the tragedy of the royal house, into which the kingdom is drawn. The role of tragic hero is, so to speak, divided between Darius and Xerxes, thanks to the ingenious idea of summoning up the spirit of the dead king. Xerxes does not have sufficient stature by himself; instead he appears in counterpoint to his father. Aeschylus represents him as younger than his forty years. He is ill-advised, impetuous and immature.

Darius can only explain his son's transgressions as the work of some daemon who had robbed him of his senses. He was sick in mind. How else could he have arrived at the suicidal notion of trying to conquer Greece by sea, and above all, as we are told again and again, of bridging the Hellespont? The daemon is repeatedly invoked in the play. Without it, the defeat of the massively superior Persian forces defies all understanding. The daemon is held responsible for distributing luck, which plays a part in all battles, in such grossly unfair proportions. We may well ask why this should be so. Darius believes that the source of all this evil is Xerxes' lack of insight and his youthful recklessness. This is evidently the case. But the comment follows on the assertion that 'heaven takes part, for good or ill, with man's own zeal' (742). So was it simply an unforgivable error on the part of the king, a case of scandalous hubris (symbolized here by the attempt to bridge the Hellespont) – or was the daemon involved from the start, in the decision to go to war? No answer is forthcoming from Aeschylus. And it would probably be too modern an inference that the daemon simply served as a convenience, to attribute the extraordinary and inexplicable events of the action to a supernatural cause beyond human comprehension.

For there was probably a powerful desire for understanding at work here, which would not make do, as we might, with a mundane explanation. Things could not simply be explained away by the limitations of a Persian king, the cunning of Themistocles, the courage and skill of the Greeks; rather, the working of a divine will was detected. Things were not fully accounted for by earthly forces, even if this dimension was relatively easy to grasp. Aeschylus makes this clear by citing a whole series of factors which doubtless conspired in events, but he juxtaposes these with divine causes. The guile of Themistocles is counteracted by the daemon, and the way that Xerxes is duped is counteracted by the envy of the gods. This does not entail the negation of responsibility; neither human merit nor human guilt is denied. But there is more to events here than simply their mundane aspect.

The focusing of earthly responsibility for the misfortune on the figure of Xerxes is emphasized by the fact that Aeschylus all but ignores the prehistory of the war. There is no mention of the Athenians having started hostilities in the first place by supporting the Ionian uprising of 500. The Persian expeditionary force which was defeated at Marathon was a response to this affront. And during that revolt, the Greeks had desecrated Sardis, so that in this respect too the Persians were merely exacting revenge in kind. Or should the destruction of Miletus have satisfied their desire for vengeance? Aeschylus was well aware of this prehistory. These were after all the most momentous 'world' events from his mid-twenties onwards.

Then there is a second major departure from historical truth: the telling of Darius' story. For not only did he indeed cross the Halys, but he also entered Europe, and did so by means of a bridgehead, which he had constructed for the purpose, not over the Hellespont, but the narrower Bosporus. And he had twice ordered attacks on Greece, both of which were broken off with severe casualties. We are expressly told, towards the beginning of the play, that his 'vast and noble army' (244) was destroyed.

By making these changes Aeschylus concentrates all the human guilt on Xerxes. The Persian empire is thus set apart from its monarch, and so removed from the theological equation of transgression and punishment which generally holds for Aeschylean tragedies. According to Greek belief and the initial fears of Darius, such hubris on the king's part might well have brought about the fall of the empire. But this would have gone against historical fact. Furthermore, Aeschylus shows that the disaster of war and its consequences, including the antagonism of the elders, was punishment enough for Xerxes. This implies that the customary chain of revenge and counter-revenge has been broken. For it had always been the case in Aeschylean tragedies, as in the myths upon which these were based, that every punishment for injustice gave rise to fresh injustice, as, for example, when Agamemnon punishes Troy for its violation of the laws of hospitality by new violations of his own. Here, though, the Greeks have twice repelled punitive attacks by the Persians, whose revenge has evidently failed. Perhaps it was historical reality which suggested that the conventional chain reaction could not operate here. In this case, any mention of the prehistory would only have caused confusion; we must ask whether Aeschylus was moved by patriotic considerations, or simply wished to preserve the consistency of his theory.

But by abstracting Xerxes' failing from the broader historical context, and rounding the action off with his punishment, Aeschylus was also extending the model of justice upheld by the isonomic polis into the arena of world events. We know from Solon that the polis could and should guarantee a life of regulated justice within its bounds, where crime was avoided altogether – or at least dealt with summarily where it arose. Thus the prolonged chain of reciprocal acts of punishment and revenge was broken. This chain, and with it the ongoing rise and fall of various regimes and dynasties, was in evidence in the Eastern world, and also to some extent among Greek tyrants; and it dominated myths too, as we see in the case of Agamemnon in Aeschylus. According to this principle, Xerxes' hubris would have had to have been a turning-point in Persian history. But here too it transpires that the transgression may be cleanly dealt with. With regard to an act which represents a single offence against the world-order and, in that it ends in catastrophe, reaffirms that order, the playwright sees the Graeco-Persian war as a parallel to the machinery of justice in the polis.

The most significant frontier within this order was the one which nature – and the gods – had drawn between Europe and Asia. But by constructing the bridge over the Hellespont, Xerxes sought to score a victory over the gods, and over Poseidon in particular (750). The tragedy reverts to this act again and again. The spirit of Darius dwells upon it. By means of this bridge, Xerxes was attempting to force both the two lands and the sea under his yoke (72, 722, 736, 745). The yoke runs through the play like a leitmotiv. The yoke of power ensures sovereignty over Asia (594). Xerxes wishes to subject Greece to a yoke (50), and it is a yoke that he seeks to impose on the two women in Atossa's dream (191, 196). The bonds of marriage are also dubbed a yoke (542), and it is this, the only natural example among them, that he destroys many times over by leading thousands of men to their deaths. His claims to mastery repeatedly collapse into absurdity.

It is, however, worth noting that the criticism is levelled not at the fact of the crossing, but at the bridging of the Hellespont. It is not so much Europe as Greece which is to stay free from Persian rule. That is why the second virgin had stood not for Asia, but for the land of the barbarians. Thus, the good and judicious King Darius could make conquests in Europe (in Thrace to be precise), and, conversely, the Ionians in Asia had freed themselves from the Persians with the help of Athens. Aeschylus does not mention this, but it was common knowledge. The subordination of the Greeks achieved by Cyrus, apparently with the blessing of Zeus, was now a thing of the past. Was this really the essence of Xerxes' punishment?

Aeschylus would doubtless have preferred a political division between Asia and Europe as clear as the geographical divide. But historical reality conflicted with this, and instead he divides land and sea so absolutely that nobody can enjoy success on both at once. The fact that the Persians relied heavily on Phoenician and Greek fleets which were well used to naval engagement was glossed over. The prime concern was not military accuracy, but a perspective on the Persian empire as a whole, and in particular its mythical foundations. Participation in the naval battle, for which they had little experience, had been no foregone conclusion for the Athenians eight years earlier. With the Persians on their doorstep, it was a spectacular procession to the temple of Athena on the Acropolis, led by Cimon, son of the victor at Marathon, which is said to have persuaded many Athenians to evacuate the city and risk naval warfare. Cimon laid aside his bridle, which he no longer needed, and took up a captured shield from the temple before joining the ship on which he would fight with it. The significance of the weapons in this symbolic act is taken up by Aeschylus in his contrast between the Greek lance and the Persian spear and bow and arrow – though by that time, the Persians had themselves most likely adopted the lance as a key weapon. Finally, we have freedom on the one side and, on the other, monarchy and the pride which subjects take in their obedience. And the fact that the freedom of the Greeks and the nature of the sea are united in being unamenable to any sort of yoke as it were locates the Greek spirit within the ranks of natural phenomena.

The world is therefore split into clearly distinguished realms and elements, which are evidently governed by an immutable natural polarity. The military effects of this – the Greek superiority at sea and the peculiar geography of the Greek world – simply go to prove the point. There is thus a double causality at work here: events can only be explained by the transgression against, and reaffirmation of, the world-order.

It is particularly significant that the different domains, sea and land, freedom and monarchy, Greeks and barbarians, are not simply seen as black and white; both have their own justification, and can claim the support of the gods. The portrayal of Darius is an obvious case in point. Yet there must be division. The frontier allows no passage. And this is exactly what is embodied in the fate of the individual, who stands before the chorus at the end, vanquished, alone and in rags, who must suffer being asked why he thinks it worth mentioning that he has saved the quiver, the symbol of his reign, and then bemoans his defeat at length and is steeped in reproaches.

The most important point about Aeschylus' *Persians* would seem to be that the war of 480 is 'repeated' in the play. This in itself may well have answered a widespread need among the Attic citizenry. Great and momentous experiences, which transform our horizons, which rise for a time high above them, doubtless have to be repeated and 'memorized' in order gradually to be assimilated and laid to rest. After all, this had been the triumph of a David over a Goliath, a fact that will have retained all its improbability for quite some time. Since then there had been nothing but upheaval. Things were bound to be in a state of confusion; much of what had been achieved and experienced could no longer simply be squared with customary knowledge, beliefs and concerns. The fact that all went according to the plan of the great Themistocles will not necessarily have made it any easier to come to terms with.

So the Athenians will have repeatedly recounted these events to themselves. Their sphere of knowledge had to develop to incorporate them. Tragedy was initially only one, rather incongruous part of this process, but it was able to make a significant contribution to the interpretative work of telling the story. For tragedy artificially reconstructed the whole state of affairs, set it in a distinct perspective and enacted it according to distinct roles – and by doing so at the very centre of public attention, it carried a particular responsibility and a large measure of authority.

It is significant that Aeschylus did not simply remove this action to the domain of the Persians in distant Susa, but rather that he involved his audience in it by virtue of the plot construction, leading from the premonitions of the chorus to the return of Xerxes; by introducing the ghost of Darius and, not least, by encouraging them to identify with the Persian experience in various ways. It was not just a matter of even-handedness; rather, Aeschylus was concerned to raise the suffering of the Persians out of the 'national', and into the general, human dimension. At one and the same moment, he let the Athenians review their victory through his powerful depiction, and transposed them into the sorry situation of the enemy. While affirming the justice of Persian rule, within its given boundaries, he reinforced the distinctive quality of the Greeks: the fact that they would never be subservient. The freedom of Athens is not only celebrated, but represented as – even proven to be – an integral part of the general order of things.

In this way Aeschylus shows the outcome to be just. Xerxes' defeat is the consequence of the violation of a border imposed on mankind by nature and from on high, a border separating both Greek from barbarian and land power from naval power. As always in tragedy, it is a question of pointing up the polarities between great forces. These apparently defined the nomological knowledge of the Athenians at that time, and were sufficiently prevalent to co-ordinate things within the framework of that knowledge. Thus, the story is understood as the disruption and reconstitution of an order established between the opposing forces. In this way, Aeschylus is able to root the Persian War within the broad context of nomological knowledge.

For us the particular interest of the play lies in the fact that this process is grafted onto a historical event. Aeschylus clearly had to respect the reality of history. He could not, for instance, introduce the opposition between Europe and Asia, as he might have wished, but had to confine himself to the ethnocentric one between Greeks and barbarians. He could not tie up the fate of the empire with that of its monarch. There simply was no extended chain of reciprocal revenge on the mythical model, for the vengeance of the Persians had recurrently been thwarted. The failure to mention Athens' part in the Ionian revolt was not necessarily a weakness, because it was arguably extraneous. The fact that Darius is rather too positively drawn may be accounted for by the specific perspective of the Persian elders; and it may also have had to do with the fact that kings tended generally to be seen in a more favourable light after their death (witness Agamemnon in *The Libation Bearers*). And the advantages were also considerable. Aeschylus was able to create a coherent picture of things within the conventions of the genre, ensuring that sense is preserved, that the world-view is in order and that belief in the justice of political and military processes and in the gods is upheld.

This also had its political consequences: if the world-order was affirmed, in as far as the individual who had offended it met with punishment, then the Athenians too would have to stay within their limitations, in the war against Persia for instance. Darius' warning 'that man is mortal, and must learn to curb his pride' (820) was meant for their ears too. And his exhortation that present good fortune should be enjoyed and 'your soul taste each day's pleasure' (as wealth is of no use in the grave) must have meant something to the Athenians. The powerful experience of defeat which Aeschylus presented to them by way of *The Persians* must have brought home to them the dangers of combat, as must Aeschylus' great lament on the pity of war. He certainly did not reject war on principle, or hold that it might be abolished, but he showed that such a terrible thing should not be embarked upon lightly. So Aeschylus had much to say to the leading citizenry of the Greek world. By placing the most important event of the time within their knowledge, he was able to regulate and extend that knowledge.

Aeschylus won the prize with his plays of 472. Shortly afterwards he was invited to perform *The Persians* in Syracuse.

On the threshold of democracy

We know little about the history of Greece in the late seventies and sixties of the fifth century. Towards the end of the 470s, there had been a conflict surrounding Themistocles, which came to a head in his ostracism. The ruling that each year a vote should be held in the people's Assembly to determine whether any prominent man, held to represent a danger to the city, should be banished for a period of ten years, had on several occasions been successfully implemented by Themistocles himself in the course of the 480s. Now he himself fell prey to it. The ostracism involved no judgement or dispossession; it was simply a matter of suspicion. The person concerned, whether rightly or wrongly, had to make a sacrifice to ensure that the city should remain free of tyranny. It was the only such ruling in world history which could genuinely halt the rise of a tyrant, for, by the time guilt may be proved, the tyrant is generally in full control and can avoid any trial. However, we cannot be sure to what extent the original model of ostracism still functioned after the Persian Wars. It certainly became *de facto* a battle to the death between the two most powerful men at any one time.

Themistocles had to go in the end because his politics diverged from those of his younger rival, Cimon. The latter concentrated on the conduct of war against the Persians and on the development and reinforcement of the League, and he operated with vigour and success. He was also concerned to protect the interests of Sparta, believing that Greece needed both its leading powers. Athens could not bear alone a yoke designed for two. Cimon clearly understood his politics not as narrowly Athenian, but as Greek. In this sense he still moved entirely within the horizons of the Persian Wars. This was the justification for his often tough policies regarding the cities of the League. He also believed that these policies would be secured by a sound relationship with Sparta. He had many friends there, and the Spartans were initially content to play a passive role, as there was plenty to occupy them at home.

Themistocles, though, thought that in time Athens was bound to come to blows with Sparta. The old supremo could hardly accept with equanimity the rise of the new power. He perceived a constant threat to the position of Athens within the League, for, any city which wished to rebel would naturally turn to Sparta for aid, and such a temptation could not be resisted for long. So, in his view at least, it was necessary to be prepared for the eventuality of war against Sparta, and to take every step to inhibit this dangerous rival. He wished to move closer to such enemies of Sparta as Argos, and if possible to forge alliances with them. It would be folly in his view to seek co-operation with Sparta, where there was only opposition. His calculations were precise. Themistocles was a passionate and able strategist; he was used to seeing through superficial appearances, customs, friendly words and gestures, and to recognizing the principles which governed affairs of state. He believed that, whatever the Spartans pretended to think and want, or indeed genuinely did think and want, was of no consequence by comparison with the *raison d'être* of the state.

The acute and ruthless determination of this way of thinking seems to have been as uncanny for the aristocrats and the landowners who held sway in the Assembly in the late 470s, as for the Spartans themselves. It opened up new perspectives, which most were unwilling to recognize. How could the League be led and war declared against Sparta at one and the same time? Should the Persian Wars be suspended for this purpose? Themistocles' sang-froid, his ostentatious, careful, and yet at the same time daring, plotting made great demands on the people. His plans were based on the sort of radical rationality, to which the Athenians were not as yet attuned. They had not objected as long as they had needed Themistocles and felt beholden to him. But the compelling figure began to fade, and the requirements of the day took over. They were ultimately ready to ostracize the man to whom they owed the city's salvation in the Persian War. When the Spartans let it be known that he had dealings with the Persians, Themistocles was found guilty of treason.

Cimon, on the other hand, was in harmony with the bulk of the citizenry. Not only did he enjoy significant success and swell the city's coffers, but he was also well liked as a character. He was helped by the fact that following him involved no conflict with the traditional ways. His intellectual stature was much more modest; his spirit was not darkened by too much thought. He seems to have relied more on his senses; he was gentler, more generous, enjoyed life to the full with an aristocratic nonchalance, and yet was an able general and admiral. He would appear to have radiated a just sense of satisfaction. So why bother too much about Sparta?

Cimon evidently conducted his political affairs in close concert with the Areopagus. The choice was obvious, for it was here that he could find the most influential and, above all, the most experienced politicians of the city, who could be of use to him in dealing with the newly expanded arena of Athenian politics.

Opportunity for dissent was limited, as all hands were engrossed with new tasks, successes and profits. A vacuum was opened up, and the first concern was to gain possession of all manner of things. Discussion of, and consensus on, Athenian policy will have caused no great problems. In addition, the existence of the people's Assembly, and the fact that decisions were reached in that forum under the influence of skilled speakers, would have encouraged solidarity among the members of the Areopagus.

While the Areopagus was able to develop a clear political line, Cimon could rely on his authority in the people's Assembly. Indeed, he had to rely on it, for contemporary reports suggest that he had none of the Athenian way with words. So the important decisions lay with the Assembly, but they were largely predetermined by the Areopagus; the aristocratic Council was probably in essence responsible for the shaping of Attic politics.

This worked well until the advent of a group of dissidents who shared the ideas of Themistocles. Their leader was Ephialtes, and the young Pericles was also a member. We know that these men wanted a new policy regarding Sparta, which led to tremendous arguments in the mid-460s. In 464 the large and wealthy island of Thasos left the League, having evidently secured a promise of support from the Spartans. But the support was not forthcoming, for a severe earthquake led to an uprising of the Messenian helots at the same time. Sparta was paralysed. When the helots dug in on Mount Ithome, holding the Spartans at bay, Athens was asked to help with the unsuccessful siege. Cimon was in favour of so doing, Ephialtes against. But Cimon prevailed, setting off with a force of several thousand hoplites.

But, besides the controversy over foreign policy, Ephialtes also pursued internal and constitutional aims. He waged a campaign against the Areopagus, and he brought several of its members to trial for accepting bribes. He would have had little difficulty here, given the customary exchange of gifts between nobles when travelling privately or as envoys; the line between *bona fide* gifts and bribes was not easily drawn. And his prosecutions were successful. He most likely agitated against the Areopagus in the people's Assembly at the same time, for he cannot simply have toppled it like a bolt from the blue in 462/1. He must have realized at some point that he could not prevail against Cimon as long as the Areopagus continued to exert such influence on political life. And he was not interested in half measures.

It seems that two fundamentally contrary points of view clashed in the figures of Cimon and Ephialtes. For all his openness, Cimon was clearly tied to tradition. Through the step-by-step processes of Athenian politics, he had gradually managed to bring about an altogether new state of affairs. But, as he viewed things from within, so to speak, and had got used to the new situation progressively, he seems to have believed that the political foundations had meanwhile remained unchanged, not least in terms of relations with Sparta. He seems to have been utterly devoid of cunning, and was even accused of being too carefree. How could he be expected to fear others?

Ephialtes, on the other hand, came into politics as it were from the outside. And he thus perceived the situation as it now really was. He appears to have recognized how extraordinarily bold and insecure, how fundamentally new, the position of Athens was. How could one remain carefree in the face of the huge disproportion between the number of the citizens and the extent of their city's domains? Around 465 Athens had suffered its first great defeat, and the loss of Thasos must have given food for thought. Themistocles' warnings were no doubt still in people's minds. So Ephialtes entered the political arena with few preconceptions. He saw the need to make careful calculations, to seek out allies wherever possible, and among Sparta's enemies in particular, to reinforce the ground already held and above all not to give anything away. It smacks of a new generation; at any rate it was a radically new spirit in Athenian politics.

In the meantime various things had changed in Athens. In the 470s the city was caught up in terrific, breathtaking activity. The fleet, so hastily constructed before Salamis, now became a regular political instrument. It had to be enlarged; docks were built; many men came from outside Athens to serve as oarsmen or to make money as craftsmen working on the new armaments. The city expanded; new buildings sprang up; and it was probably at this time that an entire new settlement was developed at Piraeus. The people's Assembly was confronted with an infinite number of problems – armaments and war, alliances and diplomacy – the business of politics burgeoned. And the fleet and army needed constant new supplies of citizens. There was much that was new and compelling.

With time, however, they became accustomed to it all, even to the success of the city. For fifteen years the life of nearly every young adult male had revolved around service to the polis. Even if this made their bonds with the interests of the city no stronger, it certainly made them more intimate and immediate. Thus new perspectives arose. In addition, the thetes class – the oarsmen – became ever more numerous. They represented an entirely new political force, coming from outside and thus able to think more boldly and more flexibly than the landowners, who until then had held sway over the Assembly. They no doubt felt that some things were ripe for change.

However keenly they were aware of the city's interests, Cimon and his friends were noble gentlemen of a traditional cast of mind. They were subject to their own political situation, the *noblesse oblige* which linked them with others of their class throughout Greece and their many friendships outside the city. The Areopagus met *in camera*. They will have sought to spare the members of the people's Assembly the finer points of political argument. But all this could only function as long as the citizens did not challenge the idea that counsel 'from above' was always in the best interests of the city. The new demands and relationships forged through action were at odds with the aristocratic order. Ephialtes and his friends were also of good family, but they clearly felt that the old aristocratic prerogatives were of no service to the city. They were more concerned about what threatened Athens, and the need for more courage to exploit fully the city's potential. The 'man who held the lowest oar' could well understand this, for he too had been granted a good measure of common sense by Zeus.

So it seems that in Cimon and Ephialtes we have the clash between the old and the new, attachment to tradition and the assertion of practical advantage respectively. One might also read for this the opposition between respect for moral imperatives on the one hand, and the simple dictates of political expediency on the other. This was more or less the context out of which *The Suppliants* of Aeschylus was written, and in which it was staged.

The Suppliants

Aeschylus' *Suppliants* was performed in Athens during the second
half of the 460s BC. The plot contains clear references to a 'popular
government', which is the earliest known instance of the people
being portrayed as the rulers of the polis. The play is actually set in
Argos, which could be significant in its own right, since Ephialtes
certainly wanted to establish ties between Athens and Argos. The
relevant passages could at the same time, however, apply just as
well to Athens. It would be reasonable to see them in the context
of the serious internal political disputes which resulted in the
Areopagus being deprived of power (462/1 BC) and which may
have stretched over a period of two or three years. Thus political
history would, to a certain extent, support the general opinion that
The Suppliants appeared in 463 BC, and it is this that forms the
basis of the present argument.

The play was the first part of a trilogy which dealt with the
Danaids, the fifty daughters of Danaus. They have fled from Egypt
with their father in order to avoid having to marry the fifty sons
of Danaus' brother Aegyptus. The goal of their flight is Argos,
homeland of their ancestress Io. They are pursued by their suitors.

This first, and only surviving, play from the trilogy deals with
the reception of the Danaids in the city of Argos. There must
have followed a battle against the pursuers which ended with the
destruction of Argos and with the death of its king, Pelasgus. The
second and third plays must have contained the dispute between
the victorious pursuers and their quarry, which finally leads to a
marriage contract. According to the myth, all the Danaids kill
their husbands on the wedding night, except for one who has
grown to love hers. It seems that this daughter is, consequently,
sharply censured; there do, at any rate, remain to us some beautiful
lines which are spoken by Aphrodite in her defence. Apart from
this, we do not know of anything else which might give us an idea
of *The Suppliants*' wider context. The significance of the play is,
however, largely dependent on knowledge of this context.

The daughters are terrified of the men, whom they constantly
reproach for recklessness and the overstepping of laws and conventions (hubris) and to whose rule they do not want to subject

themselves. The men, after they have landed at the bay of Argos, send a herald to demand that the women proceed immediately to the ships; this sort of conduct seems to confirm what the women said earlier about their suitors.

But the behaviour of the women has not yet been satisfactorily explained. They have claimed not only that the sons of Aegyptus have no right over them, but also that a marriage between them would virtually be against the law. When King Pelasgus, with whom they are seeking asylum and protection, asks them whether they are against a marriage because of enmity or because the law forbids it, all he is told is that a match is completely out of the question. When he once more tries to ascertain whether the suitors really have no claim on the women according to the laws of their home country, they say that they never want to be subjected to the power of men (or by men), even if it means having to flee to the stars. Whether they are only rejecting their cousins, or the concept of marriage as a whole, remains unclear. For the most part the latter seems to be the case, though occasionally it seems to be the former (this is assuming that the text, which has come down to us in a relatively bad state, is not misleading us). In any case, they give no consideration – not yet, anyway – to the rights of others, and will brook no attempt at persuasion (which is the preserve of Aphrodite). For them there are only power and victory (or death), just as, on the other side, the sons of Aegyptus rely solely on force. Both parties are extremely biased. The order of things is out of joint.

In their demands for asylum, the women are quite uncompromising, even insolent. First, as was usual for those who sought asylum, they call on Zeus, the god of suppliants, and on other gods. At the same time they let it be known that they would rather die than marry. If the gods on Olympus will not pay them any heed, then they will find refuge with the 'Zeus of the underworld'. They threaten Zeus that if he does not give them protection, he will get a reputation for being unjust. Ultimately they are his descendants, since he impregnated Io. John Ferguson writes that the fact that they turn to the Zeus of the underworld means that they are being little short of blasphemous.

In any case, it is obvious that they are trying to blackmail the gods. 'Children, we must be wise,' says their father in an attempt to calm them down (176). Several times he emphatically warns them to act with more modesty; they should use 'words to move tears and compassion for your need' (194). But all this is in vain. Aeschylus does everything to point up the women's impertinence and lack of moderation. Furthermore, he does not establish the father as a spokesman. Danaus, when he is not occupied with business offstage, acts more as an adviser to his daughters on the rules of good behaviour. The daughters call him their counsellor and leader. Like them, he is against the marriage, but it does not become clear whether they act according to his wishes or not. He lets them plead their case on their own, and they take it up with all the determination that youth and endangered femininity seem to put at their disposal.

In their petitioning of Pelasgus they are frighteningly certain of the relevant laws; these are laws which are constantly reasserted with the help of the gods, whether as a punishment or as a reward. They threaten him by saying that misfortune will befall him if he does not grant them their request. The gods protect those who, like the Danaids, have prostrated themselves at their shrines; and similarly, according to the picture that the women paint, those who abuse this protection will, with absolute certainty, be punished.

The king hesitates. He takes the case very seriously since he knows that if Argos takes in the daughters of Danaus, the sons of Aegyptus and all their followers will attack the city. The question is whether he should do what is imposed on him by the gods, or whether he should protect the city from what he calls 'a new war' (342). Serious difficulties threaten as a result of either choice: 'To save us all, our need is for deep pondering; an eye to search, as divers search the ocean bed, clear seeing' (407).

Pelasgus still hopes to avoid trouble for the town and for himself. But when he is told again about the punishments that will come about for his children and his house as a result of Zeus' judgement, he seems to give in. 'I have thought well; and here's the rock that strands me now: with one side or the other it must come to war' (438). His words seem to indicate that it is more important to remain true to the gods; but this is not made absolutely clear. He offers great sacrifices to the gods and in so doing he seems to be seeking an escape from his predicament. At this, the women put forward their final 'argument'. If their will is not done, they will hang themselves from the statues of the gods in the temples. They could do nothing worse. This is blatant blackmail. One might be able to disobey one or other holy law on one particular occasion, but it is not possible to countenance such an extreme desecration. The women, however, declare their intention with indescribable coldness: they allude to the sashes and girdle that they tie round their clothes; Pelasgus thinks that they want to talk about their wardrobes but the real point is eventually made clear to him. The leader of the chorus emphasizes this with satisfaction: 'Your eyes are open now; I have made you see the truth' (467).

Pelasgus sets out the whole problem again: 'I am launched upon a deep and dangerous sea where ruin lurks' (470). He tells of how bitter the losses would be if there was a war: if 'men for women's sake should soak the earth in blood' (477). But he decides to recommend to the people's Assembly that the city should take in the refugees. Since, and he has said this before, the women have settled themselves at the public hearth, it is the people, and not he, that must be responsible for the decision. If the position of the whole city is at stake, a communal decision must be made about its defence.

The people meet together at another place. We only hear that Pelasgus, using the most persuasive rhetoric and references to the threat of the anger of the gods, elicited a unanimous decision to take in the women as resident aliens (metics). The Danaids gratefully sing songs of blessing to the city. But when the herald finally comes on, they once more succumb to worry and fear – until Pelasgus appears and expels the herald from the country. Before the chorus sings its final song of departure, Danaus gives his daughters more directives as to how to behave: after surviving so well all the dangers that they have faced, they should not give themselves up to the temptations of love. 'Value chastity more than you value life' (1013).

The way that Aeschylus characterizes the daughters of Danaus is, at first sight, difficult to understand: why do they use terrorist tactics to try to impose their will on the city of Argos when they are toying with thoughts of death anyway?

The problem of seeking asylum, more than most other considerations, led to the question of what significance moral laws, sanctioned by the gods, have in the political arena. It is an issue in which the city never normally had any specific interest, but when it accepts the suppliants, it lays itself open to great danger. This shows exactly where they stand in relation to the gods. Furthermore, the Danaids' ancestral link with Argos, which is mentioned several times, speaks in their favour; and their powerlessness may also work for them in that, as Pelasgus says, it awakens compassion in everybody. Why is this not enough? Pelasgus' decision would have been more honourable if he really had disregarded the considerations of political expediency for moral reasons. But the power of moral laws seems to have been weakened: the Danaids, even if they are not actually abusing the concept of belief in god-given laws, do behave in an unduly boastful and inflammatory way.

But maybe Pelasgus' decision would not otherwise have been credible. Perhaps the reverence for the gods that he shows in this case would have been unthinkable without the fear of them that the Danaids so vividly evoke. Later, in the *Oresteia*, Aeschylus returns to the theme of the link between fear and reverence. In any case, even if Pelasgus made the decision of his own free will, it would have been problematical. If he had actually decided to follow Zeus without any pressure on him to do so, it is difficult to understand why he, or at any rate, why his city, should have been punished. Usually, mythical heroes make mistakes in relation to the gods – perhaps without knowing that they are doing so, perhaps with the best intentions, perhaps because there is no other choice; whatever the case, they do something which gives a religious basis to their fate. Pelasgus does not really do this. He just finds himself embroiled in the affair, mainly as a result of his own lack of decisiveness.

If one were to question in a similar way the motives of the Danaids, one would have to assume that the answers could only be found in the lost parts of the trilogy. It could be that in being so uncompromising in their demands, they are preparing the way for the murder of their suitors. It could be that here Aeschylus is deliberately bringing the feminine and the masculine into conflict, with the intention in the end of bringing about some sort of balance between the two. Already in *The Suppliants* we see that he ends the play with the chorus of Danaids facing the criticism of their servants. Where the daughters of Danaus call on Artemis, the protectress of chastity, to support them, the serving-maids pray to Aphrodite. Perhaps the ending contained a new beginning. Perhaps the sister who succumbed to her suitor won out with Aphrodite's help and atoned for the others, which could easily have led to a marriage. In the fragment of the 'speech of defence' that remains to us, Aphrodite appears as the embodiment of all the life and all the fruitfulness in the universe. The idea of such cosmic productivity was, at that time, thoroughly relevant and was, perhaps, linked with the start of some cult.

Relations between the sexes in Athens may have been immutable, but they were not necessarily taken for granted. Other tragedies, too, show how this social order had constantly to be reasserted or at least made comprehensible in the context of the much more questioning attitude of the Athenian democracy. On the other hand, or perhaps because of this, the whole cosmic order, the prerequisite for order within the polis, was in need of reaffirmation. The cosmic and the civic could not be separated and the radical nature of some of Athens' institutions made the reaffirmation of such principles necessary.

The broader contrast between East and West could also have played a role. The exotic strangeness of the Danaids and the sons of Aegyptus is explicitly emphasized. The fundamental difference between the two worlds is given clear expression by the misunderstandings which arise on both sides. As is the case in *The Persians*, the independence and unique character of the West is affirmed. It is also worth noting that Pelasgus is the ruler not only of Argos but of an empire that stretches westward from the lands where the River Strymon flows, to Greece. In those years, Athens happened to be conducting a war in the area around the Strymon. It is possible that the fate of Argos would have taken a turn for the better in the following two plays and that it may have faced a more auspicious future.

In spite of the uncertainty about what followed, *The Suppliants*, within its narrow political context, offers some extraordinarily interesting insights. The Athenian citizens must have watched it with extreme excitement. On the one hand, the subject of Pelasgus' decision, which figures so centrally in the play, must have been highly explosive. On the other, the participation of the people in the decision-making process must have been of the greatest relevance, especially because of the particular style in which it is described, a style which lends the subject special weight.

As mentioned earlier, Pelasgus tries first of all to avoid making a decision, by explaining that it is not before his hearth that the Danaids have prostrated themselves, but before that of the city. He is not able to decide anything without consulting the whole citizenry. However he becomes fully aware of the extent of the problem when the Danaids simply refuse to believe this and explain to him that he is indeed the responsible party and that he should prepare to accept any guilt. He clearly sees that he must arrive at a decision which he can present to the people. In a wonderful speech, Aeschylus has him express how restrictive this responsibility is: 'What can I do? Where turn? I fear either to act, or not to act, and so let events take their own course' (379). He looks for a way out by raising the question of justice, hoping, no doubt, that the Danaids might have violated their cousins' rights. When this hope founders and the women swear their devotion to the gods, he says that the decision is too hard for him to make. Even if he did have (or, perhaps, although he has) the power, he would not pass his final judgement without the consent of the people. It must not be said that he has endangered the city for the sake of strangers. The Danaids have to make clear the action which he must take by referring to the punishments that are threatened by the gods should he not comply. And after a long and meditative soliloquy, he does comply. He thus goes before the people's Assembly with clear intentions: he is no longer interested in hearing their opinions, but simply wants them to agree with his own decision.

This long process does not merely set out the general problem of the necessity of making decisions, together with the question of whether one should get involved or let things take their course. Rather, it highlights the conflict between considerations of purely earthly expediency and the observance of god-given laws. At the same time, it has a bearing on the problem of the different responsibilities of the political leaders and the people. The conflict between moral laws and immediate political expediency was not, of course, a new one. It must have arisen constantly in cases both large and small. But as a rule, this conflict would not have been seen so clearly or have been supplied with such a pragmatic solution. In the medium of theatre, however, every question must be posed in a more sharply defined way. The terrible predicament in which people can inadvertently find themselves, and which they must face alone, especially if they are political leaders, is made all too evident.

In this political context, there must be a particular point to the unwavering behaviour of the Danaids, who make use of any convenient religious view as a means to assert their own will: they pose the question as bluntly, and make the decision as urgent, as possible. The women brook no evasion and they reinforce the moral, god-given laws so much that these effectively determine the decision. They present a very tangible problem and thus they become far more dangerous. (As a rule people would have tended to fear immediate earthly dangers more than the dangers that the immortals might threaten, the hope being that the latter would pass over them.)

Since Aeschylus is using a mythical example to portray the problem of political decision-making to such great effect, we can assume that the problem must have been especially relevant at that time. Bearing in mind what we know of those years, this is not at all improbable. Decisions had to be made about the most difficult questions. Policy-making was strictly concerned with the fulfilment of its own specific aims, and this already made more difficult the problem of how to relate one's customary actions to the traditional principles of morality and belief. This tension equally arose in the conflict between Cimon and Ephialtes.

At issue were points of view similar to those that Pelasgus faces when dealing with his problem. The fundamental nature of the conflict and the severity of the rhetorical struggle against the authority of Cimon and the Areopagus, together with the new situation as a whole, would have allowed the citizens to appreciate very well the whole difficulty of deciding whether 'to act or not to act and so let events take their course', and also of deciding between the traditional conventions and political expediency. But more than anything else, the disputes of those years may have impressed on the Athenians how excessively taxing the difficulties and the consequences of these questions could be.

It is here that the other problem thrown up by *The Suppliants* becomes important. This consisted in the question of how political decisions should be reached and, above all, who should make them. In the play it seems that, in the end, it is a matter for whoever happens to be leader. The people's role is merely to endorse his decision through spontaneous approval and without the usual referendum.

But Pelasgus only comes to his decision as a result of the enormous pressure put on him by the Danaids. Before this, he found the question too difficult to answer on his own. This is, incidentally, similar to Athena's lack of decisiveness, as shown some years later in Aeschylus' *Oresteia* of 458. There, she is supposed to decide whether the matricide Orestes should be condemned or acquitted. In 458, however, the court that Athena appoints remains split over 'the question, since ultimately it amounts to whether the old or the new laws should be respected – not a question on which there could be unanimity. Perhaps one has to say that after the Areopagus was deprived of its power, unity was for a long time impossible; before this, on the other hand, unity could, because of the shadow of the fear of divine wrath, be achieved by observing the old laws.

The Suppliants makes it very clear, however, that it is possible for a leader to be overtaxed by having to come to a decision. This weakness is made even more obvious by Pelasgus' subservient attitude towards the Danaids. It may be to his credit, when he is prompted by thoughts of the threat of the gods' wrath, to cry out, 'that of all things is to be feared' (479), but before this he has let himself be pressurized to a remarkable degree. The Danaids, to his horror, bring home his predicament with a very tangible image. They have put wool-bound branches (a sign of supplication) on the shrines which stand on the hill which overlooks the city in which they want to take refuge. They demand from Pelasgus that he respect 'these gods, your city's helm, thus garlanded' (345). Several allusions could be contained in this phrase, one of which must be to the fact that the helm is the raised part of a ship where the pilot sits; the idea of a polis as a ship comes through very strongly in Aeschylus' work. The Danaids thus monopolize the place of the gods as well as that of the king.

Pelasgus could make a decision, and implement it, but this would, nevertheless, not be a victory; this is quite apart from the insoluble nature of the question which is at issue. As much as he is influenced by considerations of responsibility, prudence and good conduct, the circumstances to which he is exposed make it doubtful whether his leadership is adequate.

These doubts are in turn supported by the remarkable claims which are made about the people. The claims do not stop at the principle that those who are affected by something should also make the decisions about it (366), which in itself would be nothing new. The idea that the warriors (or, in this case, the people) should decide about starting a war, had been current for a long time. Even regarding the fact that the chorus speaks expressly (referring to the voting) about the citizens making the law (604), one could draw parallels with a much earlier testimony from Sparta. *Krateîn*, which is here translated 'to make the law', could simply mean 'to be the decisive factor', and could refer to the fact that the people's Assembly, when a matter is put before it, has to make the final decision. But what then follows – the chorus' blessing of 'The people, whose power rules the State' (699) – was, as far as we can tell, completely new.

Furthermore, in the face of the problem that faces Pelasgus, the principle that those who are affected should also decide on what is to be done must be seen in a new light. If the question is so difficult and the consequences so unknowable that an individual (and perhaps also the Areopagus) becomes helpless and loses all ability to cope, does that mean that it is impossible for anybody to take over the responsibility for others? Was there, then, no choice but that those concerned not only concur with the decision, but actually make it themselves? Does this mean that the people really did take over sovereignty (or at least show that they had it)?

There have been several objections to this interpretation, which puts a large political significance on the conspicuous, and new, emphasis on popular rule. It has, for example, been said that the reference to the necessity of the people making a decision has the dramatic function of an excuse, within Pelasgus' long excursus on how to decide. It is, however, not right to claim that there is a conflict between dramatic and political objectives; the two are very closely bound together. On the one hand the distress of the king and the impossibly excessive demands placed on him, on the other the fact that the decision of the people is so important, are simply two sides of the same coin. Even if at first it did seem to be a delaying tactic when the king says that those that are affected must decide, it is clear by the end that he really is no longer able to lay down the law himself. Thus 'popular rule' is shown to be the product of a new situation which emerges during the process of decision-making. All that the chorus does is to point out how things stand. The fact that Pelasgus rules over a whole empire (Aeschylus expresses this 'rule' with the same word '*krateîn*') only serves to make his weakness more apparent; it says nothing about the power relationships within the city. There is, therefore, no perceivable reason why one should not take seriously the completely unequivocal, apparently new, and in any case very far-reaching expression about 'the people who rule the city'. It could be said that the play is so structured as to show particularly well how this assertion was arrived at: it was due to the overwhelming demands made on, the inescapable problems faced by and the weakness shown by King Pelasgus.

How much the king is dependent on the people is shown by the fact that, in his own words, criticism is often levelled at his leadership – which makes him afraid of difficult problems. In the end, the suppliants significantly credit the people's rule with watching over the common good 'with wise forethought' (700). They state the wish that the people will hold on to power.

It would seem very reasonable to assume that, in the words spoken about popular rule, one is supposed to recognize allusions to the disquiet caused by Ephialtes. By breaking down the authority of the Areopagus he wanted popular rule to take effect; he at least (as a first step) wanted to ensure that the people recognized the importance and decisiveness of their own role – this was all that he could count on.

Brief allusions to contemporary politics are often to be found in Aeschylus' work: there are, for example, those to the newly established alliance with Argos in the *Oresteia*; to the Athenians' military endeavours in the *Oresteia* as well as here; and also, as Peter Spahn has recently pointed out, to the provisions made for building accommodation for metics (above all, for the oarsmen who were hired by Athens). This last reference is taken up in the clear-cut choice that Pelasgus puts to the Danaids: they can live in either communal or individual quarters; some of which, as he points out, belong to him, some to the public (957).

One notable speech of the Danaids to the king should also be seen as an allusion to the agitations of Ephialtes. When Pelasgus actually says that it is not to him personally that they should appeal, they start their answer with the lines 'You are the state*, you are the people' (370). The words used for 'the people' are *tò dēmion*, the substantive form of the adjective which comes from *dêmos*; it literally means 'that which is of the people'. With similar forms (e.g. *tò politikón*) it was possible to signify all of that which is most purely expressed by the quality that the adjective derives from the noun.

It is a remarkable expression: a king or a tyrant can be as absolute a ruler as he wants, but the Greeks always talk about his rule as a separate entity, and never identify him directly with the city that is being ruled. The concept of identification, which allowed it to be said by Louis XIV that he was the state, was still a long way off. Similarly, the Greeks, despite all the knowledge that they had of ancient Egypt, could hardly have subscribed to the view of modern Egyptologists that the best word to use in order to signify the Egyptian 'state' is 'pharaoh'. The context too would make the expression unlikely; even if one could identify the rule with the city, which is improbable enough, it would be completely out of the question to equate him with 'the people'. This phrase does not, then, constitute an unreasonable exaggeration. The point would be lost if the exaggeration went too far beyond what was credible. Thus, one can assume that the expression contains an allusion, and that this allusion constitutes its purpose. The expression was the ironic reversal of a very clear sentence which Ephialtes could well have used: 'All – or, all of us – are the city, the whole of the people.' This identification between the citizens and the city, a concept which Aristotle later formulates, was already well known in the fifth century. We see it, for example, in Herodotus' answer to the question of where the whole of the city was: the whole of the city is to be found in the majority.

The claim of the aristocrats, and so also of the Areopagus, that, thanks to their intellectual and moral superiority, they could best

---

* Meier translates 'polis'.

serve the interests of the city, could not be easily countered by the
wider public; Ephialtes probably relied not least on support from
the lowest class, the thetes. He had, then, to put the question
another way: the argument had to be not who could do what for
the city, but 'who' the city was; then the answer could come in
terms of the *dêmos*.

This would accord with the opinion that the questions which
arose were too difficult and too controversial for it to be possible
for them to be answered by an individual, solely on the strength
of his own knowledge of right and wrong, justice and injustice. As
both Athena and Pelasgus say, a vote is the only remaining option.
Those affected by a decision (and this view now gains new
significance) should be the decision-makers. According to the general opinion, the people's Assembly in Athens, like the one in *The
Suppliants*, had for a long time been the decisive force, but what
this meant in specific cases is open to question. What we know of
the disturbances of that time, if interpreted correctly here, seems
to point, however, to the fact that the Assembly would always be
responsible for these decisions; or, in other words, that the political
decisions would be given over entirely to the people's Assembly
(without it being subject to the authority of the Areopagus); and
this indeed is what happened. The citizenry was no longer the
passive object of an aristocratic rule that was not so much concerned with welfare as with wars and foreign affairs (which were
to be no longer managed responsibly) but an active participant in
the political process.

By seeking to endow Pelasgus with precisely the quality that no
individual – nor any body like the Areopagus – can have, namely,
complete identification with the city, the Danaids make clear the
absurdity of any attempt by an individual to make the decisions
that should actually be made by the people that they affect. Their
assertion clearly provides more evidence to support their view of
the impossibly excessive demands made on the king. The fact that
Pelasgus then influences the decision of the people (for which the
Danaids do not thank him, and for which they do not include him
in their song of blessing) is an example of tragic irony: his action
is of as little help to them in the rest of the trilogy as is the actual
decision of the people – a decision which they are at such pains
to praise. What it does do, however, is harm the city of Argos.

If this is a correct interpretation of the course of the events involving the Danaids, Pelasgus and the people of Argos, we can say that Aeschylus is using a distant myth in order to offer to his contemporaries a clear view of their own situation, not only to the Athenians but also to their allies. On top of this, he 're-enacted' a part of contemporary politics that would have sharply brought home the absolutely vital need to face up to making decisions, especially those decisions that had to do with the choice between the laws of the immortals and pragmatic expediency, and the confronting of impasses. The play would, in the end, have pointed to the answer to the situation, which lies in letting those that are affected make the decisions, indeed in letting them rule. In the end there is no one else who can take their responsibility. All of this was done within the context of a completely new situation: the citizens' place in the world was completely new, since the problem of the order of things, albeit not in itself new, was far more pressing than before.

If this interpretation is correct, Aeschylus can be credited with a considerable achievement: he attempted to inform, legitimize and give self-confidence to the citizenry. He gave the people a sense of who they were and what they were doing, and did this through the use of other methods than simple polemic. And the fact that the decision duly taken by the people had serious consequences showed precisely that the difficulties of such a situation could not simply be evaded by having those concerned make the decision. The questions were no easier for the people, but the power of decision-making was properly attributed. The Danaid trilogy, which could well have had far more political significance in its complete form, thus contributed to the situation which prevailed during the years immediately before the revolt, the most important event of the Athenian democracy.

The removal of power from the Areopagus

In 462/1 Ephialtes and his allies finally succeeded in getting a motion through the Assembly ruling that the competence of the Areopagus should be confined to cases concerning blood-ties. The right both to call officials to account and to hold council on political matters was withdrawn. Ephialtes' justification would seem to have been the need to deprive the aristocratic Council of the *'epítheta'*, that is rights, which had never been granted to it in the first place, but which it had taken for granted.

Ephialtes' success was considerably facilitated either by the fact that Cimon was absent from the city on his campaign on behalf of the Spartans, or, if he had returned by then, by the humiliation he suffered at their hands. The Spartans are said to have become suspicious of the Athenians' reckless, self-important and rebellious manner and to have sent them off home earlier than all the other allies. We are not quite sure about the sequence of events here. But it is certain that Cimon was significantly weakened at the time that Ephialtes scored his victory. Not long afterwards he was ostracized. Shortly after this Ephialtes was assassinated.

There followed a sea change in foreign policy. Athens struck up alliances with Argos and Thessaly against Sparta. The city of Megara joined forces with them and, at about the same time, they went to war with Aegina, which had belonged to the Spartan camp. Around 458 Pericles had the Long Walls constructed between Athens and Piraeus; he fortified the city's position in relation to Sparta in every way possible. The war against Persia was meanwhile continued, although we know of only one expedition, albeit an extraordinarily ambitious one: an Athenian fleet went to the support of the rebellion initiated by the Libyan King Inarus in Egypt around 460 BC.

In the various wars of the period Athens suffered severe losses. We are in possession of a list of the men lost from one of the phylai during one of those years: it names 177 men who fell in battle with the Phoenicians on Cyprus, in Egypt and at different sites in their homeland. Even if these losses were by some chance higher than average, the implication is that at least a thousand citizens, that is, between $2\frac{1}{2}$ and 3 per cent of the total, were lost in a single year.

The removal of power from the Areopagus entailed a shift of responsibility for Athenian politics to the Assembly and its Council of the Five Hundred. Although nobles still held the most important posts, commanded the fleets and armies, formulated proposals for the Council and the Assembly and sought to determine the political line, there was no longer any institution where the most pressing problems could be discussed and policies prepared by the foremost experts and most influential statesmen. The authority of the aristocratic Council was a thing of the past.

This was a significant departure. It is true that the tyrants had managed to keep the nobility from power from the middle of the sixth century. But, while the people may once have ousted the aristocracy by means of civil war, no political replacement had been found. Later on, a series of different reforms strengthened the influence of the citizenry at large. The rights of the Assembly were extended, 'people's council' established and developed and the general self-awareness and power of all citizens must have increased. At the same time the influence of public officials was cut back, and their selection was now made by lot. This also had an indirect effect on the Areopagus, which was made up of men who had been top officials (the archons). But the upper class was still well represented; thanks to the rule of tenure, its members could acquire considerable expertise, and many of the most powerful politicians would still have belonged to it.

All these changes improved the citizens' scope for opposition, but they were also able to have a positive effect on the direction and character of the city's politics. For the politicians must have taken some account of the interests of the people's Assembly, though it remains unclear just how much. After all, the aristocratic Council still existed and it may well have been able to appeal to the Assembly in such a way as to maintain its influence. This must above all have been the case after the Persian Wars, with so many new challenges arising. The phenomenal successes also meant a good measure of common cause between the aristocracy and the people.

Thus any reforms up to 462 did not introduce wholesale modifications of the political order. Conceptual history would seem to confirm the idea that isonomy was not seen as rule by the people. In as far as it was a system of rule (*archē*), it was 'government' by civil officials alongside the 'leadership' or authority (*axīōma*) of the aristocratic Council; and whatever the extent of the Assembly's influence, it was above all marked by equality in terms of political rights and by the achievement of a political voice. This did not necessarily involve an 'awareness of holding power'. In comparison with later developments these isonomies would have been termed 'mixed constitutions'.

But now there was a profound rupture, as the question of who should rule over the most powerful Greek city was posed anew, and posed in terms of a simple alternative: either the people ruled (as *The Suppliants* has it) or the nobility. It was the most fundamental alternative possible within the citizenry: whether the governed should be *et de iure et de facto* free of any institutional, aristocratic authority in their political decision-making. It was no longer a matter of who was able to exert most influence, but of which of the two fundamentally different constitutions should be chosen.

This meant the end of the authority of the aristocratic class. Individual aristocratic politicians could still enjoy considerable status, but not of right. And it could be secured only on the basis of an ability to win over the Assembly.

This is where a new dimension to the citizens' identity came into play: over and above the status and equality of citizenship, they came to have a sense of being at one with the city. Even if it was only by chance that people first started asking 'who' the city really was in this particular situation, the situation gave rise to the answer that it was nothing other than the sum of the citizens. Even if Ephialtes emphasized the insight and sound common sense of the masses, believing that they at least were not distracted by selfish concerns from serving the best interests of the city, it clearly made sense not to play off the relative wisdom of the people and the aristocracy, but to focus on a different question altogether: who is the city? This is the positive counterpart to the negative contention that the aristocrats had made poor leaders. So on the one side there was a group which sought to make the city's decisions for it (motivated by self-interest), and on the other a group which maintained that that which their opponents called the polis was in reality the citizenry, and, given that all politics revolved around the citizens, it was they who should make the decisions, free of any 'higher' authority.

Plutarch was later to speak of an 'undiluted democracy' (*ákrātos dēmokratía*). Ephialtes filled the citizens' cup of freedom so full that they became intoxicated with it. The reaction from abroad, but also in some cases from home, would have been highly sceptical, especially as the weakening of the Areopagus meant a stronger function for the thetes. And so there were plots to topple the democracy. Both the murder of Ephialtes and various reports of a conspiracy support this. In 457, a year after the performance of the *Oresteia*, various noblemen were suspected of having dealings with Sparta, which was engaged in battle with Boeotia. They were charged with inciting Sparta to march on Athens in order to overthrow the new order there. Pericles' Long Walls were also a thorn in the side of many aristocrats.

The break with the Areopagus not only turned the old hierarchy upside down but it destroyed the fundamental correspondence between the political and social orders. This must have been highly problematic for a society which took the various domains of existence to be 'homologous' in structure, holding, for instance, that the gods and the animal world belonged to similar orders of being. The tragedies bear ample witness to this. If the world order and that of the polis were seen as being in tandem, such a colossal revision of the political must also have had ramifications for the image which the Athenians, indeed the Greeks in general, had of the world order and of the gods.

If Aeschylus' *Suppliants* was not performed in 463, it probably appeared in 461 or 460 – though it might be that Aeschylus put on other plays then. If the playwrights could only complete three tragedies and a satyr-play every two years, then he cannot have presented new plays before 459 or 458. We know that the *Oresteia* was performed in 458. So he submitted it in 459, having worked on the project since 461 or 460. It was produced in the immediate aftermath of the events of 462/1 and must have been conceived as his response to those events. The *Oresteia* stands in tangible relation to the politics of the time, and in particular to what was perceived as the most momentous event of Athenian history in those decades. And there is no better evidence for the fruitful interaction between politics and art – for the political art of tragedy – than this trilogy, which, according to Swinburne, is 'perhaps the greatest achievement of the human mind'.

The *Oresteia*

The *Oresteia* is the only complete trilogy surviving from antiquity. It is composed of the plays *Agamemnon, Choephoroe (The Libation Bearers)* and *The Eumenides*.

The plot

The first play begins at the moment when the news of the fall of Troy reaches Argos. It has arrived via a chain of beacons; the poet is apparently referring to a contemporary innovation of the Delian League. When the chorus of the elders of Argos deems such a means of communication impossible, this shows not only how the old lag behind the times, but also how extraordinary was the effect of such a conquest of great distances in space for those times. The accelerated change in the Greek world found its expression here, in the conquest as it were of great distances in time, which the *Oresteia* then goes on to treat.

The chorus recalls the departure of the army and the portents which were given to its leaders. It also recalls how Agamemnon, King of Argos and commander of the force, felt compelled to sacrifice his own daughter Iphigenia, for it had been prophesied that that was the condition for obtaining fair winds. The army had been anxious and, plagued by hunger, and severe storms from the north had even battered the fleet in the harbour. Faced with the dilemma of failing the army or slaughtering his daughter by his own hand, Agamemnon had favoured the army.

The Queen, Clytemnestra, enters and describes the sequence of the beacons to the chorus. Shortly afterwards there comes a herald bearing an exact report of the Greek victory and of the great losses incurred. Finally there enters Agamemnon himself, the victor. Clytemnestra receives him with obsequious respect. She wishes to cover his path into the palace with purple cloth; Agamemnon resists; such treatment is reserved for the gods and appeals only to barbarians. He is afraid; he fears the disapprobation of the people. But his wife persists. Thus he succumbs for her sake, stopping only, as if it were merely a question of protecting the cloth, to untie his sandals, before striding over the god's 'splendours dyed red in the sea' (949). This is above his station, a transgression of the demarcation separating the Greeks from the barbarians, but also of the limits laid down for humans by the gods.

Before the door stands Cassandra, handed over to Agamemnon by the Greek army, the 'flower and pride' (954) among a mass of booty. She refuses to enter the palace, remaining silent and unyielding until she is left alone with the chorus. She then gradually reveals first the terrible, bloody history of the palace of the Atreidae, this human 'slaughterhouse' (1092) before which she stands, then the fate of the king, who is murdered even as she speaks, and finally her own imminent end. Agamemnon's father Atreus had slaughtered the children of his brother Thyestes and served up their flesh on their father's plate. Only Aegisthus, who is now Clytemnestra's lover, had been spared. The revenge which the queen wreaks on Agamemnon for her daughter Iphigenia, is also meant indirectly for Atreus, and so forges a new link in the chain of atrocities.

At the end of the first tragedy Clytemnestra steps out of the palace, only to be showered with reproof by the chorus. Her lover Aegisthus joins her and threatens to bring the old men 'to reason'. Clytemnestra probably stood on what was called the *ekkýklēma*, a small platform which could be rolled out of the palace wall, which formed the backdrop (this mechanism overcame the difficulty of not being able to show the interior of a house without much of the audience being unsighted). At the queen's feet lie the corpses of Agamemnon and Cassandra.

The second play begins with the return of Orestes. The son, who shortly before Agamemnon's home-coming had been sent to distant Phocis, comes to avenge his father. The night before, Clytemnestra had dreamt that she had given birth to a snake, swaddling it and giving it her breast like a child, but together with the milk it had sucked from her thick, congealed blood. Thereupon the queen deputed her daughter, along with the enslaved Trojan women (who here form the chorus), to make an offering at her father's grave.

Electra is at a loss what words to use for a sacrifice she so detests. The women advise her to pray: 'Let some god or man come down upon them' – 'Judge or avenger, which?' – 'Just say "the one who murders in return"' (120). Electra doubts whether this would not be an act of impiety, and the answer comes: 'How not, and pay the enemy back in kind?' (123). She bemoans her brother's absence, and at that moment Orestes appears. He plans to introduce himself to the palace as a stranger, commissioned to bear the news of Orestes' death. This is what happens, and Clytemnestra receives him and has him shown to the men's quarters.

A little later the old nurse emerges. She is to summon Aegisthus with armed attendants. In words both moving and comic she laments the passing of Orestes, who had been her charge since his birth. For a short time gentleness, the voice of caring and nurture, is allowed to interrupt the progress of bloody vengeance. The women persuade the nurse to say nothing of the armed guard to Aegisthus. He duly comes alone, with a spring in his step and protestations of mourning on his lips. His death-cry is soon heard from within the palace. A servant raises the alarm. He responds to Clytemnestra's question with 'The dead are cutting down the quick, I tell you' (886). But Orestes is already on hand; after a long dialogue he forces her back into the palace at the point of a sword. Once more the play ends on the *ekkýklēma*, with Orestes carrying an olive-branch wrapped in wool, the corpses of the slain at his feet.

However, while in *Agamemnon*, Clytemnestra and Aegisthus had been only too sure of themselves, glad and proud of their murders, in the albeit uneasy hope that the chain of violence might now be broken (1569), Orestes is overcome by madness, even as he speaks. He sees that which nobody else on the stage (or in the theatre) can see, the coming of his mother's 'hounds', the Furies, the terible avenging spirits 'shrouded in black, their heads wreathed, swarming serpents!' (1049).

The last part of the trilogy opens in Delphi; the Pythia comes out in front of the temple and reveâls the line of succession to the sanctum. In the beginning it was Gaia, the Earth, the first prophetess, then her daughter, Themis; without violence the oracle was then made over to Phoebe, who presented it to Apollo at his birth. Then, looking about her, she sings the praises of the gods who are honoured there. Finally she retires into the temple to carry out her office – and returns at once, for there she has encountered Orestes and his pursuers. And before the audience have a view of

the Furies, they are presented once more with a fearful impression
of them: the Pythia crawls on all fours. No, it is not women
that she has seen, but Gorgons, black, obscene, repulsive. 'Their
heaving, rasping breathing makes me cringe. And their eyes ooze
a discharge, sickening' (53). Finally we see them in the flesh:
together with Orestes they are rolled out on the *ekkýklēma*. They
are sleeping. So hideous was their appearance that they are said
to have induced premature labour and miscarriages among women
in the audience.

Apollo appears. He has absolved Orestes and now allows him
to depart. Hermes is to accompany him. It will be a long journey,
and everywhere the Furies will hunt him down. The shade of
Clytemnestra awakens the avenging spirits. Apollo banishes them
from his hallowed ground.

The scene then changes to Athens, to the Acropolis, before the
image of the goddess Athena. It is the only time, as far as we
know, that Aeschylus sets his action in his own city. After long
journeys on land and sea, Orestes has followed the direction of
Apollo and delivered himself up to an Athenian court. The Furies
arrive on his trail.

Athena herself appears and has Orestes and the avenging spirits
present the grounds of their dispute to her. She explains that the
case is too difficult for any individual arbiter. Neither is she in a
position to decide judgement in a case of murder. And she sees a
particular difficulty in the fact that Orestes has come seeking
sanctuary, so that he must be taken in, but that the Furies have
'their destiny* too, hard to dismiss' (476). Deprived of victory,
they might wreak heavy damage on the city. But as she has been
confronted with the case, Athena determines to set up a tribunal.

The audience can now see how the Areopagus, which has just
been stripped of its political functions, is established for all time
by the goddess. Her inaugural speech is explicitly addressed to
'the people of Attica' (681), that is, to the audience. She recalls
that the crag of Ares (the Areopagus) had once been occupied by
the Amazons, who built a new fortress with 'towers thrust against'
the high walls of the Acropolis. On this spot, once the scene of
such a threat from without, a new counterforce within will now

---

* Meier translates 'rights and obligations'.

hold court. Here 'terror and reverence, my people's kindred powers, will hold them from injustice through the day and the mild
night' (690). The goddess counsels the citizens to entertain neither
'anarchy nor tyranny', and not to expel the fearful (*deinón*) from
the city. For 'where is the righteous man who knows no fear?'
(699). Thanks to terror and reverence, however, the Athenians
have the security of a bulwark for the land and the city such as
neither the Scythians nor the Spartans can boast. (These two
peoples were renowned at that time for their long-established good
order (*eunomía*).) Athens now seems able to excel them by virtue
of its democracy – as long as it does not cast what is fearful out
of the city.

The parties have set out their respective cases, and Apollo joins
in to defend Orestes. He pleads for acquittal, while the Furies
claim that the matricide must certainly be handed over to them.
As Apollo and the Furies exchange serious reproaches, the judgement is made. Finally Athena declares that she too will cast a
vote, which, as she freely admits, will favour Orestes. The vote is
equally balanced, so Orestes goes free; he takes leave with thanks,
promising that Argos will be beholden to Athens in future.

But the Furies are outraged. They have forfeited all honour,
and their justice has been 'ridden down', as they repeatedly say.
They can no longer fulfil their duty. They have already announced
what this implies: they alone stand for the respect due to justice,
so now murder is granted a free rein. They then threaten to pour
venom on the land, to visit a plague upon it. Athena attempts to
placate them, offering them residence in the city, a share in 'this
country cherished by the gods' (869) and great honours. The first
offerings made at births and marriages would be consecrated to
them, indeed they would be responsible for the welfare of the city's
houses: 'No house can thrive without you' (895). However they
are not so easily won over. The goddess has to make four new
attempts before they submit. They do so not just because of the
offers made, but also because Athena treats them, in all patience
and deference, with *peithô*, the 'majesty of Persuasion, the spell of
my voice that would appease your fury' (885). Thus, at the end,
the goddess celebrates the *peithô* with which she could persuade
the wild recalcitrants. However, she adds, it is Zeus of Counsel

(Zeus Agoraios) who has prevailed here (970), the god, that is, of the Assembly, of the political market.

After long songs of blessing, a second chorus, this time evidently representing Athenians, accompanies the Furies by torchlight to their new seats in a cave on the slopes of the Acropolis, or, to be more precise, of the Areopagus.

Both in its detail and as a whole, the *Oresteia* is much more strongly related to politics than the other tragedies of Aeschylus known to us; indeed one might suppose that its grandeur and gravity are due not least to the profound political ferment and questioning of those years. Only one who is not aware how central politics were to the experience and thinking of Athenians in the fifth century in general and more especially in those years, could see this as a disadvantage or short-coming, or as too narrow an understanding. Seldom can one study so well what tragedy meant to its audience of Athenian citizens. Seldom is the supposition that this audience urgently needed its theatre more convincingly borne out.

Thus one must beware of impeding access to the play by applying an inappropriate concept of politics conditioned by modernity. Precisely because politics were so all-embracing in those days, it is possible to understand the play in an 'unpolitical' way, that is, from a general, human point of view. For this very reason its significance reaches far beyond politics, and beyond the historical situation of 458 BC.

Political allusions

There are striking allusions to contemporary politics and military campaigns in the *Oresteia*. There is repeated reference to the Athenian alliances with Argos. Apollo even declares that he has sent Orestes to Athens in order to establish a covenant for all time. While waiting for the arrival of the goddess, Orestes traces the range of her activities in his imagination: perhaps she is in Libya going to the aid of friends, or in Chalcidice; she eventually herself reveals that she has come from the plain of Scamander where she had to take possession of lands which had fallen to her from Troy. As one of these is clearly an oblique reference to the city's engagement in Egypt at that time, it is more or less certain that at the same time the Athenians were at war or engaged in other business in the other two places.

To explain why in Agamemnon's absence she had sent Orestes to a family friend, Clytemnestra had declared that the friend had alerted her to the dangerous situation of Orestes' father before the walls of Troy and of the further danger 'if the people rise up howling for the king, and anarchy should dash our plans*' (883); for it is human nature to trample on the fighter when he is down. It seems quite plausible to relate these words to the fall of the Areopagus; they may even contain an allusion to Cimon's absence. And why is Agamemnon referred to on several occasions as 'leader of the fleet'? It has the same topical ring about it as Aegisthus' epithet for the rebellious chorus: 'slaves at the oars' (1617), as if he had Athenian thetes before him.

But all of these are passing remarks of no great significance. It is only the references to the alliance with Argos which are of real importance, for an association with Athens' new foreign policy is clearly implied. This is, however, part of the united front which the goddess calls on her citizens to adopt towards the outside world at the close of the *Oresteia*. Otherwise we have mere 'quotations' rather than concrete attitudes, regarding the political agenda. But even these quotations show the extent to which politics permeate the play. The real political significance lies elsewhere, however, in the 'repetition' of the historical moment of upheaval, in the attempt to integrate it into the sense of things, into the Athenians' systems of order, both high and highest. But it was clear that the framework could not remain unaltered: too much had happened in the meantime. In this sense, the 'repetition' embraced something quite new, something which would nevertheless eventually find its place within the old order.

Conflict and appeasement

The Eumenides is dominated by the opposition between old and young gods. In the entry song of the chorus in *Agamemnon*,

---

* Meier translates 'council'

Aeschylus followed up the first invocation of Zeus with mention of his two predecessors, Uranus and Cronos, though they remain nameless. The power of Uranus was great, then he was smitten; nobody speaks of him any more. And Cronos too met his match. So the rule of Zeus is put into historical perspective from the start, at least as far as the past is concerned. There is no indication that he too might succumb; on the contrary. After all, his rule is relatively new.

Aeschylus now compares the ancient lineage of the Furies, the daughters of the Night, with the young Apollo. The antithesis is total: the Furies are black, Apollo and his world white, sunlit and civilized; the Furies are terrible to behold and savage in manner, neither human nor god. None of the gods would give them hospitality. Their retribution is barbaric. Apollo clearly sets them apart from the Greeks, even as they draw attention to their office, which is founded in ancient law. And they claim that Apollo undermines this by honouring the human above divine law. Apollo has Hermes, Athena and, above all, Zeus on his side, the combined strength of the 'young' dynasty.

The distinction between the two camps is manifest in the fact that the Furies defend an old right and the young gods a new one. Orestes would have fallen victim to the old spirit of vengeance. The murder of his mother would have given ample cause. If he was not voluntarily prepared to admit to it, witness should be given on oath. But granted that he did not deny the fact, the very idea of initiating a trial is seen by the Furies as a violation, since trials are meant to ascertain the course of events. And a murderer can never escape his guilt. But Athena feels that the case should be confirmed by a court. The motives should be considered, if a just judgement is to be made, rather than the mere semblance of guilt which would be conveyed by sworn statement. And she is at a loss to believe that there can be no end to the pursuit. Orestes had claimed that blood dries in the fullness of time. Besides, he had atoned for his guilt, and it had become clear on his long journey that he had committed no offence against any of his hosts (such as had always been the case with those stained with blood). So the condition for asylum in Athens was met; those who sought it could not bear the guilt of bloody deeds, as the treatment of the matter in *The Suppliants* shows most clearly. This would not stop the Furies from pursuing their vengeance further, for their claim rested not on the problem of Orestes' being besmirched, but on respect for the law.

There is much to suggest that, with this 'new law', Aeschylus was alluding to certain more recent achievements in the legislature of Attica, which had led to the development of a free assessment of evidence. Apollo had recognized the way out in dealing with judges: one must simply use 'a magic spell – with words' (82). He significantly uses the same word for 'way out' (*mēchanē*) as Pelasgus does in *The Suppliants* when he expresses his doubt. But this change in the judicial system was probably not simply introduced overnight, but was the product of a long process. The only historical parallel to the collision and battle between the old and the new can have been the conflict over the Areopagus. By arranging that Orestes is not simply tried, but that a decision has to be reached between the old and the new, Aeschylus repeats what the Athenians had experienced only three years earlier.

The proponents of the Areopagus can hardly have avoided using the same argument as that repeatedly voiced by the Furies: that its opponents were in violation of time-honoured law. For in Athens at that time the old, the traditional, would have had much to recommend it, whereas the new order had little to offer, at least in terms of the political perspective. This is one of the implications of *The Suppliants*. For the Furies argue so powerfully against the new, and the young gods steer so clear of temporal lines of argument, that we can certainly conclude that the innovators could not simply challenge the old order with claims of 'the new'. Novelty for its own sake would not win people over. This is perhaps why Ephialtes appears to have countered the conservative arguments with the assertion that the power enjoyed by the Areopagus was arrogated. What was represented as the old by the Areopagus party was to be superseded by something far more ancient.

It is also possible that the rift between Cimon and Ephialtes came about in a way similar to that between the Furies and Apollo. The conflict over a single question (how to deal with Sparta?) became so intense and dogmatic that the total structures of the two opposing orders became embroiled in the argument. But this must be a debatable point.

In any case, bias on the one side in Aeschylus fuels bias on the other. Apollo challenges the Furies' right to Orestes, because they take the murder of the mother so much more seriously than that of her husband (219). It is not only the memory of Orestes' father that motivates Zeus to take his side, but also the sight of his 'mother's advocates' (761). The two camps come to stand for more general oppositions such as that between male and female, and between the legal bonds of marriage on the one hand and the bonds of blood on the other. Apollo is unequivocally in favour of marriage and of male domination. He goes so far as to assert that the children are really only the progeny of the father, as the mother only plays host to his seed for a short time. This is why Clytemnestra's murder of Agamemnon is so terrible, a violation of the highest order, while Orestes' matricide may be justified as avenging his father. It is 'Not the same for a noble man to die, covered with praise, his sceptre the gift of a god' (625), and this not in battle but by the hand of a woman. For the Furies, on the other hand, there is no tie so intimate and binding as that of the child to his mother. Next to that, marriage pales into insignificance. Apollo and the Furies are both equally adamant that the two murders cannot be compared. But this unleashes the most deadly strife. Limited points of view pretend to be comprehensive. If Orestes was only able to avenge his father by murdering his mother, it is because the duty of revenge has been taken to perverse lengths. Questions of prestige also become involved, because Apollo sees it as a matter of honour to defend the individual who has sought his protection. Athena herself manifests allegiance to one camp when she justifies her vote for Orestes by saying that she sides with men, except with regard to marriage. Of course such conflicts, with gods intervening on behalf of their favourites, had been seen before. But here, for the first time, the world order is at stake; and the fact that the partisan god was seen physically on the stage, an appearance for which we know of no precedent, must also have had quite an impact.

Aeschylus contrives to represent these divisions in such a way as to produce 'a master drama of partisanship and injustice' (Grillparzer). New and old law alike are informed more by *parti pris* than by justice. Nor does the decisive role of the goddess necessarily guarantee the fairness of the outcome.

This conflict was not simply part of the broader struggle arising from the establishment of a new dynasty. Rather, it broke out when the rule of Zeus was already well established. For in the course of *Agamemnon* and *The Libation Bearers* the Furies are seen as faithful servants of the ruling gods, with responsibility for dealing with any murder. In the long series of punishments which, according to Apollo, threaten Orestes if he fails to effect the revenge, the Furies are naturally cited as henchwomen.

This also corresponds strikingly to the situation of Athens. Here too the primacy of the people was established long before 461 (even if the Areopagus had tended to set the tone). The two forces then came into conflict, with the result that, as in *The Eumenides*, a new order was created within the context of the same system of rule, itself relatively new.

The profound, fundamental and ultimately intractable nature of the opposition is reflected by the vote of the Areopagus. We do not know to what extent Athenians at that time held the view that there could be only *one* just order in accordance with the will of Zeus, but it is quite possible that many did, or at least that they believed the order of things was essentially a matter of truth and wisdom and not simply to be tampered with by random votes. Such an order had been sought during the sixth century, and decisions had been taken to install a just system. Knowledge itself had been developed through the recognition that popular participation in politics was necessary. It is clearly human nature to resist the idea that an established order is arbitrary in nature. And old principles still tend to remain compelling, even when particular elements no longer hold true. If faith in a *single*, just system, ordained by the will of Zeus, was still alive among the Athenians, the vote as it appears here must have had a quite staggering effect. It will have seemed, at the very least, absurd. And it threw into sharp relief the decisions just made regarding the Areopagus; there could be no doubt of the motivation which lay behind them. It is even possible that the hung vote in the play more or less corresponded to the real situation. But it is perhaps idle to speculate on this. What is crucial is that this makes quite clear the extent of the difficulties brought about by such a conflict between old and new.

The interpretation which Aeschylus puts upon the vote also serves to point up the sort of consequences such a method of decision-making might have. Such a fundamental question as the choice between an old and a new form of justice is seen to defy any individually conceived solution, and has to be put to a wider vote. And then the result could not be closer and can only be reached at all by the intervention of the goddess against the majority of earthly judges. And the hung vote, which is only resolved in Orestes' favour according to the principle of *in dubio pro reo*, ironically represents the victory of a new law.

So this is democracy. This is how things stand when the most fundamental question of who should rule is cast as a straight alternative between the aristocracy and the people. It is no longer acceptable to give everyone his due according to status (such as in Solon's time and no doubt long after that), for the popular claim on power now excludes the possibility of leadership by the aristocracy. Now it is only victory in the ballot, by however slim a margin, that can decide the issue.

This democracy is, however, also evidently given the blessing of Athena, which serves as a stamp of approval. When confronted by the problem of Orestes, the goddess was able to choose the method of the decision by due process; she did not share the inner struggle of King Pelasgus in his doubts. And where she herself has to come to a judgement of the case, she has no problems; she simply follows her own inclination. In this sense her vote has little genuine bearing on the justice of the case. But this is not of the essence; what matters is the fact that she found an institutional solution – and that she was able to cope with the consequences of the vote. This shows the particular strength of her thinking, and it is this that is decisive, this that makes the decision work.

For, according to Aeschylus' construal, the holding of the vote is not the end of the matter. Rather, there follows the reconciliation of the Furies. Their anger is a further parallel to the contemporary situation in Athens, for here too the losers will not have taken the matter lying down. Athena declares that she alone among the gods 'knows the keys to the armoury where Zeus' lightning bolt is stored' (827). But she has no wish to make use of this knowledge. What she brings about through assuaging offers and persuasion is probably more an example and a challenge than a parallel to real events. But we cannot be sure of this, or of the effect that Aeschylus achieved here. It is clear at any rate that he was at least as intent on showing the need for a conciliatory spirit on the part of the victor as on legitimating the particular decision reached by the vote in his play.

It has long been a point of contention whether the Furies are changed by being accepted in Athens and granted the title of Eumenides. They certainly gain a stable seat, new tasks and new sacrifices. While they are still meant to be feared and to punish, it is unlikely that they will continue to devour their victims alive, as they had earlier threatened to do to Orestes. When the city takes them into its service, their position is evidently changed. Even marriage is put under their auspices, and Athena addresses the leader of these creatures, who had hitherto been viewed neither as divine nor human, as a fellow goddess. So they are indeed transformed in significant respects.

Zeus' order is re-established on a new foundation, as the old is integrated, allotted a place and a function, within the new. After the schism, the terrible entrenchment of oppositions, after the ruling and the dangers which spring from it, in the end there is appeasement. Because this is recognized as the doing of Zeus Agoraios, the whole is revealed as a political process, or at least as a process bound up with political decision-making. And it is portrayed with an optimum degree of accuracy, an impressive combination of political experience, careful thought and, of course, aesthetic treatment.

This process not only shows multiple, often close connections with political reality, but the resulting consequences are clearly drawn. When Athena counsels her citizens to respect 'Neither anarchy nor tyranny' (696), she takes up, almost verbatim, the demand raised by the Furies in a choral song earlier (526). It is the only time that Aeschylus has two parties represent the same express principle with such vigour. The Furies had added that the god always gives victory and sovereignty (*krátos*) to that which 'strikes the balance'. This sounds like a denial of the requirement implied in 'demo-cracy', and is at the very least an urgent warning against an extreme form of popular rule. For this must have been understood by 'anarchy' at that time, given that it had broken free of the traditional power structures. The Furies ask: 'Is there a man who knows no fear in the brightness of his heart, or a man's city, both are one, that still reveres the rights?' (522). Athena explains that 'terror' should never be banished from the city. She says this in the inauguration speech for the Areopagus. When she subsequently promises the Athenians that they will enjoy an order superior to that of the Spartans and the Scythians, she gives democracy the highest possible accolade: for it was just this that was cast in such doubt after the Greek revolution. Now the new, practised with due moderation, is really presented as a great achievement.

Taken together, the two parallel utterances of Athena and the Furies imply that the new, when realized in this way, is the fundamental principle of the only just order. Understood in a more general way, as it is here, the principle is that moderation, just measure, is supreme, and may be applied to quite different sorts of constitution. In this way Aeschylus anchors the principle of the new within a (modified) version of the old. New and old are happily conjoined. It is clear that the inclusion of the Furies in Zeus' new order is a recipe for reconciliation with the nobility. The attempt to legitimate the new also involves its integration, although no specific prescription for this is offered.

What Aeschylus made of Ephialtes' reforms is not only a moot point, but one with little real bearing on our interpretation of the trilogy. It is of course striking that when the Areopagus is deprived of its power, Athena institutes this particular council rather than some unspecified court. There must be reasons for this. But the functions which she attributes to the Areopagus in her impressive speech are precisely those that Ephialtes left intact: those of juris-diction in capital trials. When the goddess says that the members of the Areopagus should be incorruptible, she may well be taking her cue from the proceedings which Ephialtes had successfully brought against a number of them. In fact the role which Athena envisages for the Areopagus is a considerable one. It is to keep watch over the city. This could be seen as an attempt to stress the significance of the aristocratic Council in spite of Ephialtes. But it could equally well be aimed at reconciling the nobles with the reform by confirming their very important responsibilities and honours. Finally, it is possible that, by describing these responsi-bilities, Athena was exhorting the members of the Areopagus to punish the assassination of the very individual who had challenged their regime. In short, even if tragedy had been a forum for such matters, it seems that there are no partisan positions at work in this play. Aeschylus is not concerned with institutions. Even if he did vote against Ephialtes, what was right or wrong three years earlier has little bearing here. He was much more concerned with the polis order as a whole and, by extension, with that of the world in general. And this evidently demanded a spirit of reconciliation and of consideration for all parties. How this was to be effected was not a matter for the theatre. But Aeschylus does offer an indication: the Eumenides call upon the citizens to 'Give joy in return for joy, one common will for love, and hate with one strong heart: such union heals a thousand ills of man' (985).

This formula is closely bound up with contemporary developments in political history. Friendship and enmity were being revised. The inner unity of the city had to be matched by a new relationship with the outside world. It is only logical that Athena should go on to refer to the great profit that the city will derive from the conduct of war. A united front would mean work and benefit for all, including members of the nobility, if not the Areopagus as a whole. And at least one thing had changed for the nobles: while their leadership had hitherto been a matter of course, it was now contingent upon their place within and, to a considerable extent, their contribution to the whole. The means by which individuals could now make their mark and gain influence had become quite different.

The prehistory of the polis

The Eumenides represents only the last part of the trilogy, the one closest to politics, and the point where the apparently infinite chain of revenge and counter-revenge comes to an end with the decision of the polis court. It is the end of a long story. In *Agamemnon* and *The Libation Bearers* all are at the mercy of the forces at play. And the audience can see this. The elders and the Trojan women continually bear witness to their helplessness (even if the latter do participate in Orestes' intrigue).

The rulers vary. Agamemnon is not only king by right, but he also wishes to take account of the people. Despite this, he went to war over a woman and in order to pursue the campaign he sacrificed his daughter. Under his command the Greeks committed acts of desecration, destroying holy shrines. Notwithstanding all his insight, he is ultimately beguiled by his wife and proves susceptible to tyrannical, barbarian behaviour. By comparison with Clytemnestra and Aegisthus he appears in a favourable light, for they exercise pure tyranny. Thus his memory is cherished in *The Libation Bearers*. Orestes, his legitimate heir, is given help. But the people have no influence on the business of government, however passionately they may express their wrath.

Helplessness and abandonment are recurrently expressed in the fear of the chorus, which is first and foremost fear of speaking what they know. They cryptically hint at something, which turns out to be the state of the city under the oppressive regime of Clytemnestra and her lover Aegisthus. The elders are also afraid, though, because they are in a state of genuine uncertainty. They have no real knowledge of what is going on, because they perceive things only at second hand. All decisive action is taken within the walls of the palace; it is from there that Argos is ruled. And besides these as it were empirically based anxieties, there is a third fear, which springs from religious premonition. When the doors of the palace close behind Agamemnon, the chorus sings: 'Why, why does it rock me, never stops, this terror beating down my heart, this seer that sees it all – it beats its wings, uncalled unpaid thrust on the lungs the mercenary song beats on and on singing a prophet's strain' (975). The fleet's anxious embarkation for Troy lies far in the past. Agamemnon has returned victorious. And yet their hearts intuitively sing the dirge of the Furies. And they continue: 'and it's real, true, no fantasy – stark terror whirls the brain' (985) in a dance which confirms their fears.

It is, then, not a premonition which accounts for the frenzy of the elders after they have seen the king and queen meet and enter the palace, but a knowledge which is lodged in their hearts. An ultimate law appears to be borne out in this, one which cannot be a determining factor in everyday consciousness and decision-making, but which manifests itself at best in anxieties. For there is no way of knowing when and how it will reach its goal. As the subsequent exchange with Cassandra shows, the chorus can be quite obtuse when confronted directly in dialogue with hints of a certain type. But equally, distanced as observers, they may have a sense of those anxieties which are as yet beyond their comprehension.

If the thought of the terrible losses of the war arouses in the chorus a perfectly concrete concern about the grave resentment simmering among the people, they see the root of the threat in the fact that the gods keep a keen eye on those who shed much blood. What is perhaps developing on earth corresponds to the punishment intended by the gods, and they thus have every reason to fear what breathes 'under the night's shroud' (459). Their knowledge of divine retribution renders the whole situation unnerving for them, so that they fear danger from whence, as it turns out, there is no threat. But the fear in itself is fundamentally justified. The same anxiety grips them when Cassandra mentions Thyestes' feast.

Right at the beginning of *Agamemnon* the old men had recalled what they saw as the good auguries which appeared to the army as it embarked: two eagles which had slain and were now devouring a pregnant hare. The kings of birds are, according to the seer, the kings leading the army: Agamemnon and Menelaus, the Atreidae. The omen portends victory over Troy. It also portends a dreadful violation of holy laws, for young or unborn life may not be cut short. It has the protection of Artemis. And so the goddess turns her anger upon the 'eagles' who lead the army. The seer fears that she will make all winds blow foul. And this is indeed the case. She is only to be appeased by 'another victim . . . nothing sacred, no' (151): Agamemnon must match the sacrifice of the hare's young in the hunt with that of his own daughter. The deed is the same one which the Greeks will commit against the Trojans, not simply punishing them for the abduction of Helen, but annihilating the city along with all its shrines and its 'seed' (528), both young and old. What serves as a portent for the Trojan campaign is, in the eyes of Artemis, a transgression both on the part of the eagles and of the general; she thus demands a sacrifice which can only compound Agamemnon's guilt. The guilt which he takes upon himself is the precondition for fair winds and embarkation upon the campaign. Most of the Greeks are punished on their way home for the injustice done to Troy. Agamemnon, on the other hand, is allowed to reach Argos, and only there does he meet with the punishment for murdering his own daughter.

Everything is woven together in an extraordinarily bold manner: past, present and future; gods, humans and animals. Not only are eagles guilty of taking unborn life, a father of killing his daughter and an army of annihilating a city, but various ordinances are themselves destroyed. The laws of hunting and sacrifice are broken, the borders between man and beast, culture and wildness, undone. Aeschylus' language is unequivocal and telling. Good and ill fortune engulf each other. Having at first deemed the omen good, the chorus recurrently closes its strophes with the words: 'Cry, cry for death, but good win out in glory in the end.'

This shows how thin is the line between health and sickness, triumph and defeat, profit and loss. The knowledge is particularly clear in the great songs, sung as it were from a distance. And if the herald is unaware of this, he bears witness to it in his turn when he follows up his account of the triumph over Troy by describing the demise of the fleet. And when Clytemnestra recognizes the ambivalent nature of the deed, but seeks to escape it, she is labouring under a bitter delusion. She is as much subject to the law as anybody else.

All grope in the dark, entertain modest hopes and are afraid. As Karl Reinhardt shows, they have no notion of the 'unconscious', but they do have a sense of the ambivalent, as it presents itself both inwardly and outwardly. And so they fear without at first knowing quite why.

Of course the chorus appears courageous on occasion, for instance when they criticize the terrible deficit of a war fought over a foreign woman. They make the charge to Agamemnon, albeit adding that they are being open with him only to show that he can rely on them. At first they want above all to celebrate victory, then they are outraged at the king's murder and curse the assassins. They hold up the threat of the fury of the populace, but this only goes to accentuate their impotency.

In the *Libation Bearers* fear has spread to Clytemnestra; only Aegisthus notices nothing of it, but already in *Agamemnon* he had felt only his own joy at the king's death and nothing of the enormity of the deed. Orestes and Electra are fearful too, but the chorus less so; much has changed since *Agamemnon*, albeit inconclusively.

Only in *The Eumenides* is there fundamental change. There there is light. Day breaks. As the Pythia speaks her prayer, she casts around both historically and geographically. She makes mention of the changes in sovereignty over the shrine: the three supreme goddesses are succeeded by the young god, the current lord, Apollo. And astonishingly (and at variance with the prevailing view) the transfer had been achieved without violence. Then she turns to the other divinities honoured in Delphi: gods both of civilization and of nature. They complement each other, co-operate, so that all is in order. Delphi is as it were the prelude for Athens.

Things may now happen in public. When Apollo reassures Orestes, 'Remember that. No fear will overcome you'* (88), it sounds as if he is marking a new phase in the history of fear. The fearful does come on stage and is terrible to behold, but savagery is no longer a part of human individuals – Agamemnon, Clytemnestra, Electra – but incarnate in the avenging spirits. When the Areopagus votes for the Furies with a bare majority, their threats have clearly influenced the decision. But a battle is waged against them. The action shifts to the conflict between young and old gods. The partisan way in which day and night, white and black, young and old, male and female, established law and blood-ties, are opposed is shattering in its clarity. Until the decision of the court, that is. For then, with Athena's help, they are once more made to co-operate and complement one another.

Now the problem is rather that there may be too little to fear. It seems almost as if it is in the gift of the city to decide how much fear is desirable. 'Anarchy' and Apollo's rather partisan treatment of his mortal ward seem a genuine possibility. But Athena steers things back to the middle of the road.

The trilogy also represents the historical development of thought. The goddess recognizes that the Furies have the superior wisdom which comes with age. But she also points out that Zeus has given her a modicum of intelligence (*phroneîn*, 848). This *phrónēsis* evidently stands for new intellectual possibilities. On earth it is a product of suffering. The first mention of the law set out by Zeus comes in the entry song of the chorus in *Agamemnon*: 'that

---

* Meier translates 'Let no fear vanquish your heart'.

we must suffer, suffer unto truth' (177). This paves the way for thought. Thoughtfulness, the 'sense of wisdom' (*sōphroneîn*) thus comes to humans, whether they seek it or not. This is a tremendous theodicy which informs all the terrible events which are witnessed in *Agamemnon* and *The Libation Bearers*. Divine grace is 'violent' (182) in its operation. In *The Eumenides* the process seems to be reaching its goal. The Furies celebrate the Athenians as achieving wisdom at last, 'loved by the loving virgin girl', Athena (1000).

The short excerpt from the history of the house of Atreus thus represents for Aeschylus a mythical image of the lengthy historical developments leading to the foundation of the polis. After the concatenation of revenge and counter-revenge, 'with kinsmen murdering kinsmen' (1575), comes the resolution. After abandonment to the vagaries of the sovereign's fate, and a course of events which dragged everyone helplessly along with it, comes the new citizens' regime. After a time of terror comes a new order of justice, combining openness and liberty with a necessary residue of fear, and thus of respect – an order second to none. Suffering has indeed brought knowledge. A whole history has been recreated in order to show that a single decision made within it is not arbitrary.

By setting the great decision between old and new orders within this broad compass, Aeschylus establishes its historical meaning. It is a part of the bright new world. The stress on historical differences, and especially the archaic terms of the oppositions to the new order depicted in *Agamemnon*, make this clear. In this way the decision is aligned with the creation of the polis, and the process by which the citizens achieved power is focused into a single act.

The extreme absurdity of the vote in *The Eumenides* is characterized by Aeschylus as the resolution of a long, anxiety-ridden and uncanny history of ineluctable chains of violence. It is hard for us to imagine what all this meant to the Athenians, accustomed as we are to being subject to processes beyond our ken and our mastery. The modern age is predicated upon the fact that for a considerable period of time we were able to view history as progress, yielding advantage as long as it was not treated uncritically. We can all see today what it means to lose such a faith. But the Greeks had had no such experience of 'progress'. Since the sixth century they had become used to the idea that things happened, as they put it, *en mésōi* (in their midst) and depended on their decisions; anything which could not be seen was uncanny for them. Perhaps this helped the task of removing power from the Areopagus. For what was debated there was largely closed to the public scrutiny by which the Athenians set such store, and which they were so eager to develop.

If Aeschylus contrived to enact the earthly history of the polis in such a poised and compelling manner by way of the Atreidae myth, certain questions regarding the gods are begged. It may be that Zeus differed from his predecessors in making sense of human suffering by his law of 'suffer unto truth'. But the question remains: why did he do this and how did he make them learn? And why did he require such a long process, such an agenda of suffering? After all, what did Agamemnon and Clytemnestra learn? Of course Electra and Orestes were rather more restrained, more questioning and open. Their revenge was motivated by duty rather than by the terrible pleasure which Clytemnestra takes in her bloody deed. But even if they have learned anything, they are spared nothing. It is not even clear whether they act in accordance with Apollo's will. And anyway, can the *raison d'être* of the Greeks at the time of the Trojan War have been to prepare the ground for reason in following generations? It is a possible hypothesis. But what sort of theodicy would that be?

It is certainly true that it can have been no easy task to bring people to reason. It is tempting to try to construct a theodicy on this basis. But why then were the gods themselves so involved in events? Why did Zeus crave revenge on Troy, revenge so fatal for the avengers? Why did he instigate war over a single flighty woman, much to the consternation of the elders? And as for Apollo, why does he seek not only Clytemnestra's death, but that of Cassandra too? Of course it may be that the gods had to participate so relentlessly in the terrible chain of events in order to ensure the suffering through which truth was to be gained (though this does not account for why Aeschylus fails to let them transcend events). And, setting these questions aside, how can the sudden political volte-face be explained? 'The truth still holds while Zeus holds the throne' sings the chorus in the first play, the law that 'the one who acts must suffer' (1563). But why is Orestes' suffering curtailed? Did Zeus see the light because the law of revenge had reached its most extreme form here?

This perhaps accounted for the play. But there remains a discrepancy between what is achieved within the trilogy and what points beyond its bounds. A complete theology is after all being laid out here. And within its framework the events remain somewhat arbitrary. The conflict between the two generations of gods, and the new order it introduces, is provoked by the fate of an individual. Is there not a gap here, an incongruity between cause and effect (however faithfully it corresponds to political experience), a theological scandal? But perhaps such questions are out of order. The justification of this bold historical version of the Atreidae story may simply be that it could not do without a theodicy – and that the events around 460 were in need of historical legitimation? The image of history could ultimately be only fiction, a path from reality to hope. Or perhaps it was necessary for the gods to be involved as soon as the old was superseded on earth, given the connection between events in the divine and human spheres.

The question of the gods' role is best answered by the Prometheus trilogy. The question of the relationship between the old and the new, which remains open, can be approached via yet another question. Assuming that we are indeed being presented with a piece of history, is the political import of *Agamemnon* and *The Libation Bearers* limited to their reference to the historical situation, the way in which they are a foil to the brightness of a brave new world? Did these first two parts of the trilogy have anything to say in themselves to the citizen *qua* citizen?

Repetition, problematization and currency of mythical experience

The fate which Agamemnon pursues when he starts an inconceivable and dreadful war over a woman; the fate which pursues Paris too, and razes Troy; the savage pleasure with which Clytemnestra entraps and slaughters the returning king, possessed by a daemon, driven by the curse of the house of Atreus, which far exceeds the desire for revenge, and which she tries in vain to control after the deed; the terrible fate of Cassandra; was all this simply to be seen as part of the distant past, as genuinely historical and so resolved?

Were the great choral songs of *Agamemnon* and *The Libation Bearers*, the prayers to Zeus, the vast scope of experience which they drew together around the tight structure of the action, merely to be viewed in aesthetic terms, without regard to the political framework of Athenian theatre?

After all, not long before this, the Athenians had been presented, in *The Persians*, with the picture of Xerxes being driven by a daemon to embark on the fateful campaign against the Greeks. And many of them must have seen the significance of this, given their still prevalent need to find meaning in everything. For it was not good enough to trace such a calamitous decision back to arbitrary factors, poor reasoning or bad advice. All these had played a part, but (as Aeschylus shows us) not in isolation, but as an effect of a much more profound, inward and metaphysical force. It is gods and daemons (the two are virtually synonymous) who acted in this way. 'A god plants guilt in mortals, when he is out to annihilate their house', as one of Aeschylus' fragments has it. So can the daemon of the Atreidae have been so foreign to the Athenians? Must the human and the divine not have been inextricable for them too, at least in such momentous times?

The elders' powerful laments over the 'moneychanger Ares', who sends home dust instead of men to their loved ones, must also have struck a topical note. It was after all a time when Athens was engaged in so many, often distant conflicts, and incurring such dreadful losses. However eagerly the Athenians might have voted for these campaigns in the heat of the moment, many must have asked themselves whether the aims, even when they were more substantial than recapturing Helen, really tallied with all the spilt blood.

It is hardly likely that a majority of Athenians in 458 could have believed that such events as those portrayed in *Agamemnon* were consigned once and for all to history; or, to put it more carefully, that these events did not concern them personally. The actions and the suffering, the vulnerability and powerlessness, even of those on the sidelines, the elders in the chorus, must have awoken lively associations and revived latent anxieties in many Athenians. Their own ambiguous or uncanny experiences were here embodied on stage. And they will thus have understood very well the hints of the chorus as to the meaning behind events, as these hints gave voice to their own fears.

Aeschylus' *Oresteia*, especially his *Agamemnon*, thus fulfilled the age-old function of rehearsing ancient tales, in particular the sort of tales which have so much to say about the fate of humanity and the world; these were able to render anxieties familiar by, as it were, objectifying them in the people and events of an earlier age, one from which the audience felt distant and yet which touched them closely. For in these plays they could undergo and work through things which would otherwise merely have been helplessly suffered.

Tragedy could enact these stories in an especially engaging way by confronting the audience directly with criminals and victims (and the processes by which the criminal could in turn be victimized) and, thanks to the chorus, with various ways of reflecting on and even interpreting the course of events. Even the house, which is constantly alluded to in *Agamemnon* and *The Libation Bearers*, is present on stage: the human slaughterhouse, the scene of the crime, witness to so much ignominy and itself under threat (as the symbol of the ruling house).

So this is the first thing which the *Oresteia*, and in particular *Agamemnon*, could do for the citizens of Athens: it could make the ancient stories, and with them the dark world of their origins, present and familiar. But these stories were of course rendered problematic by being filtered through the experience and needs of a new age, pervaded by the demands for reason and justice, the tensions and responsibilities of the citizenry.

This took the form on the one hand of a quest for justice. The pressure, which was exerted by the terrible events, was to some extent released by the indication that a just process lay behind them. Paris offends against the laws of hospitality. Troy takes Helen in. Aeschylus has the chorus sing of a young lion (717) which a man rears in his house to be stroked and petted by all – until it is full-grown, when, following its natural instincts, it wreaks carnage on its hosts. Wild animals naturally do not belong in houses; to seek to domesticate them is to break the distinction between civilization and the wild, and revenge is inevitable. As the Trojans committed a similar transgression, their wedding songs are closely followed by funeral dirges.

The Greeks destroyed the sacred shrines of Troy, the 'seed of her wide earth' (528), her 'young' (359), and hence they must suffer. The majority of them fall prey to the tempest as they set sail. Agamemnon atones for Iphigenia, and at the same time for Atreus' infanticide, but he must also atone for crimes against Troy, although there is no explicit mention of this. It is interesting, however, that the net (*díktyon*) which Zeus casts over Troy (358) corresponds to that with which Clytemnestra disables her victim in his bath (1115). With weighty words the chorus introduces its lesson that great wealth will soon lead to insatiable grief: 'There's an ancient saying, old as man himself' (750). But there follows a contradiction: 'But not I, I alone say this'. For bad and godless deeds may indeed breed consequences, which bear their likeness as if they were their children. This is the way of the world. It is not the 'envy' or the 'fury' of the gods, but justice which holds sway. This would have been good news for the Athenians. But the connection between transgression and punishment is such that old crimes will sponsor new ones to the misery of humanity. When the predestined day arrives, a daemon will be born in the house, irresistible and unholy, the dark spirit of daring and blindness which takes after its 'parents'. In this case the curse is inevitable, misdeeds multiply of their own accord. At the end of the song in which they had compared Helen with the young of a lion, just before the arrival of Agamemnon and Cassandra, the chorus sings this lesson.

The lesson clearly applies to Agamemnon. His guilt and destiny are already decided, as set out in the song referring to the eagles; he did what he had to do when he embarked on the terrible, senseless war, which Zeus willed. The sacrifice of Iphigenia, the way he chooses out of his doubt, is the inevitable price of pursuing the war according to Zeus' will.

Cassandra, however, is simply drawn into the death of the man who brings her home. She enters as the murder is being prepared in the palace. Thanks to her gift of second sight she can describe the events. At the same time Aeschylus commissions her to clarify the historical background: Thyestes' adultery with the wife of Atreus, which was the first link in the chain of atrocities, then his dreadful meal. He also has Cassandra intone a moving lament for Troy.

But, as much as we are aided in our understanding by Cassandra, the sense of her own fate remains elusive. Apollo had loved her; she had promised herself to him, but had then withdrawn. His punishment for her was that none of the prophecies, which he had given her the power to make, should be believed. Thus far things make reasonable sense. But why does he let her die? Whatever the reason, Cassandra makes it clear that it is he who wills her death. It shows the terrible character of a god who drives his victims 'like a beast to the altar' (1296); in the words of Reinhardt, 'An enigmatic, lethal daemon'. 'Oh men, your destiny,' she finishes, 'When all is well a shadow can overturn it. When trouble comes a stroke of the wet sponge, and the picture's blotted out. And that, I think that breaks the heart' (1327). Humans vanish without trace.

Like Cassandra, the army is drawn into the war, into death, and here too we must ask why. 'God takes aim at those who murder many' (461) sings the chorus, and the context makes it only too clear that this is aimed at the kings who led the army into war. They bring punishment, or at least the curse of their people, upon themselves.

So, in some instances one can perceive justice in action, in others not. Nor is the moral situation of individuals ever cut and dried. Many a punishment seems out of proportion. It is all too easy to make a mistake. And the course of events may make a mockery of all intentions, especially in the house of the Atreidae, where the daemon holds sway. Every member of that house must not only stand up for it, but comes to be infected by it, as it implicates them all in its fate and the chain of culpability.

However convinced the spectator might be of divine justice, it certainly moves in mysterious ways. The worst elements may be set apart by being attributed to the daemon, but there is much else. And the seer Cassandra reveals that, at least in the case of Apollo, there may be more to divine justice than meets the eye. The chorus sings, 'Make me rich with no man's envy, neither a raider of cities, no, nor slave come face to face with life overpowered by another' (471). This would seem to be the only position to take in the circumstances.

All this is performed in a city which for twenty years and more has gone to war more often and more extensively than any other in Greece, and which has undertaken more far-reaching campaigns in the preceding months and years (this under the aegis of their goddess Athena, as the final play will reveal).

Karl Reinhardt has shown how in *Agamemnon* each thesis is always supplemented by its antithesis. The herald reports the triumph over Troy and the loss of the triumphant army almost in the same breath. At the end of its victory song, the chorus turns to the suffering which the many deaths will entail, referring to the thunderbolt which hangs over extravagant glory (468). Clytemnestra's jubilation at the achievement of the murder is followed by distress, an indication no doubt of an incipient sense of guilt, remorse and fear, but also simply the reverse side of the deed. Triumph is thus always complemented by the fear which succeeds it. Victory and ill fate, fortune and guilt, are merely two sides of the same coin.

Everything has two sides to it. Everything is insecure. The ambivalence of things is apparent even in language. Again and again a word will be used which proves to apply in another sense than that intended. Such terms are used knowingly but without real knowledge. Too much happens simultaneously on an earthly and a divine level. In psychological and pragmatic terms the one level may well merge with the other – the construction is, as far as possible, realistic – but it must at the same time be grasped in theological terms. As indeed it can be.

All this is so terrible that the chorus must interrupt the narrative of the army's embarkation, at a point between the report of the portentous eagles and the sacrifice of Iphigenia, in order to invoke Zeus and sing of suffering as a means to truth. This can surely only mean that the citizens are not only to experience through these events the world as represented in mythical memories and latent fears, but also the distance from these, which has been effected by the process of learning. It casts an anticipatory light on the story to be enacted in the trilogy, as if Aeschylus had meant to weave a bright thread into the dark tapestry.

For, next to his treatment of justice, the playwright also undertakes a second form of 'modernizing' the ancient tales, that of historical differentiation. This is particularly clear in the way he presents in *The Libation Bearers* a quite different world from that of *Agamemnon*. Orestes' decision to commit matricide is made before the beginning of the play. In view of the terrible punishments which, according to Apollo, would otherwise have befallen him, there is little chance of the decision being evaded in the first place. So the long scenes at Agamemnon's grave have another meaning: Orestes is evidently in need of succour and affirmation; difficulties and inhibitions still prevail. The destructive power of the dead must be summoned up. Reinhardt recalls the 'many songs, dances, and speeches, by means of which the so-called primitives would ecstatically fortify themselves before battle, abandoning themselves to the spirits for which they would fight, and which would fight in them'. But this is a question of intellect as well as magic: the claim to vengeance must be given foundation. It is particularly bad that a woman committed the murder; the chorus lists a number of comparable crimes by women. It is also a question of the just inheritance of power and wealth being restored to the son and heir.

This is in striking contrast to *Agamemnon*; there the murder was prepared within the secrecy of the palace, whereas here it is planned before its walls and aimed at those who rule within. There we were, virtually, witness to the first murders, here to their avenging. There the daemon was at work, incarnate in the 'wildest fits . . ., the fury of the possessed' Clytemnestra (Reinhardt), here there is the simple execution of a necessity: two murders which, as far as the motive is concerned, amount to punishments, a way of putting things back to rights. If, after Agamemnon was already dead, Clytemnestra joyfully struck home a third time (1386), her son at first recoils from the murder.

In *The Libation Bearers* the twilight of *Agamemnon* has given way to clarity. While the chorus in the first play could make little of their occasional outrage, groping in the dark, downtrodden and unable to act, the libation bearers play a decisive part in the action. While the elders are only 'unconsciously' aware of the terrible things to come, here the thoroughly justified act is prepared in full view. It is clear that blood 'wants more blood' (404), but unclear how things will develop thereafter.

But above all the power of the curse which bedevils the house seems to have been broken. While in *Agamemnon* there was much talk of how the lion's way is inherited, that the child of ill deeds is like its parents, here there are not only prayers that murders from the past should no longer procreate (805), but we see that Electra and Orestes are of quite a different breed from their parents. Electra does claim that she has her mother's wolfish ways (421), but she also reveals a new conception of divinity by doubting whether it is pious to accompany a sacrifice by a plea for vengeance (122). Where is the daemon of the house now?

After tyranny was established in *Agamemnon* by the assassination of the king, there now follows, as Aeschylus makes abundantly clear, the act of liberation. The city is in a sorry state. Right at the start the chorus characterizes this in terms of loss of reverence, of fear of the gods and of respect for fellow men, all of which had once irresistibly permeated the being of the people. There remains only fear of a tyrant, and success has been set above the gods (55). In *The Eumenides* Athena talks of reverence and fear as kindred spirits (690). They belong together: the former is impossible without the latter, since fear without reverence leads to pure opportunism. Only the crudely terrifying authorities are now respected; otherwise men care only for themselves. There is no justice, no consideration, no respect for others, and above all none for the gods. It is this that must be overcome, and the champion is a sober individual who is as much concerned with the restitution of his inheritance as with revenge.

So in many ways, and not least in the way that Aeschylus differentiates between the state of affairs in the first and second play, we are made to experience a historical development. The city is involved in the fate of the Atreidae, and according to the principle of homology, or correspondence between things, the whole world is implicated in the process that leads from disorder, via the recuperation of lost forces, to the restoration of order.

The tragic events are never simply confined to the dramatis personae. The world is always on stage. The *Oresteia* is constructed around a laying down of vital, elementary demarcations, and, at the same time, the profound failure of the sort of complementary interaction between elements which is so crucial to the whole. Jean-Pierre Vernant and Pierre Vidal-Naquet, and many scholars since, have given impressive accounts of how graphically Aeschylus' imagery underscores this state of affairs. Civilization and wildness must remain separate; only in the hunt may man encroach on the wild, and even there he must respect the law that life depends upon reproduction, that unborn and infant life stands under the protection of Artemis. But here humans become the quarry, a queen is a bitch or she-wolf and the unborn and young are murdered. The unworthy treatment suffered by Electra is described in terms of putting a foal under a yoke. Agamemnon even slays his own daughter and thus tenders a 'rotten sacrifice'. What might at first seem to be arbitrary metaphors are in fact integral to a system of meaning, which stresses the all-encompassing and fundamental nature of the disorder.

Forces that ought to collaborate become estranged and do battle: young and old gods, the advocates of the male and the female, marriage and ties of blood. The light and the dark, the new civilization and the old, barbaric order no longer complement one another. Roles are exchanged, as a woman wields the sword with a man's heart (*Agamemnon* 11) and the cowardly Aegisthus acts like a woman. The relationships within the stage world, the fate of the Atreidae, stand for the structures of the actual world in microcosm.

In accordance with this, the tragic denouement must bring with it the restitution of order. The transgressor must die a sacrificial death, in order to set things to rights once more. Injustice must be atoned for, the domain of the wild and the hunt must be marked off anew; the Olympians and the Furies, reverence and fear, must once more complement one another. There must be an end to the tyranny.

It is, however, notable that the *Oresteia* adds to these requirements of spatial demarcation a temporal one. By means of the stark historical differentiation between the plays, the present is set off from the past. A line of demarcation is drawn which banishes the madness of reciprocal murder to the beginnings of time. This is particularly clear at the end, when the action moves to Athens. What the Athenians see embodied before them in the orchestra may also be imagined to be happening behind their backs on the Acropolis. Events on stage are thus shifted into a more unnerving light. World history is happening in the city. The gods too are involved. Nothing will ever be quite the same again.

This is the only time, so far as we know, that tragedy takes the institution of the polis as its subject. The polis is always implied here as being part of the route from chaos to order. For things are connected. Solon and a host of philosophers had already sought for the regulations of the polis in the cosmos – and found confirmation of their political insights. Among the demarcations and supplementations of various realms of existence, the relationship between the citizens and non-citizens must have been put to the test as well. But the fact that the institutions themselves and their inception could become part of the action was only possible because, not only individual events, but an essential part of the history of the polis is treated here: the long trek from the past to the present.

If this is so, then we must ask how the presence of the old stands relative to this history and to the new order. All that must have appeared strange and problematic from the point of view of the radical new agenda.

The presence of the old and the securing of the new: political thinking and drama

Aeschylus' *Eumenides* is to some extent integrated by the fact that, thanks to a free and thorough judicial system, thanks indeed to the institutions of the polis in general, entirely new possibilities emerge or are established. The principal among these is the capacity to make decisions about how things should happen. This is the mark of a 'progressive' spirit. But this is not to say that the uncanny spirit of the past has simply been dispensed with. It is simply that there are now new means, a new capacity, at men's disposal. Tragedy is such a new possibility: the potential to revive and represent the old myths, and thus to repeat the struggle to secure order. For order is constantly under siege, and it has to be reinforced by sacrificing those who have failed and brought guilt upon themselves. An Aeschylus fragment suggests that even supreme wisdom can fail in this way.

Tragedy arises precisely at the point in time where what Vernant has called the 'conflictual universe' poses an entirely new sort of problem. The citizens become aware of themselves as active; in the discourse and decisions of their councils and assemblies they become increasingly autonomous with regard to the religious powers that, after all, are in charge of the universe. Even if, within the domestic sphere, in their dealings with their wives and servants, land and livestock, they still follow the dictates of their old faith, it becomes more difficult for them to avow the same in public. The scope of their influence considerably exceeds its old bounds. Bold decisions have to be made in the face of uncertainty. The citizens have to judge things in a purely rational way; and as they largely lack political experience, this means purely in terms of weighing up the mutable factors of power. Indeed the wide-ranging sovereignty of the city appears to give them the capacity more or less to establish control over events.

An enormous tension is bound to develop between the notions and emotions anchored in the mythical world and the new rationality. The one questions the legitimacy of the other. This tension is reproduced in that between the theatre and the Assembly, which in its turn creates internal tensions within tragedy itself. These are all the more trenchant because next to those elements which have been reconstructed or reinterpreted according to 'modern' rationality, the residue seems all the more scandalous. In *The Eumenides* in particular, a further contradiction, which must have stretched the imagination of Aeschylus as director, arises. The raging, snorting, stinking Furies with their petrifying costumes and gestures are, at the same time, old and wise; they must be able to convey a certain dignity. Even when they are most entrenched in their partisan stance, they sing of how Zeus gives victory to the forces of moderation. Of course any chorus may perform a double role on the stage, but there is no precedent for such a discrepancy as here – and compelling reasons for this lie in the conflict between the old and the new.

This tension is, however, also that of the citizenry, as they undertake the momentous removal of power from the Areopagus and establish democracy. There must have been doubts about whether this new order would hold. However fiercely the Areopagus had been resented, it had given a measure of security as a force to be resisted. Must the 'liberation' not have seemed in some sense uncanny and the successes abroad juvenile and illusory?

It is not by chance that fear of tyranny haunts tragedies from the 450s onwards, and that just measure and thoughtfulness are so often preached. Paul Veyne suggests that, if Greek citizens at that time were fearful, it was fear of themselves, while in modern states, secured by police and governmental control, fear focuses on others: communists, anarchists and so forth. He believes that they were afraid of being unable to sustain the pressures of citizenship, that they were going too far and becoming arrogant and wilful. It was the fear of this that was embodied in the figure of the tyrant.

Nor is it by chance that the men were so anxious to maintain order between the sexes; women may have had no active role to play in politics, but the men's fears of chaos would certainly have presented a threat to the order of things. The men, particularly those from the mass of the citizenry, will probably have been only too well aware of how precarious the order was in which they had the whole say and women none, despite men's having no automatic claim to it on the basis of inherent superiority. This contributed to the tension between the home and the public arena, the family and the city.

On the one hand, Aeschylus responded to these tensions with a political lesson. For the *Oresteia* is a significant document of political thinking, in the broad, rather than the modern, theoretical sense of the word. Aeschylus takes up his place in a long tradition of both political thought and political theology, where thought and practice are closely bound up with one another.

A whole chain of insights, almost an integrated system, can be traced through the work. First there was the 'pre-political' era, where the alternation of revenge and counter-revenge held sway – the sort of automatic processes which the Greeks so feared. Then came the tyrannies, in which the necessary link between fear and reverence was broken. There followed the partisan period, which ultimately succeeded in getting old problems back on the political agenda in terms of the struggle between old and new rights. It was an impassioned struggle, as it brought into debate the whole system – or, at least for the Athenians of that time, the heart of that system: the question of who should rule.

Then there was the lesson as to political decision-making, which, against the background of what had gone before, seemed to represent a sort of salvation, even if it could lead to the absurdity of important decisions being taken on minority votes. This process offered a way out of the old impasse. The problems of the non-acquiescence of the losers which resulted from it could be resolved through compromise. Victors should be conciliatory. They should stow away their weapons. This too was no bad lesson, and it is worth noting that the rhetorical graces used to win over the other side become a political factor here.

This spirit of reconciliation and moderation is promoted by Zeus' promise of victory to the moderate, by the genuine need for preserving the old and terrible and by the memory of the sort of suffering which led to moderation. There are historical reasons for no longer going about things in the old way. Zeus has ordained it thus. The commandment that the city should submit neither to tyranny nor to anarchy pre-empts what Aristotle was later to call 'political government', that is, the particular way in which the polis properly governs itself. And the Athenians must have been conscious of their responsibility. After all, the decisive turn in events, by which Athena brings terror under the control of the citizens, is happening at once before and behind them. If Aeschylus deemed the evolution from old to new in Athens to be of a piece with the mythical struggle between divine dynasties, the Athenians will have been left in no doubt as to what was required of them.

Finally, Aeschylus clearly perceived that, in the great turning points of political history, internal and external oppositions are equally in ferment. On the one hand, with the help of the Eumenides, the city must gain control over its own houses; on the other, the citizens' internal allegiance is correlated with the enterprise of their city's foreign policy, by means of which Athena will secure their glory. What had originated as Ephialtes' plan to overturn the existing order in Athens now serves to unite the citizens. This lay within the capability of the leading city of the Greek world.

By means of this movement in political thinking, the old notions of a *single* order, according to the will of Zeus, are modified in order to incorporate the new democratic constitution. At the same time the new order finds room for the old forces. But as impressive as all this is, it only represents the intellectual strand of the drama.

As a theatrical performance, the *Oresteia* represented the uncertain, the uncanny and the chaotic, from which order has been wrung. Rather than repressing, stifling or sweeping aside the fears of the citizens, as can be done within the structures of the modern state, these were kept at the conscious level. This shows how the institutions of the polis and the theatre co-operated to make the life of the citizens so all-embracing, so full. It was a question of making sure of the foundations on which they stood. The preservation of the terrible was a way of preparing for the possibility of its sudden resurgence. They would (or perhaps could) not shield themselves from it; by keeping it before them they wanted to learn how to bear it.

But, by also serving to restore order, drama was responding to the same impulse as elsewhere, in the New Year rituals for instance, which celebrated the dissolution and restitution of order. In the Great Dionysia too, chaos had constantly to be overcome. This gives a particular slant to the fact that it was the city which here 'made itself into theatre' (Vernant). By participating in this, the citizens were able to revive their unity. And the tragedies fulfilled exactly the function which Plato attributes to festivals in general: to put mortals back on their feet, or set them to rights. This was particularly true where the tragedies were conceived as trilogies and had the visionary scope of the *Oresteia*.

The repetition of the old myths and the belief which informs them were bound to set up some kind of opposition between tragedy and, if not precise forms of political belief and action, then undue boldness or extremism. It could introduce a third party to intervene in arguments. It could remind the citizens in the audience of a quite different domain of potential reality, which will generally have been excluded from their politics. By showing that the world is fundamentally just, that misfortune is generally a punishment for injustice, and, in the case of the *Oresteia*, by seeking to locate the old order in ancient history, it could help to liberate the citizens for action.

Part of the broad perspective, which the citizens so needed, was an awareness of the full range of possibilities, especially inner ones. Tragedy was the Athenians' special way of representing the subliminal to supplement their safekeeping of the polis.

So the *Oresteia* worked in manifold and effective ways on the mental infrastructure of the Athenians – among other things, by situating the revolt historically, and significantly modifying prevailing views of the world-order, so that the revolt came to make sense. What we thus see in the *Oresteia* is simply extraordinary. Certain things are common to the extant tragedies of Aeschylus, all of which post-date 472; we cannot be sure how great an advance these represent on those written before 480. But it seems overwhelmingly likely that tragedy as we know it is quite different from the earlier form. Then there is the question of how much the Athenian revolution contributed to Aeschylus' achievement in the *Oresteia*. At any rate, the way in which he draws the gods directly into the action, ranges old against new, and so introduces historical structures into tragedy, seems to be quite new. The Prometheus trilogy apparently confirms this. In this work Aeschylus methodically takes up the question which the *Oresteia* had left open: how did Zeus' rule develop into what we see here within the horizon of the foundation of democracy in Athens?

Prometheus

The one extant play of the Prometheus legend, *Prometheus Bound*, was evidently written as the first part of a trilogy. Of the other two parts, we know only a few details; from these details, however, we can draw certain conclusions about the subject matter of these other plays. The play has been passed down under the name of Aeschylus. It is true that doubt is periodically cast upon his authorship, but the reasons that are brought forward to support such doubt only serve to show that we are dealing with an extraordinarily daring piece of work, one which is indeed very different, in various ways, from Aeschylus' other extant tragedies. However, it has not yet been sufficiently demonstrated that this is good enough reason to go against tradition and assume that someone else wrote it.

The date of the play's first performance is not known, but it is normally thought to date from late in the playwright's life. There is much to suggest that the Prometheus plays came after the *Oresteia*. It may be that Aeschylus put them on in Athens in 456 BC, though this is unlikely since he died in this year and, apparently, he left behind a number of completed tragedies which his son, Euphorion, then brought to the stage. This could well be what happened with the Prometheus plays. The numerous references to bold technical stage effects in the text of *Prometheus Bound* may indicate that Aeschylus wanted to make use of newly developed innovations. Perhaps, though, he wrote the plays for another theatre, the one in Syracuse, for example. Some textual evidence does point to the fact that the play was intended for performance in Sicily. It was there, in Gela to be precise, that Aeschylus died. If it was indeed premiered there, the play's production in Athens would have been its second; this reverses the case of *The Persians* which had its second production in Syracuse (472). The content of the play seems to me conclusively to support the case that the Prometheus plays were written after the *Oresteia*.

The political situation at the time when the plays must have been written had not essentially changed. Fears, however, had been woken as a result of the battle at Tanagra (458 or 457); there was a rumour that the Athenian nobility were attempting to persuade the Spartans to march on Athens and there help to get rid of the democracy. Whether these rumours were true or not, they bear witness to the fact that the aftershocks of the removal of the Areopagus' power were not to be escaped so quickly.

The plot

One cannot really claim that *Prometheus Bound* is full of action; in spite of this, however, it must have been extraordinarily exciting. Its characters are almost all immortals and it is set far back in the mists of time – shortly after Zeus had come to power and generations before the time in which most of the epic stories are set. This distance in time is matched by the geography; the play takes place at the end of the world where, as contemporary opinion had it, the ocean flowed around the earth. There Prometheus is chained to a cliff. Zeus has decreed that this should be Prometheus' punishment for having defied his will when he saved mankind by stealing fire from the gods and bringing it to the earth and by giving to the mortals various other gifts.

At the start of the play, we see Hephaestus hammering Prometheus' heavy chains into the rock. He is deeply sorry about what he has to do and he curses the work which is the cause of his reluctance, but Zeus' henchmen, Kratos and Bia, are pitiless, and they press for a speedy conclusion to the proceedings. The group goes, leaving Prometheus alone. The daughters of Oceanus arrive, full of pity for their friend and relative. The sound of the heavy blows on the cliff has reverberated deep into the cave where they live. Later, their father comes; he wants to help Prometheus by putting in a good word for him with Zeus. Prometheus receives him politely but with reserve; he immediately sees that Oceanus' intentions are good, but knows also that they will have no effect on the situation. Oceanus would do better to look after himself; he certainly cannot help Prometheus. It almost seems that Prometheus is implying that it is inappropriate for his cousin to act as though he could do anything to help, when the truth is that Prometheus is beyond help.

A solution can come about only after a long period of time; that is, when Zeus realizes that he needs Prometheus. Even though he is completely at the mercy of the new ruler of the world, he has something without which Zeus will, in time, not be able to survive. He knows of a danger which will threaten the chief god. Later in the play, we learn that there is a woman (or, to be precise, that there will be a woman) who is destined to bear a son who will be stronger than his father. When Zeus makes love with this woman, he will be precipitating his own downfall. Only Prometheus knows her name. To this extent, Zeus is dependent on him. However, before this has any bearing on events, an eternity must pass, during which Prometheus must suffer terribly.

He explains to the chorus what he has done for mankind and how it came about that he opposed the will of Zeus. He maintains his defiance of Zeus with such daring and lack of restraint that the women become worried, but they stay with him all the same.

Io appears. She is a girl from Argos to whom Zeus has taken a fancy. Night after night she has been dreaming such disconcerting dreams about his love that she has told her father about them. He has consulted various oracles which finally let it be known that he must throw his daughter out of his house and out of the city, otherwise Zeus will exterminate his whole clan. Unwillingly he complies, 'forced to do this by the cruel bridle-rein of Zeus' (668). The love-struck god has, however, had no thought for the poor girl. Hera intervened and set the hundred-eyed Argus to watch over her; she gave her a pair of cow's horns and, when Argus was killed on Zeus' orders, set a stinging gadfly to drive her to madness and hunt her down to the end of the world; thus Io comes to Prometheus.

He cannot comfort her but can only tell her of the immeasurably long course that she still has to run, the dangers that she must watch out for before Zeus finally 'restores sanity' to her in Egypt where he will 'with a gentle touch' make her pregnant (848). From this coupling will come the race from which stem Danaus and the suppliant women of Aeschylus' play, and which will produce Heracles who, in the following play will free Prometheus, first from Zeus' eagle and then from his chains.

Io is the only mortal to appear in the tragedy. Her sufferings correspond to those of Prometheus, though she is condemned to be constantly on the move while he is chained in one place. Also, she has had no say in what has happened to her, whereas Prometheus has actually done something which was bound to arouse Zeus' wrath. All the same, as we see, whoever is loved by the lord of the gods may be destined to suffer eternally to the point of madness. 'Does it not seem to you', asks Prometheus, 'that this king of the gods in all matters alike is given to violence? A god, lusting for union with this mortal maid, he dooms her to such journeys!' (735).

After Io has left him, there follows a short choric song and a last dialogue between Prometheus and the women. Finally Hermes appears; as at the start of the play, Zeus again determines what happens on the stage. His messenger has been sent to elicit from Prometheus the details of the danger which threatens the supreme god: it is apparent that all that has occurred throughout the play has been observed by Zeus. The daughters of Oceanus had taken this omniscience into account. Only Prometheus had not bothered about it.

Hermes wants to get everything over with quickly; he is the representative of the most powerful ruler in the world and Prometheus is a pitiful subject. If the necessity of obedience is not already obvious, his suffering should certainly have taught him the lesson. Prometheus will have none of this, and he replies with arrogant conviction. He refers to his age: he has already seen the downfall of two tyrants, Uranus and Cronos, yet the new rulers imagine that they live in an 'unassailable citadel' (956). This lackey does not impress him either – so full of bravado and yet so ignorant of the ways of the world. His misfortune is preferable to having to be in thrall to the tyrant. A long dialogue develops which reaches its theological climax when Prometheus cries, 'Woe is me,' and Hermes answers, 'those are words which Zeus has never known.'

Prometheus replies, 'but time, as he grows older, teaches everything.' Hermes then plays on Prometheus' age: 'time has not taught *you* self-control or prudence – yet'. This refers to the same *sōphroneîn* that the Athenians learn 'at last' in *The Eumenides* (1000). Perhaps, then, it is this quality which time will teach Zeus to appreciate? Perhaps the god is now playing the role that the Athenians played in the *Oresteia*?

Finally, after everything has failed (Prometheus has invoked his masculinity and declares that he will never be 'womanly' and abase himself), Hermes threatens him with terrible punishment: Zeus will cast him down beneath the earth and when he is allowed up again, an eagle will come every day to rip out his liver. The punishment commences. Prometheus is swallowed by the earth, calling still on mother earth and the heavens: 'you see how wrongly I must suffer.'

Staging

Whatever the play might lack in external action it makes up for in its internal dynamics and by its potential for spectacular production. Various references in the text point to these possibilities. Hephaestus says to Kratos, 'your speech matches your looks' (78); Kratos' mask must have brought the 'doer of violence' dramatically to life. Before the daughters of Oceanus come, Prometheus detects a sound and a fragrance in the air, 'the air whispering with the light beat of wings' (115). Prometheus says that 'whatever comes, brings fear' (127) and for a moment the audience may have thought of Zeus' eagle; but then a winged chariot comes swinging (or is pushed) through the air, probably with actual moving wings. Oceanus comes in, seated on a four-legged bird which is able to kneel on landing. He proudly explains that he has guided the creature 'by will, without any bridle' (287). There is a palpable indulgence in technical innovations; it is hard to imagine how it was all done. Finally, Hermes conjures up an ear-numbing noise as the cliff on which Prometheus is chained begins to shake and then to sink (or be dragged back) into the earth, where he will stay until he reappears in the next play. The period of Prometheus' incarceration in Tartarus would have been necessary from a technical point of view as much as anything else.

One wonders how Aeschylus as director would have wanted the mad, hunted Io, tormented, as it were, by the tarantula, to appear on the stage. Prometheus' silence throughout the whole of the first scene must have had an equally dramatic effect; it is similar to Cassandra's long silence in *Agamemnon*. Hephaestus complains about his fate, but we hear nothing from Prometheus about his. Only when he is alone does he address the gods. This is like the address of the Pythia at Delphi at the start of *The Eumenides*. But here, at the end of the world, it is other gods that are invoked, the elements themselves: the sky and the wind, the source of all the rivers and 'the countless laughter of the sea's waves' (90), the earth, mother of all life, and the sun. They are all called on to witness what he, a god, is made to suffer at the hands of other gods. After the chorus has sung its first ode, Prometheus renews his silence. It stands in clear contrast to what the daughters of Oceanus have sung: 'I weep, Prometheus, for your deadly plight' (397). Not only they, but the whole country cries out in grief – and not just for him, but, notably, for his 'brothers', the Titans, who have been conquered by Zeus. This is the first time that Prometheus has been on the side of the vanquished; elsewhere he stands alone against the new gods. All the people of Asia are taking part in the grief, and finally 'the wave of the wide Ocean roars in unison with him, the depths of water weep, the cavernous darkness of the dead world mutters under, and the holy fountains of flowing rivers weep in pity for his pain' (431). Then, after this, Prometheus is, for a while, silent. One would have thought, after all we have heard, that he has suffered enough; but then we hear of how thought and anger gnaw at his heart. He cannot get over the disgrace that has been imposed on him; it is worse than any physical suffering.

Earlier on in the play, he asks the chorus to share in his suffering: until this point, the women do not leave their carriage – it may even have been hanging in the air all this time. Now, though (and this presumably happens just before Oceanus arrives on his bird), they get out, bare-footed, onto the rough stony ground and come to him, accompanying him just as they do at the end when he sinks into the earth.

From the start, the action goes on under the watchful gaze of Zeus. Kratos reminds Hephaestus that the supreme god can see everything and will be a strict judge. Oceanus' daughters are afraid that Zeus will punish Prometheus for his insolent words, and Hermes' eventual arrival confirms their fears; we can assume that this is not the first time that Prometheus has shouted his defiance to the heavens. What is finally said in this highly charged atmosphere must have been altogether shocking, even more so since it was, if our available sources are to be believed, so new. The way that Zeus is talked about on stage is not as the most revered, the highest god of the Greek pantheon, but as a common, evil tyrant.

The political oppositions

Zeus is shown to have all the features which, in the Greek experience, belonged to the typical despot. It is not only Prometheus, whose enmity and pain may have caused him to exaggerate the truth, who characterizes Zeus in this way. The daughters of Oceanus imply the same thing: 'A new master holds the helm of Olympus; these are new laws indeed by which Zeus tyrannically rules; and the great powers of the past he now destroys' (148). They are shown to be aware of the whole situation, and they add that among the gods there is almost universal anger about how Prometheus is being punished. One can be reasonably sure that such dissent would only be expressed behind closed doors: all the gods have an interest in maintaining authority and would not want to risk losing it; on top of this, they are all afraid of Zeus. The chorus tells of how Zeus will not moderate his anger until either his passion is sated or someone else seizes power from him. Thus Hephaestus, in spite of his close ties with Prometheus, must chain him to the rocks. Presumably, such subservience stands as an example of everyone else's behaviour. Zeus will countenance only absolute obedience.

This all presents a shattering image of the father of the gods. He is despotic. He is 'in control of justice' (187); this does not mean (at least, not yet) that he is intrinsically just, quite the opposite in fact: he is, for the moment, in control of the law. Whatever he feels like doing automatically becomes just. These are the parameters of the world of the play; the law consists entirely of what Zeus wants. Thus he is said to rule by 'laws of his own invention'* (402). There could not be any clearer way of expressing the fact that what is called 'justice' in the play is not justice at all; and it is very interesting that Aeschylus chooses to show Zeus' despotism and hubris through these formulae of perverted justice. The yardstick of the polis is never very far from what we see in the play, and it is the proximity to a real situation that makes things seem so bad. Zeus is not accountable to anyone (324), and he is perfectly willing to 'annihilate' (literally 'remove from view') humanity simply because he feels like it. Others may be 'planted' in their place. This is no empty threat; Zeus' thugs at the start of the play and his lackey at the end, the opportunistic Oceanus and the pitiable Io are all witnesses to his tyranny: each of them in their own way reflects his different sides. This was no fantasy, this was the style of rule after the civil war, after the victory over the old order.

Prometheus is the only character who maintains independence of will and judgement, the only one who defies Zeus. This is seen by the other characters as perverse, not because the system is so good that it would be abnormal not to comply with it, but simply because it is not sensible to oppose the tyrant. Hermes reproaches Prometheus: 'It is plain that your insanity is far advanced' (976). Prometheus, however, replies, 'perhaps – if to hate enemies is insanity' (977). He simply wants to remain true to himself, and that makes him a rebel. Even the daughters of Oceanus think that he needs to be cured. They try every possible way to soften him: 'Bow! Pray! As always, fawn upon the powerful hand!' (937). But Prometheus will not let his resolve be shaken. What is remarkable is that the women, who are so worried about him, prefer sharing his misfortune to abandoning him. They hate nothing so much as 'traitors' (1068), by which they obviously mean the anonymous gods who, in fact, owe a debt of gratitude to Prometheus (we are told later about how he engineered their victory for them).

The person who fits the description best of all is their own father, who represents opportunism. No matter how well-meaning he may be, the end of the play shows him as a rather wretched figure. He has gone over to Zeus' side and now he asks his cousin

---

* Meier translates 'private laws'.

to 'know yourself and take upon yourself new ways, for the tyranny of the gods is also new' (309). He twists the famous Delphic commandment which states that one should recognize that one is mortal (the *gnôthi sautón*) to say that one should cower and be craven (320); this attitude does indeed seem to be typical of those who were subject to Zeus' rule in its early years.

Similarly, it becomes Zeus' desire not only to punish Prometheus, but to tame him. The words that are used to describe the chains which bind him are those that would also describe the means by which one brings a horse under control or subjects an ox to a yoke. In the end, the punishment becomes a form of torture by means of which Zeus wants to force Prometheus to bow to his will. Wherever one looks in this play, one sees a repressive hierarchy to which all must defer. But there is no evidence of a legal system as the Greeks would have understood it, quite the contrary, in fact.

Prometheus himself steadfastly refuses to accept the punishment as a valid way of making him atone for breaking the law. He has made a mistake and, indeed, has done so of his own free will and in full consciousness of his actions; this is quite unlike the mortal tragic heroes. 'I willed, willed to be wrong' he says, 'All you have said to me I always knew.' . . . 'And in helping humans, I found trouble for myself' (266).

But when it comes to 'paying the price' (112) for what he has done, it is Zeus' power, rather than justice, which subdues him. This becomes quite clear when Prometheus later demands that Zeus, if he wants to hear his secret, must first release him from his chains and then himself 'pay the price for this maltreatment' (176). Here, we are not seeing justice opposed to criminality, but the political victor opposed to the vanquished, enemy against enemy. Prometheus' opinions fall into purely political categories, as do those held by Zeus; as long as the matter is not settled, it becomes more and more a question of friendship and enmity rather than of justice.

The enmity is extreme. Prometheus and Zeus seem to reflect each other in a number of ways; both of them, for example, act and think purely as it pleases them (the Greek word for this presumption being *authādía*). Prometheus explains that wanton arrogance (*hybrízein*) must be met by more wanton arrogance (970). It is this sort of rebellious talk which sharply defines and highlights the opposition.

In addition to this, the ingratitude that he has experienced plays a special, very hurtful role for Prometheus. Zeus only managed to gain victory as a result of his help, and he even claims that it was he and he alone who 'assigned to these new gods their honours' (440). While it is not entirely clear what he means by this (he may be implying that he was Zeus' most important adviser) the role that he played in the war of the gods does become apparent when he tells the daughters of Oceanus about it. He belongs to the ancient dynasty and is associated with the Titans, who served as Cronos' paladins. But he knew that it was destined that victory in the war would only be gained by cunning and not by brute force. His cousins, being obsessed with their own physical strength, would not accept this, so he went over to Zeus' side. Zeus was wise enough to welcome this approach; he let him unfold his plan and then carried it out.

In order to make him a worthy opponent for Zeus, Aeschylus has increased Prometheus' stature as much as possible (in the old myth, he was merely a fire-thief and a cheat). He has given him a new genealogy by making him the son of Gaia, the earth mother, who is here equated with Themis, the goddess of prophecy and justice. Thus he is connected with the most important of all the original immortals, rather than merely being the son of one or other of Oceanus' daughters. The identity of his father, normally said to be the Titan Iapetus, is left open in the play. Prometheus is no longer just a loner who is friendly towards humanity, but is an exponent of an elemental power. The more fundamentally important a divinity is for life, the further back the Greeks placed its appearance in the scheme of things. In this case, one could look at it the other way round; being so ancient, Prometheus' importance can be assumed to be absolutely fundamental. He becomes a central agent in the creation not only of the mortal world, but also of the hierarchy of the gods.

According to ancient tradition, Zeus had the goddess Gaia to thank for saving his life, and Themis for ensuring the security of his rule. Aeschylus fuses the two together and has the mother pass on to the son (Prometheus) the knowledge that ultimately decided the outcome of the war of the gods. She also passed on the information on which, in time, Zeus' future will depend. The total imbalance between Prometheus and Zeus is turned into a relationship of failed mutual co-operation. Zeus has all the power and Prometheus has none at all. This is the premise on which the first play is predicated. But, in the long run, this is shown to be only one facet of the whole situation; it is later made clear that power is useless without knowledge. Thus the basic formula of the play is changed: Zeus has only power and Prometheus has only knowledge. Zeus cannot be truly omnipotent because he is not omniscient. 'Necessity' and 'fate' (*moira*) are stronger than he is and will always dominate him until he stops trying to resist them. This is the way that justice is shown to work in the face of other forces.

The piece of knowledge that Zeus does not have is primarily of a tactical nature. He only needs to know from which side danger will threaten. Even the Zeus that we see here, dealing, as he does, only with hard facts, must have been able to grasp this (just as in the war of the gods he understood that cunning would decide the outcome). But according to the play, Prometheus will not give this information until a reconciliation has been effected. Aeschylus hints that this will happen, that they will 'come to each other' (192). One would imagine, however, that if such a reconciliation is to take place, it would have to entail Zeus completely changing his style of government. He must learn a lesson and may even have to suffer in order to do so. This might be what is implied when Prometheus says, during the dialogue with Hermes, that Zeus will one day, when time grows old, learn to say 'woe is me'. He goes as far as saying that 'Zeus' neck shall bow beneath worse pains than mine' (931). Such words, as well as the ones that imply that Zeus must 'pay for what he has done' need not be taken simply as empty threats born of an impotent rage, but as a true indication of what will indeed come to pass. Presumably, Zeus' 'suffering' is a reference to his downfall, which will come to pass unless he reconciles himself with Prometheus.

This presupposes, once again, that Zeus has a specific lesson to learn. He must understand that power on its own is not enough, that he must respect what is right for other people and deal fairly with his subjects. He must free himself from the compulsion to be hostile. He must achieve something quite unheard of: he must see that he too is subject to universal laws, and consequently must pay the price for the atrocity that he committed when he overthrew his father, Cronos. Prometheus also talks about the curse of the father falling upon him (910). As was the case with Orestes, the eternal chain of atrocity followed by counter-atrocity must be broken here. In this case, however, there is no higher authority which might help to achieve this. Thus it becomes clear that Zeus himself must change radically: he must acquire a new and different way of looking at things. In order to maintain his authority, he must learn about justice and moderation.

The details of how this actually happened in the other two parts of the trilogy are not clear. All we know is that Prometheus' mother, Gaia/Themis, made an appearance, so it could be that she taught him to change. The chorus of the second play, *Prometheus Unbound*, was made up of Titans. (Zeus had evidently freed them from Tartarus, whither he had earlier banished them; perhaps this is the first sign of a change in his ways.) Prometheus himself, however, must continue to suffer. When Heracles came by, he told Prometheus about the peoples of all the lands that he had travelled through. Then he freed him from Zeus' eagle. Apollo seems to have been responsible for guiding the arrow which kills the bird; Heracles had at any rate entreated him for his help in this. He also seems to have freed Prometheus from his chains; this is, at least, what Prometheus predicts in the first play. Since Zeus, when this happened, was still very much Prometheus' enemy, and since Heracles could only stop the attacks by shooting the eagle, Apollo and he were effectively starting a small rebellion. In deciding that the cruelty had gone far enough, they both took a stand in opposition to Zeus. This must have counted as one of the decisive incidents which went towards teaching Zeus the error of his ways and, particularly, the errors of his style of government. Whether the ensuing change happened all at once or gradually, and whether the change itself, or only the effects of it, were perceptible, remains open to question.

In the last play of the trilogy, as in *The Eumenides*, the birth of a cult in Athens was celebrated, probably the torch-lit parade in honour of Prometheus. This would hardly have been merited if he had been only a god of pottery, so we must assume that his status as a major benefactor of mankind was confirmed – he is the god who awoke man's questing spirit.

All this could only have happened if Prometheus also learnt a lesson. At the beginning of the play, he too saw the knowledge that he had merely as a tool to be used for the achievement of his own ends. As far as Prometheus was concerned, Zeus could equally well achieve what he had to (by giving way) or be overthrown by 'one who will find a flame hotter than lightning-strokes, a crash to overwhelm the thunder; one whose strength shall split Poseidon's trident-spear, that dreaded scourge that shakes both sea and land' (922). For the chained Prometheus either option would be welcome. He is driven to the very limits in his hostility towards Zeus. He may well be ready to fit in with a new world order, but this new order would perforce be effected by Zeus who will have emerged as superior through the reconciliation.

Thus, in *Prometheus Bound*, Aeschylus presents us with the strongest of oppositions and the model for a radical political split. This split is taken to such an extreme, with one side having triumphed years ago and the other having been thoroughly suppressed, that reason calls out for one or other side, or both, to yield. Hermes is perhaps asking too much when he demands that this happen immediately, but one would have thought that any mortal would, without too much hesitation, try to avoid the heaviest punishment; alternatively, he would have died. But here, Aeschylus' hero is immortal. On top of this, he has a certain piece of information which, after millennia, will bring the current victor in the struggle to heel. It is these parameters which allow Aeschylus to achieve such an extreme asymmetry and such a radical split.

The historicization of Zeus and the history of mankind

Aeschylus transfers the lesson of *The Eumenides* to Zeus: victory is not, by itself, enough. In order for the process to be complete, there must first be a reconciliation with the defeated party. But there is a basic difference between the *Oresteia* and the Prometheus plays. In the former, Zeus stands above the two sides and guides what happens; in the latter he is actually involved as a participant in the conflict.

This leads to an incredibly daring proposition: Aeschylus has had the audacity to give Zeus a history. I know of no other example of a supreme deity having to undergo change in order to make his authority eternal and, indeed, to become truly just. Gods may be born and may reach a certain age and thus, to a certain extent, they might have a 'biological' development, but they do not have a history in the sense of an inner maturation. Even the remorseful God of the Old Testament is not presented so radically: Yahweh only changes specific policies. Gods certainly have to tackle dangerous situations and fight for supremacy, but, once they have won, their authority is normally established beyond any question. There may be more fights ahead and they must be strong, but the question of whether they are just or not never arises.

In this play, however, the situation seems to be reversed. Zeus' regime can only be sustained through moderation, reconciliation and, evidently, through justice. Only in this way will the succession of a fourth supreme god be prevented (the Orphics of that time believed that this new leader would be Dionysus). Paradoxically, in becoming involved with earthly history, Zeus' rule is raised above history. For this is how it comes to be no longer affected by historical developments.

It is difficult to know which would have been more scandalous, the presentation of Zeus as tyrant, or the fact that the supreme god was given a history. Essentially, though, these are two sides of the same idea. As in the *Oresteia*, the historical perspective serves a specific, exclusive function: to relegate an earlier state of affairs to the past.

In this way the theological upset which was associated with the intervention of the gods in the *Oresteia* was settled. Whereas Zeus' turn-around there was only incidental to the history of the gods and was concerned only with the house of Atreus, here it is shown as a matter of central importance. It is shown to be the event which first established Zeus' rule as long-lasting.

All in all, it seems that the Prometheus plays go far beyond the *Oresteia*. Whereas in the latter the beacons serve to telescope space, and the history of the world is reflected in just two generations of the Atreidae, everything in the former is taken to the extreme; the play is set at the end of the world and, bizarre though it may seem, the only way to get to or from the place reasonably quickly is by winged beast. The action of the Prometheus trilogy stretches over generations which, according to one source, could amount to as much as 30,000 years.

Finally, the play deals not only with the greatest, most momentous epoch in the history of the gods, but also with the history of mankind virtually from its very origins. How Prometheus was able to save the humans, 'those that are oppressed', from Zeus (231) is not made clear. It could be that Zeus was simply going to let them die out as a result of their inability to live properly; whether this is so or not, they are described as being 'totally under Zeus' power' (551), without it being entirely clear what this entails. What is made clear in the first play, and also, apparently, in the second, is the extent of the gifts that Prometheus gave to man. Aeschylus develops a whole treatise on the origins of culture, bringing up, as he does so, some very interesting – and beautifully articulated – points.

Prometheus began by planting 'blind hopefulness' in the hearts of mortals (250) so that they no longer had to be transfixed by the fear of death. Before he did this, they seemed to have neglected any opportunity to improve their lot. Clearly, the only thing which differentiated humans was their awareness of death; in every other way they were as badly, if not worse, off than the animals. Prometheus' intervention at least hoped to cancel out the main difference between them and the gods.

As well as this, Prometheus gave them fire and many of the arts and crafts. He was to thank for the powers of increased awareness and for memory 'the all-remembering skill, mother of many arts' (461). 'In those days they had eyes, but sight was meaningless; heard sounds, but could not listen; all their length of life they passed like shapes in dreams, confused and purposeless' (447). They crept like ants under the earth, not even telling one season from another.

Prometheus taught humanity about the movement of the stars, about numbers, about 'the joy of intelligent discovery' (459), literacy, how to build houses, how to domesticate animals, sea-faring, medicine and mining. He dwells for a long while on how he taught mankind to prophesy, how to interpret dreams, voices, the flight of birds, sacrificial fires and entrails. In short, 'all human skill and science was Prometheus' gift' (506), and with the gift of fire 'they will master many crafts' (254). He gave them far more than if he had simply delivered up goods stolen from the gods.

But no matter how significant all this was, the question arises as to whether it was enough; for there is no mention in the list of gifts of the ability to live co-operatively. In his version of the legend, which came a mere generation later than the play, Protagoras shows the destruction of mankind as a result of lack of political skill, mutual respect and justice – skills which Zeus eventually has to lend to them. We would be wrong, however, to assume that, at the time of Aeschylus, the importance of these social skills was not appreciated. In the *Oresteia*, Aeschylus shows the necessity of justice, respect (seen to be the companion of fear) and measured thought. It does not seem likely that he would have left all this out of the Prometheus plays, but if humanity is to receive these gifts, they must get them from Zeus. Thus, one can assume that the supreme god furnishes them with this political equipment as part of the great reconciliation at the end of the trilogy.

The destruction of all order with which the Prometheus trilogy begins is much more far-reaching and fundamental than anything in the *Oresteia*. No matter what Cronos' rule was like, what emerges after his overthrow goes against all prescribed limits and any requirements of mutual support among the various forces involved. The new ruler does not respect any sort of justice, and he recognizes only his own interests. Blood-ties count for nothing. Anyone who opposes must suffer and, if he does not back down, will be regarded as sick – and is indeed beyond the bounds of the normal. The other gods are mere tools to be exploited. Prometheus is to be brought to heel like a domestic animal. He speaks, like a mortal, of how disasters befall now one man, now another, and asks the daughters of Oceanus to 'share the suffering of one whose turn is now' (274). But unlike a mortal, his mounting suffering is not mitigated by what could be a last comfort, that is, death; a fragment that has come down to us from Aeschylus says, 'Courage! The worst suffering does not last long.'

The only human to appear in the play has horns and is pursued by a gadfly. Her father had to banish her from her home and from his city (the kernel of a whole other tragedy can be found in the story of Iacchos and Io). In general, humans are worse off than animals in that they are threatened with total annihilation. The gods behave like 'women' and only the daughters of Oceanus prefer to share Prometheus' suffering rather than remain in characterless submission; as a result of this, they will be persecuted, 'hunted', by Zeus (1072). The hunt takes place for all to see; the victims are informed of their fate quite openly.

Freaks of nature, like the earthquake at the end of the first play, are not just symbols of the disturbance of order, and they are certainly not manifestations of any subsequent execution of justice (like the destruction of the Greek fleet at Troy, or the retreat of Xerxes). Rather, they are set in motion by the lord of the earth merely as a tool of his own tyranny. Power and knowledge are clearly divided, rather than being on the same side, and this is the basis for the intensifying tragedy of the first part of the play.

Prometheus Bound is the first known example of a tragedy where an out-and-out tyrant, even if he is present only in the abstract, rules over everything that happens on the stage; in other words, it is the first enactment of the nightmarish threat that tyranny presents. It is also the first time that a rebel stands directly opposed to the tyrant. This rebel acts according to his own free will; in his own words, 'I willed, I willed' or 'I was aware of what I was doing' (266). He can only stand up to all the pressure that he is put under because he is immortal and cannot, therefore, be saved by death; this is also the factor which increases and intensifies his suffering to such an extreme degree. His predicament shows us the full extent of tyranny. The tyranny of Aegisthus and Clytemnestra in *The Libation Bearers* seems far less impressive in comparison.

But at the end, everything has to return to some kind of order, everything must find its place, the lines must be redrawn, things that depend on each other resume their complementary roles. This all happens under the aegis of Zeus; he has learnt about justice and what makes authority durable, and thus the new wisdom of the highest god leads to the breaking of the chain of atrocity which has so far marked the history of ruling immortals. The world, and especially humanity, returns to normal.

This gaining of wisdom is encouraged and made necessary by the actions of rebels: Apollo, Heracles and, most importantly, Prometheus. His suffering is a graphic example of the reversal of the old traditions. According to these traditions, Zeus should make the mortals pay for the fact that Prometheus has brought them fire and taught them the trick with the sacrificial meat. But here, the perpetrator, rather than the beneficiaries, must pay. The question is whether this is a punishment for wilfulness, theft and insubordination (acts which were actually motivated at once by philanthropy and self-defence); or whether this is the sacrifice which must be made in return for the gifts which the mortals have received. Whatever the case, Prometheus' action is repaid in the end by the establishment of a cult in his honour.

Again, as in the *Oresteia* – and nowhere else so far as we know – the old and the new are among the things required to come together and complement one another. 'Power newly won is always harsh' (35). The very novelty of rule produces despotism. Aeschylus states this eight times, emphasizing it even more than in the *Oresteia*. Here, in contrast to that play, a member of the old order (admittedly one who went over to the side of the new gods) is set up as a friend of man (*philánthrōpos*) in opposition to the immortal's tyranny. In the *Oresteia*, it was Apollo who showed the most honour to mortals. This shows the radical consequence of the fact that Zeus was now committed fully to his new regime.

In order to get away with the fundamental opposition of the old and the new, and in order to 'protect' the present, the events surrounding this opposition had to be distanced in time. Only then could the whole great process be fully worked out to the end and only then could this process be integrated into the existing, more or less stable, system of thought; without such an integration it seems that justice could not be attained. Finally, the Greeks did not see history in terms of the great periodic cycles which characterize the view of other early cultures; for them, Zeus' reign had to be ensured for all time.

The political art of the Prometheus trilogy

If one addresses the question of political art in regard to this tragedy, one should resist, as much as possible, the notion that there is a firm line drawn between the political and the dramatic content. Certainly one should not belittle the political content simply because it is often supposed that when it comes to tragedy, it is certain rules of drama that are most important. Politics and drama were not alternatives, but were intertwined. Jacob Burckhardt established that myth was a way of putting something over: 'Our difficulties begin at the point where we must conceive of the simultaneous coming into being and co-existence of objects and images: their ancient involvement. All our expressions like sense, meaning etc. thus fail, like worn-out tools, to serve us.' This applies also to tragedy, and above all to the tragedies of Aeschylus. Any political statement must arise out of the drama; drama was defined by its role as a mouthpiece for political, as well as other, sentiments.

The threat of profound disturbance, indeed of the destruction of order, the fear of chaos and of tyranny and, at the end of the play, the triumph of the new order over the transgressions which have occurred – all these come together in a form which allows for everything to be experienced and suffered and which creates a necessary distance while at the same time allowing for collective involvement in what is going on. An intellectual approach is not enough to understand the vivid portrayal of events; the action must be literally 'taken to heart'. If this is achieved, the effect of the tragedy is increased; indeed it could be said that this totality of involvement is the unique property of tragedy. But, just as the audience was made up of citizens who took a very active part in the politics of their polis, so the action, particularly when it touched so deeply on the state of the polis, was intrinsically political. The less blatantly political the dramatic context was, the more this was so.

It is within this context, in which the author and his audience shared, that the explanation for the extraordinary daring of the Prometheus trilogy must be sought. The question is: how did Aeschylus make the decision to present the story of Zeus in such a new and, in many ways, scandalous manner? This daring is in no way mitigated by the fact that, for the Greeks, Zeus was not always seen as absolutely just but could show any number of facets. His unequivocal presentation at the start of the trilogy as a common selfish tyrant could not but seem profoundly one-sided and novel to a Greek audience. Furthermore, in all of Aeschylus' other extant tragedies, Zeus is shown as the god of justice. In the *Oresteia*, where two sorts of justice are presented and the action is concerned with the change from one to the other, the result is positive for the polis and a spirit of reconciliation is implied. In this sense, Aeschylus was presenting Zeus in accordance with the image that the philosopher-theologians had prescribed: the name of Zeus was a byword for a just world order. While all the mortals and many of the gods in the *Oresteia* – Apollo being no exception – could show themselves to be quite inconsistent, Zeus, at least according to Aeschylus, was not.

So once again we must ask how it is that the author came up with the daring concept that we see in the Prometheus plays. In trying to answer this, one could point to the questions which are left unanswered in the *Oresteia*, but which are answered here in the story of Zeus. One could refer to the profound significance of the homologies in tragedy, which demand that what happens in the world of mortals must correspond to what happens in other areas: in nature and the realm of the elements. Why should the world of the gods not also be subject to such homologies? These two points are linked. Throughout the *Oresteia*, the dispute between the old and the new gods, and the change in Zeus' policies, were brought to bear on what was happening among the mortals. The fact that the victory of the new form of justice could be based on a biased decision, no matter how valid, implies that Zeus intended it to be supplemented by reconciliation.

But there is still another major step to be taken: the political experiences of the new had to be transposed onto the story of Zeus' victory, and this to an extraordinary extent. The appearance of Apollo as such an unequivocal opponent was daring enough, but then to show Zeus as such a despotic ruler was to go way beyond what was normally acceptable.

In fact, Aeschylus came up against the problem with the *Oresteia*. As soon as he had realized what the true significance of a revolution was, and had asked the question as to what exactly 'order' is and how this 'order' comes to exist in time, he would almost certainly have been struck by the difference between the Zeus of the myth, who overthrows his father, and the Zeus who, according to the philosophers, stood for all that was just in the world. This difference, once recognized, becomes a thorny problem, one that was only to be solved through a historical approach. The details of how Zeus had come to power had always been clear, but it was not the done thing to suggest that these rather dishonourable circumstances detracted from his status as the epitome of justice.

Whether these speculations are true or not, the trilogy still stands as a provocative work. The play's crucial point is that legitimacy, justice and knowledge can only be acquired by experience, if not by actual suffering, and that power cannot be durable unless it recognizes its limitations and weaknesses. All this is said to us not only for the first time, but in a story which applies these lessons to Zeus himself. Unlike in his role in the *Oresteia*, Zeus does not stand above the action here; he too has to join in the fray. Consequently, if he is to stand credibly for the whole, we must assume that he undergoes a major change. We are required to see him first as a warrior, then as a victor and finally as a peace-maker. To put it another way, we see a Zeus whose fate is, at the start, not so very different from a mortal's: it only *becomes* different from that of ordinary mortals as the play progresses.

This was not simply the consequence of the *Oresteia*, but also of the revolution in Athens to which the *Oresteia* was a response. Assuming that it was desirable not to believe in the gods as something utterly fantastical but as a very real part of the make-up of the world, then worldly experience was bound to be transposed onto Zeus; the ruling *dēmos* had no master either. In *The Suppliants*, Aeschylus had shown that all of them are the polis. In the *Oresteia*, he makes it clear exactly what he means by this; but the solution depended on him calling upon the 'old' Zeus, albeit as a young god. Now, however, he discovers that if all of them are the polis, then they must be subjected to change if their regime is to last. They may be partisan at the beginning, but, at the end, they must be co-operative if there is to be a stable government. The new reality of the ruling *dēmos* made it inevitable – at least for such a radical author as Aeschylus – that Zeus' story be seen as a parallel to the contemporary situation. Since the action of Zeus' will was perceptible in reality, he must be influenced by reality.

We are faced with a form of belief in Zeus which is prepared to take account of history: with a theatre in which the world is made into drama and in which Zeus' development can also be dramatized, when it is established that the practice of justice is a skill that must be learnt. We are also dealing with a citizenry whose fear of chaos and tyranny was ripe for examination. One must also remember that this was an early stage of democracy; the political was not yet a separate issue but an integral part of life. The citizens were not the objects or agents, but the active subjects of the political process. The unconscious was rather an ambivalent area, and so the conflict between traditional belief and the new political practice had to be constantly projected onto action. The main purpose of politics had become the organization of the polis and the balancing of the old and new orders rather than the fighting of wars; nowhere are these new concerns better or more radically explored than in the Prometheus trilogy. The new order was not sure of itself and it became apparent that the old had to be accommodated so that the new did not have to stand on its own – and, indeed, to avoid the threat of reprisal from the old order. Greek political thinking was pragmatic enough for it to be recognized that everyone had to find their correct position within the polis. Formerly this had meant that the government tended to give more rights to the broad class of effectively powerless citizens. Now they had to make sure that the hitherto more powerful class, the aristocracy, was not denied the honour and respect to which it was accustomed.

For an author like Aeschylus, the change to democracy was so radical that it could only be balanced out, in literary terms, by an equally radical change on the part of Zeus. That would make it possible to show the city as being far more in tune with the wider order of the world and the gods than it is in the *Oresteia*; such a harmonization was necessary for the legitimization and moderation of the new order. People still lived in a world of broad and multifarious connections and had to adjust their behaviour accordingly: this meant that nomological knowledge had to be extensively rearranged as well – in all the ways that are explored through the tragic experience of the Prometheus plays.

This is not to say that the victorious *dēmos* of Athens was tyrannical, or that it treated its opponents as roughly as Zeus treats Prometheus, or, indeed, that this was Aeschylus' interpretation of events. Certainly the political change was very radical: the banishment of the virtuous Cimon seems strange, to say the least, and the removal of power from a class which still effectively ruled the city may be hard to understand. But the most important parallels between Athenian democracy and the early years of Zeus' reign are not the simple ones; it is not particularly important whether the defiance of the downtrodden Prometheus corresponded to that of the Athenian aristocracy, or whether his complaint of ingratitude was meant to put one in mind of the achievements of the Areopagus, or whether the assertion that Zeus threw aside those that were once great is a reference to the removal of their power.

The Athenian audience must have seen that the oppositions within the tragedy were only very rough approximations of reality. Such approximation was a by-product of the homology between different areas of life – and Aeschylus had to presuppose the awareness of his audience in order to draw parallels between the old and the new in Athens and the mythical sequence of the rule of the gods. But it was evident, beyond this approximation, that the events of the tragedy were very much related to those of contemporary Athens. The lesson about the order of the world (that is, of the polis) was unequivocal. The point is that if the action of the play had been a more exact replica of the real situation in the polis, the play could no longer be regarded as a proper tragedy.

If Aeschylus' tragedy was actually intended primarily for a Sicilian production, its relevance would not be diminished. The tyrant who ruled over Gela and Syracuse had been overthrown in 466 BC. For Athens, Aeschylus may have wanted to rewrite some of the play; he could have risked more with an audience there. Whatever the case, we can be sure that the Prometheus that he creates in the play – and who was to come to such prominence in the modern age, albeit through Christian imagery – was essentially a product of the Athenian democracy at the time of its coming of age.

The generation of the Persian War

The Athenians must have had a great love for Aeschylus. It was not for nothing that, after his first victory in 484, he triumphed in the agon on virtually every occasion that he took part. Even in 405, a good fifty years after his death, Aristophanes gives him victory over Euripides in *The Frogs*. Here it is a rule in the underworld that the greatest exponent of every great art should be wined and dined in the 'prytaneum' and take up his seat at the side of the god Pluto. This was the prerogative of Aeschylus; Sophocles has refused to accept the honour from Aeschylus, but Euripides is out to topple the master. In a long trial the two are called upon to prove their art.

There is agreement that a writer should be judged according to his skill in making 'people into better citizens' (1009). All good writers have had 'a useful lesson to teach' (1031). So it is less a question of art for its own sake than of the contribution that the playwright can make to the 'education' of adults, as a teacher does to that of children. We learn what sort of state humans were in when Aeschylus 'inherited' them from his predecessor Phrynichus – 'pretty stupid' (910). He, on the other hand, has passed them on to Euripides as noble, upstanding warriors, only to find them transformed by the latter into loafers, swindlers and rogues (1013).

In accordance with how things stand (final defeat in the Peloponnesian War is imminent) military achievement and the problem of establishing the right sort of citizenship in the city are both to the fore. Thus the focus is on *Seven Against Thebes* and *The Persians*, plays which ring with the sounds of war (of *Arēs*), and in which Aeschylus teaches the citizens how to cope with victory (1021). He presents them with heroes, whom they can take as role models. The 'high-flown', often barely comprehensible words, which Euripides mockingly attributes to him, were only of a piece with 'the noble themes and noble sentiments' (1059). Euripides, on the other hand, cast kings in rags (and the rich had accordingly dressed up in rags themselves, in order to avoid forking out for the common good). He taught the citizens how to speak (both in argument and idle gossip); they were able to move freely at the level of his tragedies, for it was their own; and he taught them a rational and systematic way of keeping house, based on personal advantage. The home was to be set above the city, self-interest above the general good, in total opposition to Aeschylus. So finally, Dionysus, who presides over the court, decides to take Aeschylus up out of the underworld, so that he can come to the aid of his troubled city.

Of course Euripides has many good points, and Dionysus, as

the lord of the great festival, announces that he takes greater pleasure in his plays, with their urbane wit, rhetorical brilliance and clarity. However, he must give priority to Aeschylus by virtue of his superior *sophíā*, that is, above all his wisdom. It is as though this expresses a yearning for the dramatist of a generation which had prevailed in the Persian Wars and laid the foundations for the glory of Athens. Aeschylus would seem to stand for his entire generation here.

It is hard to say to what extent Aristophanes is right in his judgement; to what extent the citizens really modelled themselves on the stage characters and were formed by the works of certain playwrights. We should perhaps err on the side of caution, and simply conclude that tragedy had an extraordinary, if fluctuating, influence, an influence which is corroborated by Plato and Aristotle, who view things from a similar perspective.

Nor should we generalize from the particular needs of the Athens of 405. The overriding concern at that time was to promote courage, moral strength and the leadership of the city, so that the two tragedies of war, and the lessons which they apparently imparted, had immediate relevance. All else paled into insignificance: questions about the justice of the victory over the Persians, the decisions in *The Suppliants*, the extreme partisanship of old and new, and the establishment of order in the *Oresteia* and the *Prometheia*. The impression to be given was of a fervently patriotic sort of tragedy, not one which cast doubt and dealt in ambivalence and uncertainty. So Aristophanes bears witness to only one aspect of Aeschylean tragedy.

However, without elaborating the differences between Aeschylus and Euripides, it is certainly the case that, at least in the late trilogies, Aeschylus was able to achieve something which apparently eluded his successors. He could locate his world within a grand, historical scheme of things, transcending the many conflicts. This is particularly true of the *Prometheia*, but also holds to a lesser extent for the *Oresteia*. He pursued this scheme both in the fine detail and in the broad sweep of his world. For he was able to match his profound questioning of things with an exceptional talent for finding radical solutions.

And it seems to me that the particular character of his generation was one, though certainly not the only, important source of this ability. It was a generation which was exposed in an unusually forceful fashion to formative experiences, which individuals will naturally have interpreted in various ways, but which were also bound to bring about a powerful sense of community.

Aeschylus was about fifteen years old when the tyrants were banished from Athens and Cleisthenes' reforms began to be introduced. He will have been among the youngest whose names were included in the lists of the new demes and whose military training was defined by the new order. At any rate, his life as a citizen began at just the time when isonomy was beginning to function in Athens, and when the city was scoring its first great military and foreign policy successes. He was about twenty-five when the Ionian revolt broke out and the Athenians determined to become involved. There then followed the anxious years in the shadow of possible Persian retribution, until 490, when their expeditionary force was defeated at Marathon. Aeschylus was now thirty-five and took part in the battle; it was this fact that figured in his epitaph, not his tragedies; his brother fell in the fighting. Aeschylus was in his early forties when Themistocles finally succeeded in getting the fleet constructed, these being the tense years before the second Persian attack. He also fought at Salamis, and experienced the establishment of the maritime League and the escalation of Attica's political and military operations in the Aegean. When power was removed from the Areopagus he was just over sixty.

These had been decades of great difficulty and danger, putting immense strain on the men of Athens; but they had also brought almost continuous success, at first in spite of expectations to the contrary, then outstripping all expectation. And internally the new political order was developed, as Athenians gradually acceded to a full awareness of their citizenship, and the citizenry came to be identified with the city. It is hard to say to what extent members of Aeschylus' generation, especially the younger ones, might have harboured doubts about all this; whether the hopes for the restoration of the aristocracy, or even a tyranny, extended beyond the confines of certain families. It may have been that, in the period before Marathon, the idea gained currency that the old tyrant, who had been given refuge by the Persians, might have been able to help the city in its predicament. But this in itself represented no objection to the principle of isonomy. And the city had of course retained the Areopagus, which, after 480 at least, had a considerable hand in policy-making.

Rarely has a generation achieved so much as that of Aeschylus in Athens. In many ways its successes exceeded its wildest dreams, and it must often have seemed, not least in the heady 470s and 460s, that the ultimate goal had been reached.

The arguments over the Areopagus must have thus caused all the more profound turmoil. We have no idea of the size of the majority for the reform, and whether, as would seem likely, it was the older men who met the proposals with scepticism. Many individuals must have been torn by the matter. Over a period of decades, starting with Solon and increasing under Cleisthenes, new ways of reinforcing the position of the middle classes *vis-à-vis* the aristocracy were explored. Although the continual granting of new political rights jeopardized the balance of power, it would appear that some sort of equilibrium had always been maintained. Now, all at once, the aristocracy was disenfranchised. In place of isonomy, which had always presupposed a certain equilibrium, came the democratic order. These events, the definitive breaking of the homology between the social and political orders, the phenomenal expansion of human capability, must have made an extraordinary impression on Aeschylus' generation. And though precious few tragedies survive to support such a hypothesis, I believe that Aeschylus felt challenged only in his last two trilogies to incorporate both the prospects and the dangers opened up by the new into a grand mythological framework. Given the radical novelty of democracy, he felt the need to include the old and the new in the system of complementary factors, without which no just order may be sustained. The conflict of old and new was to be not only resolved, but also relegated to the past.

And this could hardly happen without the gods. The *Oresteia* is not the first instance of Aeschylus enlisting their help, witness the appearance of Aphrodite to guarantee reconciliation at the end of the *Danaids*. What is so different about the *Oresteia* is the partisanship of old and new gods, and the broad historical horizon which this necessarily opened up. The gods thus became much more profoundly involved in things, so much so that human knowledge of them is transformed by worldly experience. This is why Zeus is ultimately given a history.

It cannot have been by chance either that, a few years after the fall of the Areopagus, Aeschylus placed a genuine tyrant centre-stage for the first time, as was so often to be the case in later plays. It seems certain that, at the moment when the Areopagus could no longer be relied upon, the insecurity which accompanied the absolute responsibility shouldered by thousands of citizens became virulent. With no other safeguard, the threat of tyranny was close at hand. It seems most likely that it was a complex sense of identification on the part of the *dēmos*, together with the individual experience of power, which suddenly revived the ancient bugbear of tyranny.

Perhaps members of Aeschylus' generation had a particular need of tragedy, and especially in those years when they became aware of how much they depended upon certain forces (for instance, the fear which goes hand in hand with reverence) and certain energies which they had to direct against themselves. And these could hardly be taken for granted any longer.

Only a poet of that generation could probably treat the prehistory of democracy as a unity. The principle that earlier generations must suffer so that later ones may learn, which made for such an unconvincing theodicy, might none the less have convinced those who had put themselves so utterly at the disposal of the polis and who saw it as *the* just order according to Zeus' will. Consumed as they were by it, they would have had no objection to seeing earlier generations being consumed in the same way. This represented a different possibility alongside the conventional fate of individual houses, whereby injustice had to be atoned for in the third or fourth generation. The logic of this was different anyhow, as the later generations had generally shared in the misbegotten fruits of their ancestors' injustices.

It certainly seems that Aeschylus' extraordinary desire to find encompassing meaning in both spatial and temporal terms, and the phenomenal tensions which he thereby sought to treat, were the product of his generation's experiences, especially in the latter years. Later generations, such as that of Sophocles, grew into the new situation. Of course they too underwent radical changes and were continually confronted with the discrepancy between old and new, which here too became the stuff of tragedy. But they were no longer witness to such monumental revisions of the general order; they could no longer, for the most part at least, hope to solve all problems through such an order. In broad terms, the focus of questioning shifted from the order of things to humans themselves.

Aeschylus' generation was after all bound up with myth in a special way. In their childhood, the Athenian horizon was hardly jostling with fascinating, earthly matters. Regardless of their usefulness in interpreting things, the many mythical tales were therefore bound to be more engaging than in later times, when they had to compete for attention with so much else.

If Aristophanes is correct in supposing that Aeschylus suited his words to the superhuman format of his heroes, then the fact that he finally indirectly brought Zeus himself to the stage, reveals the other side of his simultaneously very modest and very ambitious attempt to 'grasp' the whole in the huge, cohesive structure which is presented in his tragedies. As far as we know, Zeus never again 'appeared' on stage in tragedy in this way, and certainly not directly. Nor is there any evidence of a Prometheus play after Aeschylus. Perhaps it is this that accounts for the unparalleled adulation which this great tragedian enjoyed in his native city.

6

SOPHOCLES

We ought now to look briefly at two plays by Sophocles. Coming a generation after Aeschylus, they serve as an example of a quite different sort of tragedy and thus point to the extraordinary diversity of the form. They should also confirm that there is a strong political sensibility at work in the plays of Sophocles. This is particularly important because, although a political component is recognized – however inadequately – in Aeschylus and Euripides, it is not normally credited to Sophocles.

Ajax tends to be regarded as Sophocles' first extant play; it is usually placed in the 450s BC. The production of *Antigone* on the evidence of a report that establishes at least a chronological link between its performance and Sophocles' election as *stratēgós*, has been put at about 440 BC.

Although *Ajax* cannot be linked to any particular political situation, it is reasonable to assume that there is a connection between *Antigone* and the conflict brought about by Pericles' building policies. This conflict ended with the ostracism of Thucydides, son of Milesias, the main political opponent of those policies.

In Athens at that time, a stronger, more energetically organized resistance to the leading politician of the democracy seems to have emerged. It was centred upon the Athenian nobility whose members, in their capacity as diplomats and sometimes as generals, were often responsible for contact with the allies of the city. This contact continued to be based on family ties and mutual hospitality, and these old-style aristocrats must have been particularly put out when the funds from the maritime League were used for the development of the Acropolis. It was their friends who had to pay the money (since taxes were not demanded of the lower classes within the allied states), and the tension created by having to explain this to them must have been great.

Apart from this, the new policy precipitated a new stage in Athens' independence from the communal Greek conventions. Its self-importance and the emphasis on its own interests are reflected in its use of funds. With varying degrees of success, it used everything within reach to improve its prestige and appearance. The city freed itself from tradition and broke with much of its past in order to become the hub of activity. It was, no doubt, quite natural for a tragedy submitted in 441 BC and which Sophocles presumably worked on in 442/1 BC, to examine the questions which arose from this situation.

Ajax

The plot

Ajax, who according to legend was the second great Greek hero in the war against Troy, has been defeated in a contest for the weapons of the dead Achilles. A court has awarded them to Odysseus. The Atreidae – Agamemnon and Menelaus – the leaders of the army, should have enforced this judgement; at any rate Ajax wants to exact his revenge against them and against Odysseus; indeed against all the foremost Greeks. At night he creeps away; Athena comes to him, apparently to help him, but in fact she sends him mad. In this state he comes across the cattle that the Greeks have captured, some of which he slaughters (along with the herdsmen), carrying off the others. Back at his tent he furiously sets upon the animals and starts to beat one of them to death, imagining it to be Odysseus.

This is the point at which Sophocles begins his play. Odysseus, out spying for information, creeps up to the tent. The goddess appears and tells him what has happened and wants to show him his enemy in all his deluded, shameful misery. Odysseus resists (he is worried about seeing or being seen by Ajax) but the merciless Athena calls the hero out. Ajax tells her what he imagines he is doing and, without knowing what he is talking about, he thanks her for her help.

The chorus is made up of the crew, soldiers and oarsmen with whom Ajax travelled to Troy. As children of Erechtheus (201) they are Athenians, as is Ajax whose home, Salamis, belongs to Athens. Without their leader they are frightened like 'timorous doves' (140) and effectively helpless. The rich and the powerful are most in danger, with envy always on their heels. 'Ay, but where would the little be without the great, when it comes to saving a city-wall? – Little and great together is best. The great do well when the little are there to help them. – Which is more than fools can understand, like those that clamour against you now'*(158). The men guess at which of the immortals has taken Ajax's reason; they know that he would never have done anything so senseless in his normal state. From then on the god-sent frenzy (185) is again and again spoken of in tones of horror. A daemon led Ajax to do what he did (243).

After the choric song, Tecmessa, Ajax's slave and lover, the mother of his son, steps out of the tent and tells the men what has happened. Hearing this, they grow even more worried; as followers of Ajax they fear the enmity of the Greeks. When Tecmessa says that Ajax has regained his sanity, hope is rekindled. But the direness of the situation reasserts itself as soon as he realizes the implications of what he has done and sees what a laughing-stock he will be for the Greeks. To the amazement of the others, he breaks down and weeps. Finally the scene within the tent is revealed by means of the *ekkýklēma*: Ajax in the middle of his bloody sacrifice. He starts a long lament.

For him, light has become darkness and the murk of the under-world has become his only brightness. He has been disgraced (426) and is no longer worthy of the help of gods or mortals (400). The gods, the Greeks and the whole country are now his enemies. Should he return home? But how can he contemplate presenting himself 'empty-handed with no prize' to his father, who had once won such great renown (462, 434)? Perhaps, then, he should mount an attack upon the Trojans? But that would please the Atreidae. No, he must do something that will show his father that

---

* Meier translates 'until they have a taste of it themselves'.

he is living up to the family name. A nobleman must live honourably or he must die honourably (479). He chooses the latter.

Using the story of her own sad fate, Tecmessa tries to dissuade him from his course. She was free, a member of a wealthy house, and now she is a slave. This was dictated by the gods, and by Ajax who killed her parents, and she complied with their will. Now, since she has no one else, she has the right to claim his protection. Their son, Eurysaces, is threatened with slavery, and then there are Ajax's parents in Salamis to consider. 'Can any man forget what happiness has once been his? Love must breed love. Not to remember kindness is to be called no longer noble' (520).

Ajax summons his son; if he is of the same mettle as his father he will not shy away from the butchery. He must get used to his father's brutal world. He then gives his son the famous advice: 'May you be everything your father was, but less unfortunate. Then you will do well' (550). Ajax decrees that his stepbrother, Teucer, should bring him up and take him home to his grandparents so that he can look after them in their old age. He is to inherit the great shield which has brought Ajax such fame. The other weapons are to be buried with him.

All other words are in vain. Ajax has decided and needs no further counsel. The *ekkýklēma* is taken off. Now the chorus sings of Salamis, of Ajax's great deeds, of his loneliness, his madness, the curse which hangs over him and of the sorrow which his parents will feel.

But then Ajax comes out of the tent. He seems transformed and he speaks a soliloquy (often inaccurately referred to as a 'speech of deception'). To begin with he talks of the long, immeasurable drift of time that brings all things forth from darkness into light and then covers them over once more. There is nothing that might not happen in the course of time. It can even destroy the strongest oath and the most steely intent. Ajax himself has been 'made soft' (literally 'womanish') for his woman's sake. He wants to go and cleanse himself in the water and to bury his sword. In future he will bow before the gods and will learn to respect the Atreidae. They are in the position of power and one must do as they say. 'I have learned my lesson . . . there is no power so sacred, none so strong as to defy all rank and precedence' (669). Winter gives way to summer, night to day, the tempest lays the groaning sea to rest, almighty sleep must free what he has bound, he cannot hold sway for ever. 'Must we not learn this self-discipline (*sōphroneîn*)? (677). One should never forget that enemies can become friends and friends enemies. In conclusion, Ajax declares that he will soon be redeemed. The chorus is satisfied by this and gives thanks for the fortunate turn of events; they call for a dance of joy. Tecmessa seems to have salvaged some hope.

But everything in this speech is equivocal. Those who hope that Ajax has chosen life must conclude that he has successfully struggled to do so. The audience must at least be in some doubt about his decision; and even knowledge of the outcome would not necessarily prevent such doubt. Every sentence and word shows simultaneously that Ajax wants to commit suicide. He says nothing false. On the contrary, much of his speech seems to be directed more towards death than life. The word for 'cleansing' pertains more than anything to the washing of a corpse; the sword is to be buried in his own body, and his obedience to the gods and to the Atreidae will be consummated in death.

In the meantime a messenger has appeared, sent in all haste by Teucer. He has been told by a soothsayer that Athena's wrath would only fall for this day upon Ajax, who must consequently be confined to his tent and guarded. Incidentally, we learn why the goddess is angry with the hero. His thoughts and aspirations have gone beyond what is fitting for a mortal. When his father had sent him off to the war with the words 'go out to win, but win with God beside you', he had boasted that whereas others may have need of the gods, he had not (765); and during battle he had similarly rejected Athena's help. When she hears of all this, Tecmessa knows that she has been fooled by Ajax. Hurriedly they set off to find him.

At this point the scene changes. The audience sees Ajax by the sea. He has stuck his sword in the ground and is now calling on the gods, first on Zeus and on Hermes who guides the dead to the underworld, then on the Furies to take revenge on the Atreidae and next on Helios to make known his fate at his home. He asks death to look him in the eye. Ajax gives a final salute to the daylight, to his home and to glorious Athens, then he falls on his sword. Normally in Greek tragedy the moment of death is not seen on the stage, but here the audience are full witnesses of the suicide.

Thus far the tragedy has taken up 865 lines. Another 535 follow the death of the protagonist. Only a small number of these are concerned with the lament of Tecmessa and the chorus. The great majority deal with an apparently new set of problems which are in fact very much a part, perhaps the main part, of the old ones. Teucer appears. His first concern is for Ajax's son who, he is afraid, may be seized by the enemy. His lament follows, and very soon the subject is not Ajax's death but his own unhappy situation. He is worried about what his father will say; Teucer is only the son of a captive slave-girl, and he will be suspected of killing Ajax for his inheritance. If this is the case he will be banished.

Menelaus finally intervenes and forbids the burial of the corpse on the grounds that Ajax has betrayed the army; his body will serve better as food for the birds. Menelaus is triumphant. The Atreidae could not rule properly while Ajax lived, but now their control is complete. He then comes out with a stream of common-places: the man in the street (and we note the political implications (1071)) must obey his superiors; fear must rule in the city to preserve order and in the army so that it may be led in a level-headed (i.e. obedient) way (1075); when insubordination and libertine behaviour are the order of the day, a city will be thrown off the right path and into the abyss. He repeats his advocacy of the necessity for fear and says that it should arise in time to have an effect. Finally he returns to the reversal of power: once Ajax was great, now Menelaus is.

Teucer comes back at him strongly. Ajax was never subservient to the Atreidae but lived as his own man. He maintains that Menelaus is nothing compared to his father (1114). Menelaus taunts Teucer in turn because of his origins. They both work each other up with violent accusations. Towards the end Teucer shouts, 'Never insult the dead; you're bound to suffer for it' (1154).

Menelaus and his followers withdraw, and Tecmessa and Eurys-aces appear. Teucer has the boy kneel as a suppliant before his dead father and tells him to stay by the corpse. The chorus bemoans the fate of Troy and curses whoever it was that started the war. Till now Ajax had protected the men from fear in the night; now no one knows what will happen. They long to reach Sunium from where they can greet the sacred city of Athens.

Then Agamemnon appears, ranting about the argument with Teucer, about which his brother has just told him. He regards the 'captive woman's brat' as nothing, and he is shocked that such a 'slave' should express dissatisfaction with a supreme commander. He also speaks disparagingly of Ajax, who is nothing to him. In the debate about Achilles' weapons, the majority of the judges had ruled against him and their decision should be respected; otherwise the law has no meaning. (It is, after all, the just and not the strong who stand most steadfast and prevail.) Teucer should see reason, remember who he is and get a freeman to represent his case; the king does not understand the speech of barbarians.

Teucer, in reply, complains of the ingratitude of the Atreidae, and he lists Ajax's deeds. Then he defends his mother, who was the daughter of a king, and attacks Agamemnon's forebears: his grandfather, who was indeed a barbarian, and his mother, who was Cretan. Then he asks how Agamemnon can censure his family when his own mother had let herself be ravaged and his father had made his brother eat his own children. Teucer, 'the slave', maintains that he is a nobleman, and as the son of noblemen (1304) he will do his duty. He would rather die than abandon his brother's body. He finishes with a veiled threat of violence.

Just in time Odysseus arrives. He tries to mediate and says that if Teucer has only insulted Agamemnon he can be forgiven. Above all, the laws of the gods and of justice dictate that Ajax must not be denied a proper burial. Ajax was indeed Odysseus' worst enemy in the army, but one should not fail to do honour to his memory. Agamemnon is utterly taken aback: 'what has a king [literally, a tyrant] to do with piety?' (1350). He insists that, if he holds office, even a nobleman must obey an order. Odysseus replies that Agamemnon should still be able to 'respect a friend's good counsel' (1351). For him Ajax is still, above all, a member of the nobility. He criticizes the king's intransigence and Agamemnon finally gives in, but with the implication that he has not been won over and is only trying to please Odysseus.

The end of the play follows quickly: Teucer and Odysseus become friends, although the former refuses the latter's offer to help bury Ajax, on the grounds that it may offend the dead. Odysseus respects this. The chorus brings everything to a close with the words: 'Many are the things that man seeing must understand. Not seeing, how shall he know what lies in the hand of time to come?' (1418).

A concern shared by all

There has been much discussion as to why the tragedy goes on for so long after the death of the hero. Reinhardt writes that the 'genuinely great figure, having suffered an admittedly deserved fall' has then to suffer the 'ingratitude, the pettiness, resentment, meanness and arrogance' of those false and overblown characters who make up the other world which triumphantly survives him. However, the tragedy has Ajax as its central reference point at all times, and it is clear that he is just as important after his death as when he was alive. What is more, a person's interests, quite apart from their desire for fame and remembrance, are not completely finished with their death, but only with their burial. In the case of Ajax this is a crucial factor. He can remain independent of the help of others in suicide as much as he could in victory, but thereafter the problem of his unhappy relationship with others, the social and open side of his life, remains unresolved.

The role of the burial, which is as central here as it is in *Antigone*, cannot be explained simply by the special care that the Greeks took with corpses. It is much more to do with the characteristic passivity of the time directly after death, when a person is totally reliant on, and at the mercy of, others. Hope as he may to find some escape in any other situation, here he must depend on the respect of the living for the ancient, unwritten laws, the will of the gods, according to which the dead are to be treated with reverence. Even the powerful Ajax, who thought he depended on nobody, cannot be responsible for his own corpse. He acknowledges this problem when he calls on Zeus and Hermes to bring Teucer as quickly as possible to help him to his final rest; this is after he had rejected Athena's help when still very much alive. As it is, we see that Ajax's will is only done with the aid of his worst enemy. Otherwise the Atreidae, the real power-holders, would have seen fit, as Creon does later in *Antigone*, to throw the dead traitor to the birds as a terrible example to others; to them his ambitions make him worse than the worst enemy.

Odysseus' arguments are particularly interesting. The first thing that he says is that if Agamemnon prevents the burial of Ajax he would be contravening the law of the gods, which must apply to everybody. For Odysseus, however, as for Antigone, there are other particular reasons which seem to determine his whole course of action. Ajax was a nobleman and, more importantly, the greatest warrior after Achilles. It is this which would seem to Odysseus to make his burial inviolable. But in the end he puts forward a quite different argument: 'some day I too shall need that office' (1365). Agamemnon retorts, 'Ay, there you have it: every man for himself.' 'Whom should I serve if not myself?' asks Odysseus in reply. At this point Agamemnon leaves the field to him out of friendship, but in no way convinced in the matter.

The question remains as to how Odysseus, having secured Ajax's burial, will ensure his own. The mutual obligations that exist between the living cannot exist between the living and the dead. Odysseus can place his hope only on the fact that if one does something for someone else, one might be treated in a similar fashion in the future. Anthropologists call this generalized mutuality: in the end the generality will give what the generality has received. Thus it comes about that certain conventions, like the laws of the gods, are always valid. What Agamemnon dismisses as Odysseus' egotism is at the same time a service to everybody. He is indeed serving his own interests, but they are the interests of anybody in the face of death. In this way his behaviour makes his position superior, because of its generality, to that of Agamemnon. It is a new way of bringing about a common good, by renouncing self-interest and the divisions between friend and enemy, positive and negative.

One may ask whether arguments similar to the one between Agamemnon and Odysseus have occasionally arisen in the rest of Greek history. One may even ask whether a similar question arose in the political arena of the mid fifth century. Whether this is the case or not, Odysseus very clearly asserts a basic solidarity with all people that transcends immediate hostility. In other words, he has marked a boundary beyond which enmity must cease: 'when there was a time to hate, I hated him' (1347), but then no longer.

Teucer replies, 'You have stood alone in his defence, refusing to be party to gross outrage offered by the living to the dead' (1384); and twice we find the words 'in the greatest need' (1151, 1306) referring to a plight which cannot be ignored. With this, Odysseus' humanity takes on a character which is on a higher level than any pragmatic justification, based on kindness or strict observance of the laws of the immortals, for the burial of the dead. He not only insists that whatever has to happen will happen, but refers to an interest that binds all humanity in its weakness, and this in the face of an overreaching political capriciousness which seeks to use the dead for its own purposes. He gives a more profound answer in response to a new sort of questioning. Odysseus must defend anew the old laws because they are being undermined by a political claim which is essentially a desire for revenge cloaked in political necessity. As a realist, he does this by reference to a vested interest.

But it is not only in a few lines towards the end of the play that we encounter the notion of an 'essence', in which Odysseus finds rooted a last manifestation of human solidarity. It is strongly expressed in the very first scene, where Athena assumes that Odysseus would look upon his enemy's misery with the same malicious glee that she does: 'Now you can laugh at him; won't that content you?' (79). But he does not willingly indulge in this *Schadenfreude* because he recognizes the human wretchedness which is so expressive of the wretchedness of his own existence. No one was as strong as Ajax, and no one was more prudent than he, nor more capable of doing the right thing in an emergency. His sudden fall shows that none of us are anything more than shadows. In it Odysseus sees a comment on his own fate more than on that of Ajax. Throughout he is thinking above all of himself, but by doing this, as we see in his response to the downfall of his enemy, he expresses his humanity.

It is typical that Agamemnon should use the same word 'shadow' when referring to the dead Ajax in his argument with Teucer: 'That man is dead now – just a shadow – and yet you seem to count on him to protect your impertinence' (1257): the man is as negligible to him when he is dead as he is to Odysseus when he is still alive. It is also worth noting the way that both the Atreidae and Teucer dub each other 'nobody', so sure are they of themselves and so ignorant of the truth about human existence. They are weak because of their misplaced confidence. Odysseus' insight, on the other hand, is explicitly praised by Athena, who at the same time makes clear the consequences: 'beware of uttering blasphemy against the gods; beware of pride, puffed up by strength or substance. Know that all things mortal hang in the scales; one day can tilt them up or down. The gods love goodness, and abhor all that is evil' (129).

Odysseus, then, shows a remarkable ability to see himself in others; he is not confined by a strict adherence to notions of friendship and enmity nor by his own interests, but can see things from a perspective beyond such narrow bias. He judges not only from the standpoint of the individual, but as part of a common humanity. He knows about the power of the gods and sees how selfishly and coldly they interfere. One can only properly take their power into account if one realizes how weak one is oneself; only then can one, in a quite new way, become great. Odysseus is able to forgive, he recognizes the boundaries of behaviour and he can demur, but he is also compliant; he expressly wants to remain loyal to Agamemnon and he upholds his own contradictory opinion only on this one issue. He also recognizes the consequences of his judgement and is thus ready to do what is necessary at the end. Had Ajax remained unburied, the world would not have recovered from the confusion we have seen, and the gods would have had to punish the Greeks. It is not that Odysseus thinks this far ahead, but in doing what is right he nevertheless brings about the desired state of affairs. His thoughts and actions thus set him apart from Ajax as well as from the two Atreidae.

The breakdown of the individual's striving for autarchy

Sophocles made Ajax into an almost paradigmatic version of the ancient hero. He is big and powerful and has single-handedly done the most incredible deeds.

Central to his thinking is the concept of honour. It is this which drives him to live up to his father in terms of renown and which makes it impossible for him to accept the decision of the court. It is unclear what this decision was based on, and if one only had regard to Ajax one could suppose that it did not, in fact, have anything to do with manipulation on the part of the Atreidae but was based simply on the superior claim of the much-travelled Odysseus over the great hero of past battles. At any rate, in the end even Odysseus says that Ajax was the greatest of the Greeks after Achilles (1340). The judgement then was wrong, and consequently Ajax must have his revenge.

When his honour is threatened he forgets any responsibility to his wife, son, parents or followers. The fact that others may need him means as little to him as any notion of his own reliance on others, gods or otherwise. He does not think as humans should. In the end, he does not realize that man and woman, parent and child, high and low, are bound to each other; that there is a duty to grant and return favours to one another, and that humans have the gift of memory and thus of gratitude. It is not only Tecmessa who calls attention to the fact that he cannot be a true nobleman if he does not remember the kindnesses done to him (522). Teucer also establishes that remembrance of and gratitude to Ajax were quickly dispelled (1266). He has obviously been treated in the same way as Tecmessa.

Ajax is an absolutist and he thinks and behaves as if he were completely self-sufficient. He thinks he can treat Athena as though she were an 'ally' (117); the word he uses here is the one that Menelaus later uses to emphasize Ajax's subservience (1053; to which Teucer objects that Ajax was his own man (1089)). It is also the word used for the allies of Athens who have lost their independence.

Ajax's greatness is fascinating. Everything else seems pitifully small in comparison; and especially because of the fact that the tragedy does not end with his death, one has constantly to review one's opinion of him. Initial shock and horror give way to the overwhelming impression created by his downfall; and at the end one has to respect and admire his actions. The baseness of his opponents constitutes a background against which he seems even more impressive. Only Odysseus is able to overcome him, and then only in a quite different, rational, citizen-like way!

There is only one point at which Ajax could be seen to have fallen out of his role, and this is during the wonderful speech that Sophocles gives him when he leaves his tent to go to the sea-shore – essentially the most important point in the whole tragedy. But he shows in this speech only that the all-encompassing process of change that is characteristic of everything in the world binds him too. Only in a rash moment of compassion could he become 'womanish'. Surely the Ajax we know cannot really want to exercise a religious respect for the Atreidae (this is what is implied by the word that he uses here). That would be a gesture of unthinkable subservience. After all that has happened, how could he possibly abase himself before the gods except by killing himself? At the same time this is the only way that Athena will be placated.

What actually happens in this speech is that Ajax, in the face of death, adopts the same distance towards the world that Odysseus does. He recognizes its laws and frames them in the great, majestic imagery of the cycle of the seasons and the passing of day and night, of storm and the eventual loosening of the bonds of sleep. He already 'knows' that friendship and hostility are not permanent and perhaps also 'suspects' that he can only come to final rest with the help of his worst enemy. From this, he draws what for him is the right conclusion. It is not the only possible conclusion, because there is also Odysseus' conclusion which aims for a world order that sees the individual as one among many. But it is the only one that remains to Ajax. He sacrifices himself. Only by doing this can he demonstrate the newly learnt prudence that is so pleasing to the gods. He thus heals the great rift that he caused in the order of the world. But he does not simply restore the old order; he leaves behind a world that will never see his like again, one in which he could play no further part.

Sophocles does not explicitly say that Ajax is the representative of a world different from the one we see at the end of the play. Only at first does he concentrate on the individual consumed by self-interest, then he moves on to the other, 'social' side which is there, whether he intended it to be or not, at one and the same time. The change from one to the other corresponds to the change from a heroic to an unheroic mode of speech. The question is whether it is the old and the new that are being opposed by this change or simply two sides of the same human condition. Unlike Aeschylus, Sophocles denies a specific historical perspective (or does not recognize it). But perhaps in Ajax's behaviour he saw an all too telling parallel with the behaviour of Athens towards other cities.

History is present in Sophocles' tragedy in as much as it is a reflection of the time in which it was written and, as far as we can make out, its heroes face problems which are informed by the problems of that time.

Before anything else, one should insist on the fact that the all-encompassing experience of a changing world which provides a background to the whole play (and which presumably constitutes its topicality) is invariably voiced by the protagonist: and he is the representative, if one may make such historical differentiations, of the old world. In this way this experience achieves a certain authenticity. In the ambiguity of his great speech, Ajax justifies Odysseus' position as much as his own. His words illuminate both parts of the play, and his greatness is considerably enhanced by the fact that he is able to express this recognition.

The failure of authority

In the second, 'political', part of the play, the Greek army at Troy comes broadly to represent the city of Athens. The armaments tribunal uses the terminology of the Athenian courts and various terms denoting leadership and authority are taken from contemporary life. Agamemnon and Menelaus use arguments which are based on the principles of the polis. The talk is of priority and power, eminence and lowliness, and of the claims that the members of noble families derive from their antecedents.

Agamemnon and Menelaus do not quite conduct themselves like tyrants but as rulers who are weak and who do not want their weakness to be known. Menelaus stops arguing with Teucer because 'I'd be ashamed to have it known that I was wasting words instead of using the power I have to force you' (1159). He is not only too weak to exercise force, but too weak to win the argument with words (which has to do with the fact that he is in the wrong; 1125). It seems like a distortion of Athena's behaviour in *The Eumenides*; she was so convincing in her case that she did not have to use Zeus' weapons to help, even though they were available to her. Agamemnon is afraid that if he and his brother do not rigidly stand by their refusal to bury Ajax, they will be seen as cowards (1362); Odysseus counters by saying that they would in fact be seen as just and reasonable men. Before this he urges Agamemnon not to resort to force and intimidation nor to throw aside what is right out of sheer vindictiveness towards Ajax (1334).

The Atreidae only recognize absolute authority and obedience. They have no regard for Odysseus' 'laws of the gods' (which are the same as what, in *Antigone*, are called 'unwritten laws'). They understand friendship but do not feel any gratitude for what Ajax achieved. Rather, they are filled with a desire for revenge. They want to exercise a power over the dead Ajax that they were never able to impose while he was alive. They utilize what political knowledge they have as an instrument of their obsession. They use the right to do wrong.

Menelaus' speech about a state's need for fear harks back to *The Eumenides*; but there, the unleashing of fear is occasioned by the punishment of a living person rather than by the maltreatment of a corpse. If the Atreidae really did manipulate the judgement against Ajax – which would seem to be the case, judging by how they behave – then Agamemnon's insistence on the principle that judgements should always be upheld would seem to indicate that the authority of the institution has become debased to serve the triumph of personal caprice.

The hollowness of their claims is evident when they reproach Teucer on the grounds of his ancestry. The implication here is that being of good stock is a prerequisite for political standing. If Agamemnon counts himself as a wise and just ruler, he is greatly mistaken. He shows himself unworthy of such an appellation when he refers, as an example of how to rule, to a man who enforces his will upon an ox by using a whip. He obviously does not know whom he is dealing with. And Menelaus irritably rejects the democratic freedom to choose how one behaves (1081), a freedom represented here for the first time. Athenians must have recognized their oligarchic and tyrannical tone. Menelaus seems to reinforce this when he addresses his call for obedience in the 'common man' so unsuitably to Ajax. His speech is only superficially similar to Athena's warning in *The Eumenides*.

A major characteristic of the rule of the Atreidae is that they tend to view everything in strict terms of friendship and hostility rather than recognizing the whole. This is seen particularly clearly in the fierce arguments that they both have with Teucer, each of which ends in stalemate. The adversaries adopt ever more irreconcilable positions, the division being made even more obvious by the short commentaries provided by the chorus. None of them yields an inch to the other. Teucer even threatens that his opponents will be destined to remain unburied if they refuse to bury Ajax now. Each attaches unwarranted importance to his own position and judges others according to that model. The archaic principle of helping one's friends and injuring one's enemies is applied to the limit. Consequently, any just and reasonable admission that an opponent may be right must appear as weakness. So it is that Agamemnon only gives ground when his friend Odysseus declares his own 'selfish' interest in Ajax's burial. This capitulation, if taken literally, is particularly irresponsible, in that he backs down merely in order to do a favour for a friend, where earlier he had said that to do so would be to threaten the well-being of the whole army (that is, of the city). Perhaps Teucer is capable of becoming friends with Odysseus, but this amity cannot be extended to those who have derided his dead brother.

The Atreidae, then, are hardly less wrapped up in themselves than is Ajax. Admittedly they respect their friends, whereas he had no regard for his. But they are as isolated in their style of rule and in their friendships, as he was on his own. And whereas he was powerful in life and in death, they are weak and mean. That is the difference. Basically the two brothers stand in their own way as much as does their great enemy. Thus order is by no means completely restored by his sacrifice. Only Odysseus can cope with the resulting problems, we are left with an idiosyncratic configuration of characters.

A third option

In letting Odysseus rise above all the arguments, Sophocles establishes him in a third position which is quite distinct from that of the antagonists. He transcends their conflict because he embodies something quite different and quite new. This is seen not only when he comes on in the two great scenes at the beginning and the end. His presence can also be detected right in the middle of the play during Ajax's great monologue. His behaviour represents the other response to the recognition of the impermanence of worldly existence. In his flexibility we can see a certain feminine quality which contrasts with all the unyielding and self-defeating masculinity. He has learnt to be level-headed and knows that friendship and enmity cannot be permanent or absolute, but must adapt.

His thoughts and actions correspond closely to the great, all-embracing rhythms that govern the world. It is this recognition of universality that enables Odysseus to feel such a broad solidarity with humanity. Only in this context does the demarcation line between the mortals and the gods start to play a tangible role. Our insubstantial and tenuous existence is revealed in its true light, and it becomes clear that even the strongest must at times be prepared to cede the high ground to others.

Later, Euripides introduces the cycle of day and night in *The Phoenician Women* as an example of democratic equality at work in nature. There too, rulers and ruled alternate. One should perhaps not be concerned by the fact that the concept of equality is lacking in *Ajax*, for the image of change undoubtedly refers to a democratic model. In *Ajax* the emphasis is more on the position of great figures within a democracy, where everyone is supposed to be just one among many. Even in nature, nothing can dominate for ever; equality must eventually be established.

Athena alludes to this in her observation that physical and economic superiority do not constitute the right to rise above one's station (130). This point is reinforced in the conspicuously strong expression of doubt about whether the behaviour of the Atreidae is just (1093) and by the lack of substance behind their arrogance (1120, 1228). All this, plus the remarks made by the chorus about the envy that is brewing in the lower ranks, constitutes more than just a set of general aphorisms (which were already commonplace among the Greeks). The Athenian theatre-goers of the middle of the fifth century must have seen in it clear reference to contemporary issues.

Odysseus' superiority is based above all on his recognition of how weak the individual is. For him it is the co-operative rather than the competitive virtues which are most effective. He favours attempts at living together rather than the absolute imperative to assure personal ascendancy, to conquer and rule. Nowhere in literature before Sophocles' *Ajax* do we find such a thorough championing of co-operation: we are told that one must understand that an individual is just part of a whole; we might need now one, now another. The system of relationships is quite different from, if not opposite to, a simple structure of friendship and hostility: 'friendship is but a treacherous anchorage, as most men know' (682). Everyone, not least the highest and the lowest, relies on everyone else. One must be able to forgive and to put violent verbal exchanges in perspective. Like the harsh winter, the night, the turbulent sea and sleep, one must be able to withdraw when the time is right. A man's worth is not determined by his breeding but by his thoughts and actions. One must concentrate on one's relationships and on the general climate (*kairós*) which, in such a changeable world, is so important. Here the whole experience of life in a Greek city-state is evoked. It is also interesting to note that Odysseus, just like Antigone, keeps his opposition to Agamemnon to the point in question. He is not a revolutionary but remains well within the bounds of the established order (which, unlike Antigone, he manages to do successfully).

By recognizing his own weakness and lack of importance in the face of the great pattern which governs the world, he becomes aware of the 'laws of the gods'. Ajax is too arrogant, and the Atreidae too grasping, to bother about this. But these laws mark out certain boundaries and correspond to the interests of humanity. They give meaning to co-operation and solidarity.

Odysseus might not be the only one to express these, the play's crucial insights, but he is the only one of the characters who heeds the lesson which they constitute. They allow the play to go beyond the stubbornness of the Atreidae and the hopelessness of their argument with Teucer. They are the foundation on which the polis must stand; the principles that the Atreidae call on, no matter how just and wise they may be (1091), are not sufficient in themselves. By obeying the more profound principles, Odysseus assumes the role in *Ajax* that Athena does at the end of *The Eumenides*. He stands for a new phase in the evolution out of the ancient era: the phase where a polis recognizes its conditions of existence.

The political art of Ajax

We may ask exactly how relevant *Ajax* was to the political reality of the time in which it was written, but we do not know the exact date of the play's appearance, nor details of the internal and external political problems of Athens at that time. At best we have the clue of Pericles' law of 451 BC that allowed full citizenship only to those whose parents were both Athenian. This could be what is referred to by the remarks about non-Greek – or non-Athenian (that is, Cretan) – ancestry; it could also be the point of Agamemnon's telling Teucer to find someone else to represent him. Blood and free birth obviously play a major role in Teucer's argument that enslavement is a sad fate but does not signify a lack of honour. We do not know, however, how much all this is based upon actual incidents.

In the character of Ajax one could see a representation of Athens, which itself laid such importance on independence, treated its allies with such contempt and which, in its foreign policy, hardly lived up to the play's message of co-operation. When the chorus laments the terrors of the war and, like Ajax, longs for a return to Athens, it could be taken as a contemporary allusion (1193, 1219). But more than anything, it seems likely that the play would have prompted discussions and political arguments about the relationship between the leaders and the people in Athens; about the conceit and arrogance of the nobility; the calls for unremitting obedience on and off the battlefield; the amount of freedom that an individual should be granted; perhaps also about revolt against political decisions.

Whether this is so or not, it is surely always relevant to champion the virtues of democratic order, to assert that the leaders and the common people need each other and that a conciliatory nature is necessary for the sake of unity. Similarly it cannot be a bad thing to comment upon and justify the existing order, on the one hand through the use of exemplary action, on the other hand through the tragedy of once great and powerful figures, who since ancient times have stood as archetypes, but who are now 'impossible', no longer having a place in the world. The likely outcome of this is that events within the city are shown to have a meaning within the greater frame of the universe.

In interpreting *Ajax* it becomes obvious that one is dealing with a highly political play. Sophocles uses the story of the hero's fate in order to examine the alternative to his way of life. After the tragic fall come the politics: of conflict and of levelling. He shows the weakness of those who seem strong and the strength that comes from apparent weakness when one knows oneself and one recognizes the universal laws (and, of course, the fact that one is linked to everyone else). In the face of the temptation to be selfish, this is the alternative of reason (*sōphrosýnē*) that Athens constantly struggled to assert in its foreign policy and its internal government.

Most of the 'lessons' contained in the play are old ones: the criticism of the nobility and the call for *sōphrosýnē*; the doubt about how firm friendship is; the lesson that rise and fall, joy and sorrow, follow each other etc. There are repeated echoes of Aeschylus' *Oresteia*. But quite apart from the fact that old lessons must be constantly updated, there was much that was new in the play when it appeared: the idea that the laws of the gods are based on the interests of humanity; the concept of a common human interest and the intense awareness of the infinite possibilities of time, the frailty of all relationships and the transformations that can dissolve the greatest powers. These things are not found in this form in earlier literature.

A feeling must have arisen that certain areas, which till then had been regarded as inviolable (in spite of any individual transgressions), were now fundamentally under threat. This would have stemmed from the encroachments which were made as a result of the gradual growth of the empire and the despotism that was characteristic of Athens' internal and external relations. It would seem that the play is charged with the experiences and tensions of the politics of that time.

The instability of relationships and the ebb and flow of power are very much part of the ancient Greek experience (and, since Anaximander, very much part of the Greek concept of justice). But here they are emphasized so strongly, made to have such an influence on the fate of Ajax and are ultimately so bound up with the 'modern' character, Odysseus, that this would seem to point to the fact that the mutability of existence was at that time experienced anew. This indicates that a change was taking place: all the above factors were influencing the general state of affairs in Athens.

In any case, *Ajax* chronicles the change which had been set in motion since the time of Aeschylus and which Sophocles' generation was witnessing at first hand. Aeschylus had placed his hopes for a solution to the problems of the polis in its institutions, and certainly in a conciliatory stance on the part of Athena; even the profound upheaval of his own time was, for him, reasonable in the context of the whole history of civilization and the history of the Olympian dynasty. For Sophocles, however, everything is unsure and subject to change. Democracy can no longer be guaranteed to solve the internal problems of the city, because problems also arise in the new order. This is not a criticism of democracy but a recognition that it too is only a human institution. It becomes clear in *Antigone* that the problem is not now with a particular order, but with rationality itself.

Sophocles had, then, to initiate himself in the arena of the new, more profound questioning. The ethical claims to humanity in the polis and beyond had to be newly accounted for and developed further. In a certain sense we can see here a new, universal ethos and we can certainly see the attempt to redraw and clarify the political boundaries.

There is much that indicates that *Ajax* was an attempt to make people aware of the problems associated with the ethics and the intellectual infrastructure of Athens. Whatever general observations may be made about the effects of Greek politics on the Athenians – a certain change in, or even insecurity about, traditional models and ideas in the face of a new sort of behaviour and experience – all this seems to me to be explored here. This examination is carried out in a medium which is instructive without seeming overtly didactic. The effect is indirect but all the more forceful because of its foundation in sensual experiences and identifications. The play is about reassessing one's view of certain things and it aims to promote and reinforce a lesson which had been learnt from observing the state of internal politics, in fact to influence the fundamental principles of a volatile citizenry. In order to make the right decisions and take the right actions in such stressful times, the people have to think clearly, and the play's intention was to take on some of the intellectual burden.

Where Aeschylus was compelled to engage Athena to reconcile the factions after the great struggle between the old and the new justice, the struggle here is brought to an end by a mortal. A man, it must be said, who is beloved of Athena, but who seems to have no need of her help: he knows the lesson that she teaches almost better than she does herself (primarily because he has learnt the difference between mortals and gods). On the other hand this perception might be the result of, as well as the reason for, Athena's love.

Antigone

The story of the house of Labdacus ends with the argument about the corpse of Polynices. The ill-fated marriage between Oedipus and his mother Jocasta produced two brothers and two sisters. Eteocles took over the leadership of Thebes, and Polynices gathered an army in Argos in order to overthrow him. The two brothers kill each other in the battle, and Creon takes over the city. He decrees that Eteocles, the defender of the city, should have an honourable funeral, but that the traitor Polynices should be left unburied for the birds and the dogs to tear apart. When this ban is contravened, he enforces the penalty of death by stoning – traditional for those who support a traitor.

The play begins with a dialogue between the two sisters. Antigone is determined to give Polynices the necessary honour. Ismene is distressed because she does not think that women should oppose the will of men. One must bow to whoever is strongest and obey 'those who stand in power'. The gods of the underworld, to whom the dead should be given, will forgive her because she is under constraint. Antigone counters that, in the long run, she will have to honour the immortals far more than any mortal. She storms out, expressing hatred for her sister.

The chorus is made up of the pre-eminent elders of the town. Their first song concerns the newly won victory. Creon has called them to a meeting. He praises the loyalty that they have always shown to the throne of Thebes. He acknowledges that a just ruler must heed the best advice and that they should not let fear prevent them from speaking; rather they should openly join in the fight against any disaster that might threaten the city. One should do everything possible for the city and not let regard for friends and allies get in the way of this duty. It is this that makes a good citizen. 'Such are my standards (*nómoi*). They make our city great' (191). He now says what he has decided about the treatment of the dead brothers. The one who helped his city is to be honoured, the one who sought to destroy it is to be punished. Creon has set guards around the corpse. The elders should never side with anyone who might break his orders – a necessary warning, since the lure of profit leads many astray, even when the penalty is death.

At that very moment a sentry arrives who, after some prevarication, announces that the body has been sprinkled with dust, which constitutes a proper burial rite. There is, however, no trace of the perpetrator. The chorus thinks that it must be the work of the gods (278), but Creon cuts their speech short: the gods would never concern themselves with a dead person who in life wanted to destroy their land and their laws. He is far more worried that the deed was carried out by opponents of his regime, who never keep 'their necks beneath the yoke, loyally submitting to their king' (291). They must have bribed the guards who, the king threatens, will be tortured until they confess. The guard remarks on how terrible it is that one empowered to make such pronouncements can be so mistaken (323). After he has thanked the gods that he has been saved for the time being, the stage is cleared and the chorus begin their first song.

This is the famous *pollà tà deiná*: 'Numberless wonders, terrible wonders walk the world, but none the match for man' (332). The key word here can also be translated by 'awful', and its meaning ranges from 'admirable', 'great', and 'powerful' to 'terrifying'. It rightly comes at the start of this recitation which stands as the most powerful portrayal of the contemporary awareness of man's abilities. The chorus lists some of mankind's technical achievements: the ability to navigate the seas in spite of terrible weather, agriculture, hunting birds and animals, fishing and the domestication of animals.

'And speech and thought, quick as the wind, and the mood and the mind for law that rules the city – all these he has taught himself' (355). He can provide shelter for himself against the wind and bad weather; he is always resourceful and is never at a loss when confronting whatever chances. Only from death will he find no rescue, although he has found remedies for the most desperate plagues.

This is then summed up: equipped with measureless ingenuity and skill, mankind forges onwards, now for ill, now again for good. When he observes the laws of the land and the justice of the gods he becomes '*hypsípolis*', 'highly political', of the highest as far as the city is concerned; the opposite of this is '*ápolis*', 'unpolitical', against the city, not able to live in the city – the state of someone who is wedded to wrongdoing out of sheer recklessness.

Human greatness is an ambiguous quality. It can be used for the betterment or to the detriment of the polis. It produces essential tools but cannot guarantee that they will be used reasonably.

After the song the sentry returns with Antigone, whom he has caught red-handed as she was re-anointing the corpse. He is sorry that he has to disturb her in her grief, but he always puts his own skin first.

Antigone does not deny that she has heard about Creon's order – or 'law' as he likes to call it. Her explanation is that 'it wasn't Zeus, not in the least, who made this proclamation – not to me. Nor did that justice, dwelling with the gods beneath the earth, ordain such laws for men. Nor did I think your edict had such force that you, a mere mortal, could override the gods'* (450). She is not at all scared of the death penalty: finding herself in the cursed position of being a daughter of Oedipus, an early death would be a blessing to her. She will never accept that her brother should remain unburied.

The chorus criticizes her inherited intransigence. Creon calls it 'the stiffest stubborn will' (473). He is furious and refers to the reins with which one tames the wildest horses and the humility that is the proper lot of a slave. He takes it as a terrible insult that Antigone is now boasting about what was already a terrible

---

* Meier translates 'that a mere mortal might transgress the unwritten, immutable laws of the gods on the strength of it'.

deed. Above all he feels that his manliness would be threatened if he gave in to a woman. In spite of his kinship he declares that she, and her sister with her, must be punished with the most dreadful death. During a fierce dialogue, Antigone claims the greatest possible honour and glory for her actions. She says that the old men would support her if fear did not keep them quiet. In order to strengthen her argument she uses the same words that Creon used to exhort the chorus to speak up if necessary at the start; and, with hindsight, it does indeed seem a bitter irony that at this moment they would do better to follow his exhortation rather than bow to his will (if they had known better). But they keep silent, which Creon takes as a condemnation of Antigone. He asks her whether she is not ashamed of differing so much from them (510). He insists that only one of the brothers should receive the honour of a funeral: 'Once an enemy, never a friend, not even after death' (522). She protests: Hades demands the same rights for everyone.

Ismene is brought on, and she declares that she wants to die with Antigone. Antigone again coldly rejects her. Full of loathing, she explains: 'Live your life. I gave myself to death long ago, so I might serve the dead' (559). In the end Creon orders his thugs to take the sisters away.

In their second song, the chorus sing of the *átē*, the destruction, with which the house of Labdacus is afflicted. One sorrow has unstoppably followed another and now the last one has been provoked 'by a senseless word, by a fury at the heart' (603). They sing about Zeus' power which no mortal can 'override'; the implication seems to be that somebody has expressed such hubris (perhaps Athens itself). They speak, too, of a law, just as the chorus of *Agamemnon* once did. But now this law is not 'learn through suffering', but 'no towering form of greatness enters into the life of mortals free and clear of ruin'* (613). Hope can be both a help and a delusion. Foul is fair to those whom the gods have damned; they spend only a short time free from *átē*, from destruction. They say nothing more about man's potential; that is only one side of the coin. What is now being said of the house of

---

* Meier translates 'Nothing in the life of mortals goes very far free from destruction'.

Oedipus will in the end be generally applicable. There is very little room for manoeuvre.

The next scene sees the entrance of Haemon, the son of Creon, whom Sophocles makes Antigone's betrothed. Creon fears that his son will fire angry reproaches at him, but Haemon declares 'you in your wisdom set my bearings for me – I obey you' (638). This gives Creon the opportunity to start a long, paternal and statesmanlike exhortation. Orderliness begins in the home – which means that he cannot give any regard to his niece, the bride. Only those who rule their homes well are fit to rule the polis. Such a man will give good commands and take them too (669). Creon also touches, though this seems rather unmotivated, on what democracy teaches about the necessary exchange between ruler and ruled. Much of what he says, nevertheless, would have been quite acceptable and in line with the thinking of the day: the diatribes against anarchy, the disorder which women threaten and the necessity of male rule and of obedience. Perhaps he goes too far and is too absolute ('that man the city places in authority, his orders must be obeyed, large and small, right and wrong' (666) but a similar phrase is to be found in the writings of the sage Solon (fragment 27).

The leader of the chorus finds that what Creon has said is reasonable, but qualifies it by adding 'unless old age has robbed us of our wits'. Haemon is no more capable of contradicting his father than they are, but he does start to suggest that there may be an alternative course of action. He hears what the people in the town are saying – something that his father is too removed to be in contact with. The people are mourning Antigone, praising her action and bemoaning the injustice of her punishment. Protesting his love, he begs his father not to be so single-minded about what is right and what is wrong. 'Whoever thinks that he alone possesses intelligence, the gift of eloquence, he and no one else, and character too – such men, I tell you, when you spread them open, you will find them empty' (706). One must be able to learn, to be adaptable and not to overstep the mark. It would, of course, be best to be born infallible, but since this is not really possible, it is best to listen to those who have good advice.

The leader of the chorus concurs with this, but Creon is incensed: he will not be schooled by such a young man. He is back to his main argument: should one admire a rebel? Is Antigone not suffering from some sickness? When Haemon talks again of the people, the essential component of the city of Thebes, Creon does not argue that they have taken Antigone's side, but he asks whether the polis has any right to tell him what he should do. He is now completely beside himself: 'Am I to rule this land for others – or myself?' Haemon argues, 'it is no city at all, owned by one man alone.' 'The city is the king's, that is the law.'– 'What a splendid king you'd make of a desert island' (736). To this Creon has no reply, except to say that Haemon is blatantly taking the woman's side. As long as he holds his rule to be sacrosanct, he cannot be wrong. 'You expect to be listened to but not to listen,' says Haemon. His father retorts, 'You will never marry her, not while she's alive.' 'Then she will die – but her death will kill another.' Creon takes this as a brazen threat, which leads Haemon to say that it is no threat but simply a phrase which is intended to 'combat empty, mindless judgements'. He storms off.

Creon rescinds Ismene's death sentence but decrees that Antigone be walled up alive in a cave. The chorus sings of the power of Eros. They see Antigone being taken to her death and cannot hold back their tears. She bids farewell to the light and calls on the city and the elders to bear witness to her death. Then she gives the puzzling declaration that she would never have broken the law in the way she has for anyone but her brother: not for a husband or even for a child. She could always get a new husband or child, but, since the death of their parents, her brother is irreplaceable.

This is all said during a dialogue with the chorus. They acknowledge the renown and praise that she has received. She is going to her death as a mortal, but as a law unto herself (*autónomos*). 'It is a great thing for a dying girl to hear' that she shares the fate of an immortal like Niobe. They mean this as a comfort, but she takes it as mockery. They then become more critical. She has gone to the last limits of daring, smashing against the high throne of justice. They later reassert that to honour the dead is to show devoutness, but authority will brook no transgression. Her own blind, passionate and self-regarding will has led her to destruction.

'My reverence only brands me for irreverence,' declares Antigone. If what Creon wants is just in the view of the gods, then her suffering will lead her to an understanding of her sins. But if this is not the case, then those who do her such injustice should suffer no more than she must (924). Creon wants to get it over with quickly. The chorus sings its third ode, in which it once again testifies to the terrible power of fate.

After this, Tiresias, the blind soothsayer is led on by a boy. He had wanted to observe his birds, but they were in a frenzy. He tested the burnt sacrifice but it had putrefied. Dogs and birds had strewn the altar with pieces of Polynices' corpse. He tells Creon that 'it is your high resolve that sets this plague on Thebes', and he tries to make him follow better counsel. All men make mistakes, and if one tries to amend folly, one can change things for the better. Presumption (*authādía*), however, damns a man to stupidity. But Creon will not be told, he feels attacked from all sides and he will not listen to Tiresias, whom he accuses of being corrupted by money. He presumes to say that even if the eagles of Zeus take the corpse up to the throne of god, he would fear no dishonour and would see no reason to bury the body. After a long argument, in which Tiresias predicts what will happen, the seer goes.

Creon finally becomes less sure of himself. 'It's a dreadful thing to yield, but resist now? Lay my pride bare to the blows of ruin? That's dreadful too' (1096). He is not yet totally convinced, but the leader of the chorus puts pressure on him. Tiresias has never been wrong before. The king is at last persuaded. 'I shackled her, I'll set her free myself. I am afraid . . . it's best to keep the established laws to the very day we die' (1112). He is presumably referring here to the old unwritten principles, some of which we have seen him transgress. He certainly now seems to be prepared to acknowledge justice and, in the act of setting Antigone free, to reinstate it.

The chorus now sings its last ode, this time about Dionysus, the patron of Thebes, on whose help they call. But it is too late. At that moment a messenger arrives. First he laments the fickleness of fortune and refers to Creon's deserved greatness and the services he has done. But 'now all is lost'. When a man has squandered his true joys, he is as good as dead' (1167). Earlier Antigone said, 'I gave myself to death, long ago' (559), and now Creon is in the same position. His queen, Eurydice, comes on and we hear what has happened. The king had Polynices buried after praying to the gods of the underworld for forgiveness. One of his followers had then heard a loud cry coming from the cave in which Antigone was immured. Antigone had hanged herself and Haemon was lying at her feet. Creon begged him to come out, but at this, he tried to attack his father and then plunged the sword into his own side. The messenger concludes his story by saying that Haemon has proved that, for a man, lack of judgement is the greatest evil. He doubtless means this to be a comment on the effect that love had on Haemon, but Tiresias has only just spoken of this concept of 'lack of judgement' in regard to Creon; after the queen has made her exit and Creon has had his son carried on to the stage, we hear that Haemon's death is in fact the result of his father's rather than his own, failing. The chorus finally grasps what has happened: 'Too late, too late, you see what justice means'. Then we hear of the death of Eurydice. In a long lament Creon acknowledges his guilt. 'Take me away, quickly, out of sight. I don't even exist – I'm no one. Nothing' (1325). He longs for death. But Antigone's wish that he should suffer nothing worse than she is not fulfilled: 'For mortal men there is no escape from the doom we must endure' (1337). To live on is much worse than to die. At the end, the chorus is left alone on the orchestra. It deems wisdom to be the greatest part of happiness. One should respect the gods and refrain from speaking rashly. Thus one learns reason as one grows old.

Sophocles' *Antigone* tells us more about the political nature of Greek tragedy than most other plays. The characters are drawn and the action set out in such a way, the language is so rich and so replete with associations, the enigmatic Greek religiosity and the general humanity (which still has a clear message for us today) are so vibrantly present, that a political interpretation of the drama would seem to be severely reductive. And yet the fact remains that *Antigone* is again and again presented in our theatres as a political play. These days especially, it is seen as a drama of revolt against the power of the state. One cannot avoid finding political implications throughout the text; indeed they are the strongest force at work in the play.

As in *Ajax*, the fate of a traitor's corpse is the main problem. Not to bury it in home soil accorded with Athenian law. Sophocles would have also seen an offence in this, as not burying the corpse would lead to a disruption of the whole order of nature; in Hades the same law applies to all. Above all he was of the opinion that antagonism must be limited by human solidarity. Athenian law did not in itself rule against the burial of traitors, and there is no reason to suspect that the Athenians would have objected at all to such a thing.

In contrast to *Ajax*, however, the body here is not in the hands of a friendly party but in those of an enemy. And there is no Odysseus to sort out a compromise or to bring a third, universal option to the argument.

The one person who has the wisdom to do this, and who in his own way does do this, is the seer Tiresias; but he cannot quite succeed. Odysseus was only successful because he had Agamemnon's friendship, but Tiresias is doomed to failure because Creon declares him an enemy, or, more precisely, a corrupted tool of his enemies. The same happens to Haemon, whose reasoning is closest to that of Odysseus. Thus no solution is found before all the parties involved have ended up either dead or irredeemably stricken, which is worse than dead. Only when it is all over can the chorus learn at least something. But even this only comes from age – and who can tell how much must be endured before then!

In *Antigone* the characters' various prejudices and interests are particularly extreme and comprehensive, and Sophocles brings them into conflict with each other in order to set them out as clearly as possible. At first, Creon acted as a king should. He saved the city – although we are not told how – and used to listen to Tiresias' advice (994, 1058, 1162). He has, then, conducted his affairs well until now. The way that he confronts the elders may seem rather odd to us, but his demand for openness is nothing new; the principles on which he lectures them, and later Haemon, presumably correspond to a great extent to those that were enforced by the Athenian democracy.

The insecurity that leads him to fear enemies who do not recognize his authority is obvious. This is the result of a monarchical system, and it causes him much anguish. Perhaps it also has something to do with the seriousness with which he treats his position. He is undoubtedly a conscientious ruler; it is this which determines his instruction to leave Polynices unburied, and he believes that everything must be done for the good of the city. On the one hand, his thinking is steeped in the old distinctions between friends, who are to be helped, and enemies, who are to be hurt (643); on the other, it is strongly influenced by the interests of 'his' city. Clearly this means that he must judge people according to how they relate to the city. Finally, he is revealed, at certain points in the play, to be an enlightened man. Thus we see that he will pursue whatever he thinks are the city's interests to the bitter end. This is where his first mistake lies.

It is not yet a bad mistake. As Tiresias says, to err is human. It only becomes serious when he refuses to listen to advice about how to remedy the situation. Creon's fate becomes nothing less than a parable about what happens in such circumstances: he cannot take seriously anyone who questions his decision – even if, as in the case of Haemon, it is done with the best of intentions and out of a desperate filial love. Such doubt only serves to trigger off all sorts of defence mechanisms: the chorus's suggestion that it may have been a god that sprinkled the corpse with dust prompts his first fury. He recognizes no alternative interpretation of events. He suspects anyone who tries to change his mind of being corrupted, either by money or by love. He allows nothing to touch him.

In the long dialogue with Haemon he finally reveals himself as a tyrant. He certainly has not been a tyrant from the start, but we now see how a ruler who has made one wrong decision, and who sticks to it against all better judgement, becomes more and more unyielding, until he is completely incapable of normal communication. The exchange between father and son is one of the most significant monuments of political thought. Haemon takes the Athenian ideas about the city-republic as obvious truths and he gradually emerges as the counter-force to the tyrant: his father's style of rule is suitable only in a land without people. In a city, on the other hand, it is not enough to speak, order and obey; it is also necessary to listen, learn and pay heed to others. It is not possible to rule *against* the citizenry.

There can be no question that what is shown here with oppressive reality will have been copied from the Athenian democracy. Because of this it has often been asked whether there might have been something of Pericles in the portrayal of Creon. When he is first mentioned, by Antigone in the eighth verse of the play, he is referred to by Pericles' title, *stratēgós*. And Pericles too was enlightened. He had made Athens an unprecedented centre of all activity and, like Creon, he had established service to the city as pre-eminent over personal friendships. We hear from his rival, Thucydides, that he had a great many friends among the Athenians and their allies and tried to pay more attention to these allies. So, like Creon, Pericles could well have used this to argue that it is of the greatest importance that one's relations with the city are favourable (209). Apart from this, we know that Pericles transgressed certain unwritten conventions at about this time, which led to his being taunted in contemporary comedies as a despot and a tyrant.

Antigone is a new sort of 'hero'. She is, of course, a king's daughter and sure of her way; like other Sophoclean heroes she is often characterized as 'intransigent' (the same word is used to describe Ajax). But throughout the play she is in an extremely weak position; and unlike Prometheus, Ajax and Orestes she does not question the authority, or the existence, of the autocrat who is in conflict with her. She does not think of murder or revenge, but wants to comply with authority for the most part. She only feels compelled to disobey Creon on one point; and even here she is not absolutely sure whether she is in the right. All the same, she cannot do otherwise, she must bury her brother.

Sophocles provides very particular motives for her actions: her puzzling, even dubious, love for her brother; the deep and unavoidable misfortune which has made her a daughter of Oedipus and which leads her to desire death (perhaps she is inescapably destined to die); and finally the uncompromising, severe character that she reveals so clearly in her treatment of the weak, vacillating Ismene. All this enables her to live up to the laws which she calls on in her confrontation with Creon. From the start, she knows that she is more beholden to the gods than to humans. But the fundamental nature of her righteousness is only brought to the fore when Creon makes his demand for obedience. There are ancient 'conventions' (*nómima*) – the term she uses in preference to 'laws' – which are unwritten and unchangeable and which were made by the gods back in the mists of time; these supersede all laws made by mortals.

Sophocles couches the orders that the king gives in a variety of very revealing terms. Often they are simply called *kḗrygma* ('proclamation' or 'message'). Creon himself likes to call them *nómoi*. This is the ancient Greek term for a custom, convention or law. It is used to mean the laws and rules which have been handed down from generation to generation. But since the word once meant 'justice', it could also be used for the growing amount of new laws that were created from the sixth century onwards (and for which there is another word: *thesmós*). The more that justice is determined by written laws, the more the main emphasis of the concept moves away from that which is unwritten. Here in *Antigone*, we see for the first time that justice is defined so much by civic laws, that the unwritten laws must be specifically characterized as such.

There is no mistaking that Creon misuses his decree by calling it 'the law'. There is a lot of evidence to suggest that in using this sort of vocabulary, Sophocles wanted to make clear the real situation (which was, perhaps, only newly apparent): justice had now become a matter of free-willed – indeed potentially free-wheeling – decision-making. It is not only the specific content of Creon's decrees, but also the increasingly influential legislative powers of the Greek people's Assembly which are at issue. This is why Antigone says that she undertook Polynices' burial in defiance of 'the people's will' – as though it really was a matter of their laws (907).

There is also some reason to believe that a real contemporary problem is reflected in the conflict between Creon and Antigone. The subject of the conflict is not only the limit of policy, but also of polis legislation, and this concern could easily have been prompted by the dispute about Pericles' building policies. As we know, Pericles' rival, Thucydides, son of Melesias, had organized his aristocratic supporters in a completely new way in order to make them a more influential and meaningful part of the people's Assembly. By doing this, he hoped to halt the harsh, inconsiderate power politics which were being practised by Athens in its dealings with its allies and which disregarded so many traditional 'conventions'. In a certain sense he was trying to set a new agenda. The war against Persia had been brought to an end, and the alliance made less sense than hitherto; Athens' immense self-assurance and selfishness were ever more apparent. In 443 Pericles defeated Thucydides, son of Melesias, who was made the subject of an

ostracism and had to leave the city. It is not, then, unreasonable
to assume that the problems of the limits of policy and legislation
were at this time viewed in a new light.

The chorus' first ode, which is about the awesome potential of
mankind, also relates in particular to the Athens of those years.
The pride in man's abilities reflects a widespread feeling. Whether
this pride is refuted in the rest of the play, as has recently been
claimed, is more debatable. If we look at Creon's conversations,
language would indeed seem to be quite limited in its possibilities.
What the ode claims for mankind's navigational skills does not
seem to apply to the ship of state, and the word that it uses for
man's thoughts points at the same time to his arrogance. All of
this, however, serves to confirm the ode's concluding sentiments:
both good and bad use can be made of these abilities. This
depends, on the one hand, on where one stands in relation to the
law, and, on the other, on whether one can keep within the
accepted limits. The latter was the danger that Athens faced; the
city was well known for its rashness. There is every reason to
believe that the utterances of a man who wants to get on by
infringing Zeus' authority are meant as an allusion to the behaviour
of the city. It is here that the danger of breakdown, which is
obvious in the play, is seen as a possible result of mankind's
immense potential. No other play or historical source bears such
impressive witness to the awareness of such potential. The
expression of 'undreamt-of capabilities' shows how new this awareness was: there is no question that here was something to be proud
of.

However, in implying that man's abilities may lead to great
danger, the song points to an awareness that may have been
sparked off by Pericles' strong-willed 'self-aggrandizing' attitude to
the polis and by his readiness to use his allies' money to adorn
the city. In those years many new, risky ventures were undertaken,
which was probably a great cause for concern.

It was, then, a new, relevant and urgent problem: who could
guarantee the wisdom of decisions made by a person who had
such room to manoeuvre? Such a policy-maker can, as we have
seen, completely convince himself of the wisdom of his folly, in the
face of the strongest objections. The council of the rich and powerful (843, 940) elders hardly represents an independent point of

view. Even at the end, when they show pity for Antigone, they curb their acknowledgement of her worthiness with criticism of the disobedience which has led to her punishment. It could be that they are worried, but nowhere do they let this show. Their main driving force is clearly a profound empathy with the monarch and the necessity of obedience to him, and an antipathy towards anarchy (*anarchíā*). But we are told that the people bemoan Antigone's fate. We do not know whether this is out of admiration for her courageous and independent action or because they feel that her brother must be buried. Perhaps Sophocles wants to show that the will of the people (their wisdom?) is just. In any case, no one, not even the son or the seer, manages to influence Creon.

Who, then, should guarantee the good sense of decisions? It is hardly a matter for the constitution, for such a radical experience would present difficulties for both the democracy and the people's Assembly. There was no place for any feeling of superiority over the tyrant on the part of the democrats. The play proposes only one answer to this question: one must hold firm to the laws of the country and the justice of the gods – to the written and, above all, to the unwritten, laws. We see that this is what Creon has learnt when he declares his desire to restore the power of the 'established laws', the necessity of which he is significantly 'afraid of'. This is the wisdom that the chorus comes to learn at the end of the play.

Over and above this, *Antigone* implies another example of the sort of behaviour that is characteristic of Odysseus in *Ajax*; but Creon is not capable of such behaviour for most of the play. In the dialogues with Haemon and Tiresias it is, however, made clear that one should be accommodating and let others have their say. Just as Odysseus knew that a citizen is one among many, Creon should realize that there can be more than one point of view and that only after discussion can good decisions be made. A wealth of contemporary experience must lie behind such literature; Sophocles must have breathed the breath of democracy and felt all its inherent difficulties when he formulated the idea that a man is empty if he only believes in one opinion. Such a man does not know how to deal with the multiplicity of possible opinions; the breadth of his experience does not match that of democracy. The question arises, as it does in *Ajax*, how much the city of Athens is supposed to be reflected in the portrayal of an isolated, intransigent individual.

But there is, perhaps, another point as well: Antigone, despite her noble birth, is effectively powerless and is basically in the same position as an average citizen. She is not a revolutionary and is normally as acquiescent as anyone could wish. It is in regard to only one issue that she is disobedient, and that is because she recognizes a higher justice, one with which she is determined, admittedly for quite personal reasons, to comply. She acts, then, both lawfully and unlawfully, faithfully and disloyally, at one and the same time. But she surely also represents a model of the sort of independent, unorthodox thought which brings certain points of view, indeed necessary ways of thinking into force. She adopts precisely the removed stance – towards the influences, for example, of the people's Assembly and the general feeling in the city, and towards the prejudices of contemporary politics – which is necessary to bring them into question. Perhaps a city relies on such 'citizens', despite the risks they must run and despite all the one-sidedness and stubbornness that form a necessary part of their character. This is not because they are always completely right – Antigone's case is not so clear-cut – but because things do not progress if everyone thinks and behaves as compliantly as someone like Ismene. The great admiration that the people of Thebes, as well as the chorus of elders at the end, show for Antigone, perhaps echoes the awareness that such citizens are necessary.

This would indicate a new concept of civic responsibility: liberation of the individual within the community, a liberation which, along with many others, corresponds to that achieved by the Sophists. We know of similar convictions, expressed at a later time by Socrates and by the priestess Theano, who disobeyed a civic resolution which required her to curse Alcibiades. She maintained that her role was to pray and not to curse.

It is interesting to note that Sophocles portrayed this concept of civic responsibility in the actions of a woman, someone who stands outside male society, someone who can have no ambition within such a society, and whose actions and behaviour are consequently completely alien to Creon. This restricts her capacity to be an example to the rest of society, as do her unusual motives and her stubbornness. But whereas the great heroes of Greek tragedy usually appear to make the figures of the ancient heroes problematical by showing that they no longer have a place in the new society, Antigone, who is apparently so powerless, could be said to create quite the opposite impression.

What is certain is that Sophocles' *Antigone*, like his *Ajax*, is saturated with politics from beginning to end. It provides the context for the main conflict, distinguishes the different parties and figures largely in all the arguments and motivations. We can only assume that this pervasive political content is largely based on the specific issues of the day.

Admittedly, one cannot look at the political aspect in isolation, which is what Creon does; his absolutism in this regard is not to be imitated. There are certain boundaries which must be respected. The politics of the time were firmly rooted in the world of the gods, of both those above and those who inhabit the underworld. They were also rooted in the constant recurrence of transgression and ruin which must in the end be atoned for, in this case by the disobedient Antigone (even though she wanted to be the one who reclaimed justice), by Haemon (whose death also struck Creon and yet whose lot was happier), by Eurydice and finally by Creon himself, the 'living dead' who has to live on through everything. Thus there is sufficient sacrifice to restore order. Since the Greek audience experienced the portrayal of this process as it happened, from the proud entry of the new king to the complete collapse at the end, one can perhaps hope that they came to see reason more quickly than the chorus of elders.

Whether this is so or not, with *Antigone* Sophocles confronted the citizenry with a picture of itself, partly with its actual circumstances, but mostly with an idea of what could happen. He made clear, with unerring realism, where tyranny lurked among them (and among their politicians and leaders). He showed how threatened the position of reason and rationality was and how disastrous it is to go beyond the boundaries that Athens, which sometimes seemed to want to take issue with the power of Zeus himself, had constantly tried to overstep. The myth, which for the most part Sophocles seems to have invented himself, must have hit home with the Athenians precisely because it was so extensively modelled on reality.

Because Sophocles put all this into the mythical past, however, the events would have seemed distant enough for the audience to be open to what he was trying to say; in this respect, the play would not have seemed to be about the politics of Athens or of the contemporary world at all. Thus the citizens were relatively free to appeciate everything that went on in it. They were not offered much comfort by the events, but plenty that they would recognize and remember. Thanks to the vividness of the language and, above all, of the performance, a great impression must have been made.

Thus the familiar but captivating medium of tragedy could be used again and again to explore freely political matters which would otherwise be too daunting and unyielding. The citizenry is opened up to the whole seriousness and dubiousness of politics, their politics. That the need for such a process prompted the writing of such impressive works as *Antigone* would seem to point to the fact that it had an absolutely vital role to play among the citizens of Greece.

7

THE POLITICAL
FOUNDATIONS OF
CLASSICISM

If the art of Aeschylus and Sophocles, and of Euripides too, was
so political or, rather, so attuned to the more profound problems
of the Attic citizenry, to the mental venture of their politics, how
is it that it can still have such a fresh and powerful effect on us?
That it can strike us as being Classical?

We do not have to know exactly what their art meant to the
Athenians in order to gain access to it, understanding of it and
enjoyment from it. What then do we have in common with the
Athenians; or what is so special about tragedy; or where does its
common, direct appeal for the fifth-century audience and for us
lie? For the art of most peoples and periods does not strike us as
being at once Classical and so readily accessible.

What is true of tragedy applies equally well to other products
of the fifth century: the comedies of Aristophanes, the historical
accounts of Herodotus and Thucydides, the work of the great
sculptors. It also goes for the architecture of the temples and
propylaea; the fact that we can only view them in truncated
form, and have great difficulty in imagining how they and their
surroundings can have appeared, is not in itself an argument
against their accessibility. Nor, after all, do we know exactly what
the tragedies looked and sounded like – the masks, the movements,
the dance, the pipes, the rhythms of the language – not to mention
the fact that we can hardly put ourselves in the place of the
Athenians of that period, and are at best able to venture certain
opinions about their reception of the works.

But a book dealing with the political art of Greek tragedy, its reference to the polis, cannot but concern itself with the question of how and why these works retain their appeal for us, whether they are really so essentially accessible in themselves or whether our European culture has taken up too much from the culture of the Greeks for it to strike us as strange. We have no right to regard modern Europe as the goal of world history, and our values and ways as universally applicable. If we take medieval and above all modern Europe to be so strongly influenced, both directly and indirectly, by the Classical world, if we assume that they could never have come into being without it, then there is all the more reason to assume wide areas of historically determined common ground between the Greeks and ourselves. After all, our notions of mankind and its destiny are informed by Greek experience, and their mythology is much more familiar to us than its Germanic equivalent.

It is none the less the case that there must have been something special about the 'Classical' century (though Classical rhetoric and philosophy only developed in the fourth century). Something must have shaped the products of those decades in a particular way, in order for them to maintain their abiding and peculiar fascination, in a manner unparalleled by most other epochs even from our own history.

This 'Classicism' cannot merely have been the product of the chance meeting of many individual talents. Rather, social group-ings must have existed which particularly encouraged individual talent, enabling it to be realized in new ways. These can surely be sketched out. For Renan's talk of the 'Greek miracle' recognizes the extraordinary character of this age, but should not be taken to preclude further attempts at explanation. If this 'Classicism' was grounded in a 'miraculous', momentous coincidence of factors, then these must be seen within the broadest temporal and spatial context. The conditions for it arose on the one hand out of the centuries of history, which charted the development of the peculiar Greek character, and on the other out of the political developments throughout the Mediterranean, in the time leading up to the Persian Wars.

As far as we know, the formation of any culture is bound up with a thorough reconstruction of world-view, of the way in which time is organized and, not least, of artistic representations of the key elements of reality and the key human types, according to the guidelines set for example by the prevailing hierarchy. Forms are thus developed which make particular achievements possible, and at the same time set limits to their grandeur, requiring precise sorts of specialization, so that even the monarch must come to terms with the constraint 'without which one may not constrain others'. However much cultures open up for their members, they also restrict the scope of their activities, indeed of their thought. In the great culture which went before or existed alongside Classical Greece, the model established by the monarchies (with the co-operation of the priesthoods) was so entrenched in the social structures that the transition to a republic or a democracy was impossible. Only modernity has opened up such possibilities, probably thanks to the mutual permeation of Greek and Christian elements, which were installed in the modern state from the start and above all created the potential for opposition to religious forces.

As with all of these cultures, the Greeks had to develop the sort of all-embracing apparatus of institutions, ideas, philosophies, beliefs and meanings without which any higher, differentiated form of civilization cannot exist. And they had to formulate their own identity. However, as monarchies had no chance of gaining power in their midst, there was no radical reformation of the body politic, which might have required the collaboration of all towards a single cause and created the sort of ideology which rulers cultivate in order to secure the basis of their rule among their subjects. On the contrary, we observe that the burgeoning activity of the Greeks, which set such startling change in motion and created such new forms, was curiously directed outwards, into new areas, leaving the old ones more or less untouched; or rather, leaving them to their own devices, for they clearly had to change in some ways.

First, the enormous new dynamism was aimed at distant places, with the continuous foundation of new cities, covering virtually all of the Mediterranean west of Greece and reaching well into the Black Sea to the north. In Greece itself, on the other hand, few new conquests were made, and there was little need to reorganize the citizenries to meet the demands of intensive warfare. Nor was much energy devoted to intensifying the economy. To an astounding extent, the polis societies were spared the repercussions of the new activity, however much it affected them indirectly. The most important new development in the poleis was that of a public arena, a communal space for the most important groups within the city, one characterized by leisure, sport and social recreation. By virtue of the darker side of life, and its necessities, being excluded from this sphere, a spirit of gaiety also came into being, together with the ideal of grace in appearance, behaviour and discourse. The public life of the various cities was mutually reinforced by the movements of travellers, singers and rhapsodists. This public sphere also included politics, of course: the conflicts between aristocrats, the usurpations of tyrants, the uprisings of the exploited classes and occasionally civil war.

The ideal which largely held sway here was that of autarchy. In spite of sociability and conflict, individuals stood more or less in splendid isolation. The keen interest in competition, sporting or otherwise, is characteristic of the general principle that it was more a matter of outdoing others than of serving the general good by specializing in one's allotted tasks and securing influence. So it was, relatively speaking, more important to develop individually than to gain power, and the 'competitive' virtues were accordingly much more strongly developed among the Greek aristocracy than the 'co-operative' ones.

This aristocratic world developed a particular brilliance, and it remained in many senses exemplary throughout the history of Greece. It seems most likely that at an early stage it gave substance to the Greeks' need to determine who they were and established the direction in which their need would be satisfied. This need must have had a peculiarly important and influential effect for a nation whose existence was so far-flung and largely limited to points on the map. While some of its settlements shared frontiers in Greece itself, many were separated by vast distances, bordering on all sorts of peoples, highly cultured and 'barbarian' alike. Yet it was a nation which must have set the utmost store on preserving the essence of its character. We know that oriental influences had an enormous effect on the Greeks over a period of time, but these ultimately only served to mediate knowledge, myths, images and ideas. The Greeks assimilated what they had a use for, but essentially remained unchanged, to all intents and purposes maintaining their previous course. That which united them in spite of everything, and accounted for their individuality, lay to some extent in their shared gods, their language and certain historical memories, but the area in which they intensified and reinforced this sense of unity was that of their life-style, which led to a first flourishing in the Archaic, aristocratic culture.

However, as this culture was ultimately the preserve of a select few and, instead of permeating the life of the cities, it set itself apart, albeit at their centre, it was bound to remain politically very weak. It was based upon the suppression and exploitation of the commons. Many of these people fell into debt and were sold as slaves. This led not only to an economic, but also, in the long run, to a moral and political crisis: the ethos of the aristocrats was too weak, the bonds between them and the masses too insubstantial, to avoid the creation of a moral vacuum between the upper and lower classes, which could only aggravate their contentions.

The result of all this was a series of uprisings and civil wars, culminating in attempts to secure a civic position for the middle classes, to pitch their increasingly powerful political voice against that of the nobility. The public dimension of the cities was accordingly extended and took its cue from the mass of the citizenry, who perhaps lagged behind in cultural terms, but were able to set the pace politically. Public life came to be virtually synonymous with that of the citizens. This involved a considerable intensification of the polis, which followed upon the reorganization of the military into the phalanx.

Whatever impulses might have been at work among the citizenry at large, they were predominantly dictated by political concerns, that is, by a spirit of rationality. The laws of politics and civil existence had to be recognized and disseminated, and these must have seemed rather abstract. For the new political thinking could not attach itself to the interests of a monarch, directing things from the centre, but rather it had to enable the citizenry to function without a monarch. They had to recognize the conditions of civil life and to change or recreate them where they were faulty, in order that the citizens themselves could become the centre of the whole. Faced with such a challenge, it was clearly necessary to reason in a more general and detached, a less self-centred, way. It was necessary to underpin their reasoning by seeking out analogies in the cosmic order, indeed to conceive of the cosmos as operating according to the same laws as the polis. And finally, if they wanted to draw the middle classes into the political process – as indeed they did – they had to make this reasoning accessible to them. Nietzsche speaks at one stage of an '*agonistic* feeling, which seeks to prevail before a public, and must be comprehensible for that public. (Which is why such different individuals bear *exaggerated* allegiance to "what is common to humans".).' He also sees the 'awakening *sense of reality*' as 'itself a consequence of the agon'. Of course, for 'humans' we should read 'citizens' in this case. But in a sense this makes little difference, because the culture was so fundamentally grounded in public discussion. It evidently not only had to make itself comprehensible to the populace, but had to incorporate their perspectives, indeed had in a certain sense to identify itself with the generality.

Max Weber once said that the ability to be astonished by the way of the world is the premise for asking questions about its meaning. In this case an entire citizenry must have asked such questions, varying of course from individual to individual, but in such an overt and intense way, that all must have been affected by it; in exactly the same way the lack of orientation, the need for a sense of equilibrium in such strange times and the anxiety, which must have resulted from this, will have affected everybody.

It was a long process, taking at least two and a half centuries, before the Greeks developed an institution of authority which could fulfil the role of the monarch in other high cultures, namely, to establish new foundations for communal life. Individual aristocrats, co-operating closely with the lower classes, now achieved what neither the aristocracy in general nor the tyrants had attempted or been able to achieve. The achievement was a limited one, for women, non-citizens and slaves were excluded, but it none the less achieved a civic body embracing high and low, based not on the homogeneity of classes but on community of interest within the polis. Divisions remained of course, not only between citizen and non-citizen, but also within the lives of the citizens: a demarcation prevailed between the domestic and the public domains, and by the same token between the ancient and the modern, between the still powerful sense of the irrational and the developing force of reason. But by being subjected to such tensions (not to mention those provoked by the many political conflicts) and at the same time to such terribly difficult decisions, these citizens developed a many-sided, all-embracing and problematic world. Many questions presented themselves; the culture of public discussion ensured that these were duly formulated. If the respective answers cannot have been simple, they were at least possible, and possible in a way that we could call 'Classical'.

For I would contend that this is just where the basis of Classical Greece lies. To put it in simple and general terms, it sprang from the fact that a series of answers, which were already latent in Greek history, could now be given in a new and virtually perfect form, a form which derived from and responded to a *general* state of affairs, *general* requirements, and was thus itself general. The answers were formed by the spirit of reason which suffused the citizenries, which, notwithstanding the superiority of many individuals, was common property, and which set its sights on permeating the world at large. For the political world in which these men met and in which they had to operate could more or less be held in view, and seemed increasingly to follow inner laws which were paralleled in the cosmos. And external problems too could be mastered, though here it was Athens which took the lead, just as it became the cultural centre of this world.

The fact that the spirit of reason was so general and so successful, so concrete for the majority and so abstract for a minority, operating in new fields such as the recording of history, Sophistic theorizing, philosophy and various sciences, set the whole tone of life in Athens and contributed at the same time to the openness and accessibility of its culture.

Of course many things came together to set this tone and make possible the Classical culture of the fifth century. But this was just what had been prepared by the Greek imagination, the powers of conception, creation and reasoning developed in the Archaic era, which now, under the particular conditions of the new century, were raised to a new, perhaps less charming, but definitively 'Classical' level. The aristocratic Kouros and Kore were superseded by the long series of Classical representations of man, in the course of which Greek artists gained control over the design of the human body – in the same way as the citizens did over that of the polis. The two processes clearly corresponded to one another. And the sculptors now began to transcend the level of mere variation of types and to mould the human form *per se*, in such an ideal and consummate fashion, that we find it barely credible, though it was evidently true to the times. Polyclitus tells us that, on the strength of exhaustive measurements, he was able to work out a golden measure, a canon for the human body; he seems to have realized this model in his Doryphoros (Spear-bearer). This sculpture as it were expresses in the highest form the equality of men, of the citizens of the polis. Polyclitus voiced the citizens' answer to the question: who is man?

This presupposes the model of the citizenry in which every individual could lay claim to totality; or, as Pericles puts it in the Funeral Speech in Thucydides: 'It seems to me that each of our men, graced with skills for most things, stands as a self-sufficient personality.' 'Self-sufficiency' (autarchy) clearly implies being able to square up to any demands. And even allowing for Pericles' exaggeration, there must be a genuine grain of truth in his statement. These citizens represented together the whole of the polis; they were not discrete components of a clockwork mechanism of state, members of a society of specialists, and thus of necessity individual in a one-sided way. Behind the communal ideal lay that of the aristocrats. But it had become much more comprehensive, and it evidently had to be represented. The visual arts, too, would help to show the citizens who they were.

On the great frieze of the Parthenon, the Athenian citizenry even had itself depicted in a festive image of the Panathenaic procession. The horsemen and the virgins are mainly drawn from the nobility, but they stand for the whole citizenry; the image and its select models give better expression to their grace than they could have managed in real life. Yet they were clearly not so distant from this ostensible grace, the superabundance of power which inspires levity and elegance, that they could not find it credible and thus amenable to perfect depiction.

Of course in all of this reality is heightened. But the ideal which a society sets for itself also has claims to reality, at least in those epochs of its history when that which it has striven for is fulfilled. And that was clearly so in this case, which is why the ideal could be formulated and figured in such a way that it still compels even today, in spite of all the distance and scepticism we may feel. If it seems to us more like a dream than anything else, we should none the less assume that the dream came close to reality at that time.

It would be fascinating to trace the development in the representation of the gods in the fifth century (sculpture and tragedy show striking parallels here); to show how the experiences and problems which the citizens of the fifth century had with themselves and with their gods are marked out here; to show how the 'higher humanity' of the gods corresponds to that of humanity itself; or indeed to argue that the architecture of the Parthenon perhaps does not directly express the spirit of Athenian democracy, but is certainly evidence of what that democracy enabled, or encouraged, a great architect to plan and to construct. And there is a host of other examples covering many different areas of activity, which ultimately amounted to that 'sense of capability' which characterized the fifth century. This awareness is equally a product of the fulfilment that eventually came to the political problematic of the polis after such protracted efforts, and it was provided by the citizenry at large. This is not to overlook the part played by Athens' successes and the new, rash and ultimately fateful dynamism of its foreign policy. 'The self stepped out, and stepped down' is the striking way in which Gottfried Benn formulated this development.

If we are not to suppose that Greek Classicism, the simultaneous production of so much that was extraordinary and of lasting effect, was a matter of coincidence, then the only conclusion is that it can be explained in terms of the state of affairs in the fifth century, and in particular the situation in Athens. This being so, can we really make do with the idea that the times merely made it possible, rather than actively promoted it? That the impulse which arose out of the political circumstances simply came to rest in the arts and sciences, and was not rather involved in a system of multiple interactions? That the Greeks, the Athenians in particular, did not *need* this art? It seems hardly likely.

It seems to me, on the contrary, that Greek Classicism is in itself a further argument for the case that the Greeks were in need of art, and of course of tragedy in particular. They may not necessarily have been fully aware of this, though the significance of such an institution as the performances at the festival of Dionysus can hardly have remained obscure.

It is of course hard to get a clearer idea of the problems that the citizens of Athens (at least the generations of Aeschylus and Sophocles) had with their ethical and mental infrastructure. But it seems to me beyond doubt that the tensions and the disorientation they encountered should not be underestimated. And it seems equally clear that problems sprang from their political dealings which could not be solved in political terms, and yet had to be solved somehow if the political activity was to continue. Jean-Pierre Vernant has pointed out that the citizens, who were just beginning to see themselves as more or less autonomous in their actions, were faced with the problem of the extent to which man is really the source of his own deeds; and in this way they became involved in many other associated questions and ambiguities. There can, at any rate, have been no such thing as a routine in matters of fundamental importance for the citizens of these early generations. Nor can there have been a delegation of responsibility; they did not after all elect representatives, but continuously came to their own informed decisions in matters of war and peace, life and death. Politics was also still deeply rooted in religion; questions of morality and world-view everywhere entered into the political consciousness of the citizens and were not to be silenced by any particular ideology. And yet debate in both the Council and the people's Assembly will have had an increasingly pragmatic bearing. Thus there developed a yawning gap between received ideas and present circumstances, between religion and morality on the one side and politics on the other. The tensions were innumerable. And this situation must have thrown up great problems which could nowhere be 'discussed' in public – except, that is, in the arena of tragedy.

For the public enactment of problems was of huge importance, given that everybody was affected by them, everybody caught up in the same constantly shifting situation; given also that the Attic citizens were not equipped with anything like the spiritual resources with which modern societies have learned to come to terms with so much. They had no tradition down through generations of a Christian model of conscience, no churches or schools. The Athenians were much more reliant upon others than upon themselves. There were no institutions which might have taken some of the strain – except again for tragedy, which could not only serve to teach through the authority of its dramatists, but also simply re-enact so much, make it clearer, set it in a general perspective and open it up to discussion.

It was after all a time-honoured requirement among the Greeks that things should be considered 'in their midst', in the public eye. They were suspicious of anything which went on in secret and sought to evade their knowledge. So criticism had an important part to play, not for the sake of objection, but with a view to introducing perspectives which might otherwise have been overlooked (though of course this was bound to have its limits). Thus, the citizenry which initiated so many wars also wanted to hear heart-felt lament at the pity of war. This was the essence of direct democracy. The work on the ethical and mental foundations of their politics, the arguments over the questions which politics provoked for the citizens, especially in collective terms, had to be conducted in public. When Thucydides has Cleon criticize the Athenians for their passion for listening to debate, this does not necessarily just imply a particular aesthetic propensity for the pleasures of competition. It can equally have sprung from a sense of lack of orientation, not just in individual areas, but in terms of their nomological knowledge as a whole, a lack of orientation which tragedy was tailored to address.

The interpretation of the individual plays should have shown the extent to which tragedy helped the Athenians to work through difficulties, threats and uncertainties, which would otherwise have hampered them in their thinking, feelings and actions, and also the extent to which it helped to incorporate the questions and needs unleashed by politics into broader perspectives, and so assisted the development of new points of view, of a new nomological knowledge. For example, in the *Oresteia*, the parallels between the present and myth served simultaneously to legitimate the new order of 461 and to subject it to a new conception of the old divine model. Tragedy was thus in a position, at least during the first few decades after the Persian War, to add, as it were, to the stock of meaning, which was of such importance to the Athenians: that store of expectation of sense, which makes it possible for what is experienced and done to be situated within general structures of meaning, which liberates the sort of energetic and open questioning which can fulfil the expectation and resist the customary temptation to bow before questions with a resigned shrug of the shoulders. In a time where so much was new, the order of things so bold (and directly dictated by the citizens), the successes so dizzying, the quest for sense, reasons and ordering must have been urgent – and so too were the answers which would regenerate the stock of meaning and the ethical ground of politics. The questioning might easily have run riot. With so much up for discussion, the relationship between the sexes must also have gained significance, indeed the range of separations at the heart of the city, at the heart of the home, which set the citizens off from all others. It was a time of expanded horizons, and probably remained so until the onset of the Peloponnesian War. In the decades following the Persian War, tragedy must have encountered radical questions, tuning and retuning the balance of large parts, if not the whole, of the whole order. The pressures were enormous, and it stood up to these magnificently.

It was to the great advantage of tragedy that it could rehearse contemporary questions in the distant shape of myth. Pain, terror and insecurity strike us quite differently when they are held at a distance. We are less threatened and so freer of inhibition. Matters of enormity can become familiar and be considered openly. Unconscious ideas and anxieties can take shape, projected into conscious fantasies (what Bruno Bettelheim has shown for fairy-tales holds true for tragedy in many ways as well). So the works of the tragedians contributed to the ability of the Athenians to come to grips with many of the problems which beset their mental infrastructure, so that the basis of their existence could be kept clear. Tragedy introduced a tendency to train the mind in situations which could so easily have led to repression. It countered complacent self-confidence by instead leading through questioning into a genuine sense of the self – and thence towards the integration of the citizenry as a whole.

It was thus that tragedy could be the citizens' answer to the question of human destiny. Popular and high culture coalesced here as they rarely have. If, as Jacob Burckhardt held, the need for poetry in the world has never been so intense as it was for the Greeks, then this is nowhere more true than in the case of the Athenians and their tragedy. It was evidently only under such circumstances, confronted with such demands and questions, that the Athenian tragedians were able to write in the way they did.

And this applies to Aeschylus, Sophocles and Euripides, who each found the highest potential for tragic expression for their respective phases of Athenian history in the fifth century.

It would clearly be desirable to trace this much more exactly than has been possible within the thesis proposed here of the political art of Greek tragedy, limited as it has been to a few examples and to the time-span between the two great wars. The thesis rests on the argument that tragedy, that 'part of a most significant cult within the polis', as Burckhardt has it, which 'was no entertainment for a bored and cultured elite, but . . . a great festive event for the whole citizenry', was a no less urgent need for that citizenry than their (other) political institutions, given that they were propelled into a totally new situation, one which allowed of no routine, and brought with it such great possibilities, but also great dangers.

'The Athenians came to their fruition because they faced demands on every side; their requirements were not narrowly confined. But all these requirements were *general*' (Nietzsche). If the most diverse things, the darkest and the brightest, converged here in a moment of the most intense vitality – then the artistic responses to this are surely bound to strike home too for other ages.

FURTHER READING AND NOTES

The line references are kept to a minimum. In the case of longer quotations the reference is to the first line only.There are references to the Aeschylus fragments 352 and 391 (according to Nauck's numbering). Fragment 394 is cited for *Ajax* and 381 ('Where power and justice bear a single yoke – which then is the stronger?') with regard to the conception of just power encountered in the *Oresteia* and *Prometheia*. The Thucydides' quotations come from 1, 70 (the Corinthian's speech); 2, 35ff (the Funeral Speech); 2, 65, 9 (Pericles); 3, 38 (Cleon); and 6, 18, 6f (Alcibiades). 653d is cited from Plato's *Laws* and chapter 3, 80 from Horodotus.

For general information on the political and constitutional history of the age, Edouard Will's *Le Monde Grec et l'Orient I* (510–403*BC*) and John Kenyon Davies' *Democracy and Classical Greece* (New Jersey, 1978) are recommended. Jacob Burkhardt's *History of Greek Culture* (London, 1964) is also of great interest. For further details of the citizens' identity, the consciousness of ability (including references for quotations) and various other problems concerning the character of Greek citizenries, see Christian Meier, *The Greek Discovery of Politics* (Cambridge, Mass./London, 1990), and Christian Meier and Paul Veyne, *Kannten die Griechen die Demokratie?* (Berlin, 1988). An essay of Veyne's in *Annales* 37 (1982) is also cited. Greek political thinking is discussed further in my essay on 'The Emergence of an Autonomous Intelligence amongst the Greeks' in *The Origins and Diversity of Axial Age Civilizations*, Shmuel N. Eisenstadt, ed. (Albany, 1986), pp. 65–91. I give a full account of the reforms of 461 in 'Der Umbruch zur Demokratie in Athen' in *Epochenschwellen und Epochenbewußtsein*, R. Herzog and R. Kosellek, eds (Munich, 1987). The reference to the 'espace civique' comes from Jean-Pierre Vernant, 'Espace et Organisation politique en Grèce Ancienne', *Annales* 20 (1965).

Material on the tragedy festivals is found in Arthur Pickard-Cambridge, *The Dramatic Festivals of Athens* (Oxford, 1968). The technical problems affecting audience reception of tragedies are discussed in B. Hunningher, *Acoustics and Acting in the Theatre of Dionysos Eleutherus* (Amsterdam, 1956).

For useful general accounts of Greek tragedy, see Albin Lesky, *Greek Tragedy* (London, 1965), H.D.F. Kitto, *Greek Tragedy* (London, 1961), and John Ferguson, *A Companion to Greek Tragedy* (Austin/London, 1972). Karl Reinhardt's books *Sophocles* (Oxford, 1979) and *Aeschylus als Regisseur und Theologe* (Berne, 1949) were of considerable importance for my argument.

Political interpretations of the tragedies are limited for the most part to – often highly hypothetical – relationships between the texts and the historical events of the time. An example of this is Anthony J. Podlecki's *The Political Background of Aeschylean Tragedy* (Ann Arbor, 1966). Victor Ehrenberg's *Sophocles and Pericles* (Oxford, 1954) judiciously traces allusions to Pericles and his politics in Sophocles' tragedies. I have given an account of the place of the *Oresteia* in the history of Greek political thought in the essay on *The Eumenides* in *The Greek Discovery of Politics*.

Studies undertaken by the school of Jean-Pierre Vernant have adopted a quite different approach to the social contextualization of tragedy; for instance, J.-P. Vernant and P. Vidal-Naquet, *Myth and Tragedy in Ancient Greece* (1981), P. Vidal-Naquet, *The Black Hunter* (Baltimore, 1986) and Charles Segal, *Tragedy and Civilisation: An Interpretation of Sophocles* (Cambridge, Mass./London, 1981). They are above all concerned with establishing evidence of the deeper structures of Greek thinking in tragedy, for example the boundaries between civilization and the wild, the significance of sacrifice and hunting and the general importance of polarities and ambiguities in the social reality of the Greeks. These studies have helped to clarify much in the texts. I have gratefully assimilated their conclusions, but feel that it is now time to develop the arguments further, as much of their work is too schematic, with scant regard for the history of the times. There has been no real attempt to establish the true meaning of the structures of thought and imagination, to decide whether they are simply unconscious or are consciously applied, and how they are related to the political language which must have been in circulation at that time (and which is documented a little later in Herodotus and Thucydides). This scholarship should be explicitly set within the context of what we know of the Greeks in the fifth century BC.

My own approach differs from scholarship to date, briefly, as follows. I believe that I have brought the particular character of the Attic citizenry and of their situation in the fifth century BC into sharper focus. As far as I am aware, the problems of nomological knowledge and of the mental infrastructure have not so far been treated in their historical context. The observations of Vernant and his school are too concerned with deep, general structures, while those of political interpretations are largely confined to superficial accounts of events and ideologies. By focusing on the mental foundations of the political, I believe I have been able to open up new perspectives on the tragedies (even if there is much in my interpretation that is not novel). The results of this study are summed up in the thesis that Attic democracy was as dependent upon tragedy as upon its councils and assemblies (and indeed probably many other products of its classicism).

It was more or less inevitable that the concerns of political thinking should loom large in the interpretation of the texts. We can no longer reconstruct accurately what the spectators might have gained through their experience of the action and the multiplicity of emotions and identifications aroused. I cannot say how helpful Aristotles' theory of catharsis might have been here. Even if, according to Herodotus, the whole theatre burst into tears during the performance of Phrynichus' *The Capture of Miletus*, this need not have been a typical response.

It remains an open question to what extent the performances of tragedies might have exerted a magical power. They were certainly able – and this is particularly evident in Aeschylus' *Persians* – more or less to revive an event in the drama between protagonists and chorus at the festival of the Great Dionysia. They created a new reality out of the event and its interpretation, 'conjuring' things into a certain order.

INDEX

accommodation, public and private, 95

Achilles, 167, 172, 177

acoustics (theatre), 59

Acropolis: extended, 29, 167; store for public money, 57; theatre and temple on, 58, 61, 75, 105; in *Eumenides*, 105–7, 131

actors, 52, 60; number per play, 59; payment, 56; prizes, 56; training of voices, 59

Aegean, island cities of, 24; Athenian influence, 2, 24, 162; Persian influence, 12, 24, 68; shipping in, 51; Spartan activity in, 24; *see also* Delian League

Aegina, 9, 98

Aegisthus, in *Agamemnon*, 103–4, 108, 111, 117, 119–20, 131, 153

Aegyptus, 84; sons of, 86, 89

Aeschylus, 1, 5, 60, 62 ff.; compared with Sophocles and Euripides, 161, 178; dating and number of plays, 54, 101, 136–7; death, 137–8; directed his own plays, 141–2; effect on today's readers, 204; epitaph, 162; fought at Marathon and Salamis, 162; his brother, 162; influenced by his own generation, 159–65, 213, 216; informs and teaches citizens, 97,

134; military training, 161–2; political connections, 62, 94, 97; popularity, 159, 165, 168; primacy and successes, 53–4, 78, 159; praised by Aristophanes, 159–60; on stability of polis and popular rule, 93–4, 100, 186; theology, 73, 122–3, 149–55; on tyranny, 154; use of history, 77, 121–4, 161, 178; use of myth, 91, 97; use of symbolism and language, 92, 160, 165; on war and suffering, 78, 77; on world order, 116; *see also* individual plays and trilogies

Agamemnon, King of Argos: portrayed by Aeschylus, 73–4, in *Agamemnon* 102 ff., 117–20, 122–3, 126, 129, 131, in *Choephoroe*, 78, 117, 129, in *Eumenides*, 111; portrayed by Sophocles in *Ajax*, 167, 172–5

Agamemnon (Aeschylus), 102–4; depicts suffering, 121; political importance, 123–4; reflects general helplessness and Athenians' fears, 116–17, 124–5; secrecy of murder plan, 129; theodicy, 121

agon (contest), 47, 50; at Great Dionysia, 60; of poetry and song, 45; as term used by Nietsche, 209; tragic, 45, 59

Index by Sonia Argyle